KEY ACCOUNT MANAGEMENT

For free online support material please go to the Kogan Page website:
www.koganpage.com/kam
Password: KAM52773

KEY ACCOUNT MANAGEMENT

TOOLS AND TECHNIQUES FOR ACHIEVING PROFITABLE KEY SUPPLIER STATUS

4th edition

PETER CHEVERTON

KOGAN
PAGE

London and Philadelphia

Publisher's note
Every possible effort has been made to ensure that the information contained in
this book is accurate at the time of going to press, and the publishers and authors cannot
accept responsibility for any errors or omissions, however caused. No responsibility for loss
or damage occasioned to any person acting, or refraining from action, as a result of the
material in this publication can be accepted by the editor, the publisher or any of the authors

First published in Great Britain in 1999 by Kogan Page Limited
Second edition 2001
Third edition published in Great Britain and the United States in 2004
Fourth edition 2008
Reprinted 2010

120 Pentonville Road
London N1 9JN
UK
www.koganpage.com

525 South 4th Street, #241
Philadelphia PA 19147
USA

ISBN   978 0 7494 5277 3

British Library Cataloguing-in-Publication Data

A CIP record for this book is available from the British Library.

Library of Congress Cataloging-in-Publication Data

Cheverton, Peter.
  Key account management : a complete action kit of tools and techniques
for achieving profitable key supplier status / Peter Cheverton.-- 4th ed.
      p. cm.
Includes bibliographical references and index.
  ISBN 0-7494-5277-3
  1. Selling--Key accounts. 2. Marketing--Key accounts. 3. Customer
services. I. Title.
HF5438.8.K48C47 2008
658.8'04--dc22
                              2008003543

Typeset by Saxon Graphics Ltd, Derby
Printed and bound in Great Britain by MPG Books Ltd, Bodmin, Cornwall

Contents

Foreword by Professor Malcolm McDonald   *x*
Acknowledgements   *xii*
Preface   *xiii*
Preface to the fourth edition   *xiv*
About the author   *xv*

And it was all going so very well...   **xvi**

PART I   DEFINITIONS AND PURPOSE   **1**

1. **The challenge**   **3**
    Strategy or tactics? 5

2. **Why Key Account Management: aggressive or defensive?**   **8**
    The journey 8; The reasons 9; Your own journey 12;
    The rewards 13; Application exercise 15

3. **What is a key account? An investment**   **16**
    The perils of 'sizeism' 17; The investment 20;
    Does everybody know? 21; Application exercise 22

4. **What is Key Account Management?**   **23**
    What's in a word? 23; Managing the future 23;
    Where to start? 24; The importance of balance 25; Guessing,
    or making the future? 28; Sanity checks 28; A working
    definition 30; The KAM model 31; Application exercise 33

PART II   ANALYSIS: OPPORTUNITY AND VALUE   35

5.   **Knowing the market, knowing your value**   37
     The opportunity chain 37; Complex networks 46;
     Application exercise 51

6.   **Knowing the people, knowing your value**   52
     The 'opportunity snail' 52; Penetrating the snail 55;
     Putting 'chains' and 'snails' together 59; Application exercise 61

PART III   RELATIONSHIP MANAGEMENT   63

7.   **From 'bow-ties' to 'diamonds'**   65
     Three approaches to selling 67; The KAM journey 71;
     Charting the course 74; Application exercise 90

8.   **Contact strategies**   91
     The customer's decision-making process 92; The customer's DMU
     (decision-making unit) 93; The analytical tools in the DMU toolkit 94;
     Using the tools in practice 105; The action tools in the DMU toolkit 108;
     Application exercise 113

9.   **The human factor**   114
     Logic or emotion? 115; Building rapport 116; Application exercise 120

10. **The good, the bad, the sad and the ugly**   121
     The bad story 121; The sad story 123; The ugly story 124;
     Hindsight, or foresight? 126; The good story 126;
     The second good story 127; Application exercise 129

PART IV   ACHIEVING KEY SUPPLIER STATUS   131

11. **The purchasing revolution**   133
     What's in a name? 134; Reasons for the 'purchasing revolution' 137;
     Application exercise 140

12. **Supply chain management: seeking value**   141
     Escaping price... embracing value 143; Escaping the limitations
     of the 'snail' 145; Application exercise 148

13. **Purchasing organization: rationalization and centralization** 149
     Supplier rationalization 150; Centralization of the purchasing
     organization 152; Rationalization and centralization: is it good
     for us? 157; Application exercise 159

14. **Supplier positioning: managing suppliers**   160
    Making time to manage suppliers 160; Supplier positioning
    models 161; Using the analysis 163; Why measure spend? 164;
    Why measure risk/significance? 166; Managing suppliers 167;
    Positioning is one thing – but life goes on 177; Behave appropriately,
    but plan your escape 178; Application exercise 180

PART V   ACHIEVING STRATEGIC SUPPLIER STATUS   181

15. **Being of strategic value**   183
    Times change 183; When customers 'snap' 184;
    When customers merge 186; Being of strategic value 186;
    The diagnostic toolkit 189; Application exercise 191

16. **How are they growing?**   192
    Growth and risk 192; Growth and the product life cycle
    (PLC) 196; Application exercise 201

17. **How do they aim to win?**   202
    Porter and competitive advantage 202; The customer's
    money-making-logic 205; Application exercise 207

18. **What drives them?**   208
    Value drivers 208; Implications for the would-be strategic supplier 210;
    Identifying the drivers 211; The cultural match 214; Application
    exercise 216

19. **A shared future?**   217
    The shared-future analysis 217; The competition 221;
    Application exercise 223

PART VI   THE VALUE PROPOSITION   225

20. **The customer's total business experience**   227
    Identifying the customer's TBE (total business experience) 229;
    Application exercise 235

21. **The customer's activity cycle**   236
    Completing the exercise 239; Involving the team 242;
    Involving the customer 242; The activity cycle in practice 243;
    Application exercise 247

22. **Measuring the value**   248
    Using the right language 249; Understanding the circumstances 249;
    Understanding the cost in use 250; Providing the measure 250;
    Application exercise 252

23. **Making the proposal**   253
    Managing change 253; The proposal analysis 255; The 'CICS'
    questioning strategy 257; Application exercise 259

**PART VII   TARGETING: CUSTOMER CLASSIFICATION AND
DISTINCTION**   261

24. **Customer classification**   263
    Steps 1 and 2: Objectives and market segmentation 265; Step 3:
    Assemble the classification and selection team 267; Step 4: The 'KAISM':
    classifying your customers 269; Step 4.i: Customer attractiveness
    factors 276; Step 4.ii: Relative strength factors 280; Completing the
    analysis 281; Key accounts and multiple business unit suppliers 284;
    Should we tell the customer? 285; Application exercise 286

25. **Customer distinction**   287
    Step 5: Customer distinction strategies 287; Step 6: Communication,
    alignment and implementation 293; Application exercise 294

PART VIII   MAKING IT HAPPEN: PREPARING FOR KAM   295

26. **Sins and requirements**   297
    The sins 297; The requirements: *making it happen* 299;
    Application exercise 301

27. **Leadership and organization**   302
    Leadership: managing change 302; Organization and structure 309;
    Application exercise 315

28. **The skills required**   316
    Team leadership 318; Coaching 324; Political entrepreneurship 326;
    Some frequently asked questions 326; The wider team's skills 330;
    Application exercise 332

29. **IT systems**   333
    Too little or too much? 333; The vital requirements 334;
    CRM: curse or saviour? 335; Application exercise 341

30. **Measuring customer profitability**   342
    Four 'almost truths' of customer profitability 343; Giving discounts
    for volume 347; Measuring profit after *all* costs 348;
    Application exercise 353

31. The key account plan   **354**
The purpose of the plan 354; A key account plan template? 355;
Some 'must haves' 357; A sample running order 359;
Sharing it with the customer? 361; Luck or judgement? 361;
A few last tips 362; Application exercise 363

32. Tracking progress   **364**
Measuring the tangibles 365; Measuring the intangibles? 366;
Comparing key accounts? 366; Measuring the implementation
of KAM 367; The performance map 367; The KAM 'health check' 369;
How will you know when you get there? 370; Application exercise 371

33. Getting further help   **372**
The weblink 373; The INSIGHT KAM training programme 373;
The global challenge 373; Further reading 374

Index   _375_

Foreword

Good books on Key Account Management are rare. One of the reasons for this lies in the past, in the way that Key Account Management (KAM) has been defined and described. The past 40 years have been characterized by a view that KAM is mainly a selling task, albeit at a high level, and that the responsibility for its implementation rests almost entirely with the sales team.

Yet all our research at Cranfield School of Management indicates that, above all else, it is this mentality that prevents the forging of mature, trustworthy and profitable relationships. Key Account Management is not a sales initiative, it is not something you do *to* customers, and key account strategies will require the full support of the business.

Key Account Management is a team effort and, more than that, it is a business-wide effort. Our research has shown repeatedly that major clients want more than a sales–buyer interface and they want more than a traditional salesperson managing the relationship. If suppliers and customers are to forge significant relationships, as businesses, then both sides must look to new ways of managing those relationships.

Relationships are at the very heart of KAM. They provide the source of information and understanding that can be built into added-value activities. They also provide the foundations for long-term business based on mutual trust and confidence. If you care about customer retention then you should care about KAM.

So let's escape the trap of the last 40 years – KAM is not something we do *to* customers, it is something we do *with* customers, and perhaps the greatest single motivation for developing Key Account Strategies is that the customer is looking for new ways of working alongside key suppliers.

Purchasing organizations are looking more and more to the techniques of supply chain management as a means of prioritizing and managing relationships with significant suppliers. Those suppliers must respond with customer-sensitive strategies that will touch on everything from the people involved to the systems and processes used, and even to the structure and organization of the supplier's business.

Key Account Management provides the strategic base, the processes and the disciplines to handle this situation, alongside those other common challenges – globalization, market maturity and customer power.

The purpose is clear: the pursuit of competitive advantage. The days are long gone when major customers would tolerate average, overpriced products and services. Being a 'pimply me too' just won't work any more.

Competitive advantage puts you in a position to succeed, but there is more that you need to do. There is the question of profit. Most companies, if they are honest, are not able to measure the profitability of their key accounts. Many companies, once they determine to measure these things, often find their largest customers to be their least profitable. Very few companies measure the long-term returns of customer retention – annual results are often all that count. Key Account Management should be seen as the route to profitable key supplier status – the challenge of understanding profit must be taken head on. This book will provide the help required.

Peter Cheverton has used the Cranfield research to great effect. I have worked closely with him for many years and have respect and admiration for his work as a trainer and consultant with major clients. The task of implementing Key Account Strategies is far from easy, and Peter brings a combination of clarity, experience, enthusiasm and common sense to the task. This book is an excellent distillation of his experience, building on the Cranfield research and producing the essential guide to global best practice.

Please be assured that reading this book will be a rewarding experience.

Professor Malcolm McDonald

Acknowledgements

Without doubt the biggest thanks must go to the excellent clients of INSIGHT Marketing and People with whom I have worked as a trainer and consultant on Key Account Management over the last 15 years. I know for sure that I have learnt as much from their experiences as from any other source.

Professor Malcolm McDonald of Cranfield University School of Management has been as generous as ever with his support for this book, providing access to his own researches as well as encouraging me with my own.

My colleagues at INSIGHT have been kind enough to allow me the time to complete this book, and I thank them for their endless suggestions, and for putting up with mine!

Preface

This book is designed as a practical guide to implementing Key Account Management strategies. Wherever it has been helpful to use real examples of good and bad practice to illustrate important points, this has been done. Many of these examples come from my own experience in working with clients of INSIGHT Marketing and People, an international training and consultancy firm. Wherever possible the companies involved are openly discussed, but, for reasons that I hope are obvious, this is not always the case. In some of the more anonymous cases, details may have been altered slightly, either to aid clarity, or to protect the not so innocent!

I am pleased to be able to say that my training and consulting work brings me in contact with far more examples of good practice than bad, but the purpose of this book has not always permitted such a ratio. I hope that my own clients will forgive me for not filling these pages with more stories of their undoubted excellence in this field.

Please regard examples of good practice as merely examples, not role models, and those of bad practice as ways of illustrating the warning signs that line the route towards Key Account Management (KAM).

Preface to the fourth edition

KAM has been with us long enough for the basic theory to be much less of a surprise or a challenge than in times past. The burning question of the moment is much less why or what, but how.

This new edition, a complete rewrite of the earlier third edition, takes as its focus the issue of implementation and the task of 'making it happen'. The supporting weblink has also been revised with this focus in mind.

THE APPLICATION EXERCISES

Most significantly, a series of 'application exercises' have been added at the close of each chapter, to help the reader translate the theory to the real world of their own particular KAM challenge.

Some of these exercises can be tackled single-handedly, but for many it is strongly recommended that you should gather together with those colleagues working on the same KAM challenge, and by so doing advance your own practical implementation: truly 'making it happen'.

About the author

Peter Cheverton is a founding Director of INSIGHT Marketing and People, a global training and consultancy firm specializing in Key and Global Account Management. He has developed an international reputation as one of the leading experts in this challenging area, working 'hands on' with clients in Europe, the Americas, AsiaPacific and Africa.

As well as being the author of this book, now in its fourth edition and used as the standard text by several business schools, he is also the author of *Global Account Management*, *Key Account Management in Financial Services*, *Key Marketing Skills* (2nd edition) and *Understanding Brands*.

Peter spends most of his time helping clients with the implementation of KAM strategies, and regularly presents INSIGHT's *Key Account Management Masterclass* around the world, including London, Aberdeen, Glasgow, Dublin, Paris, Brussels, Amsterdam, Stockholm, Gothenburg, Malmo, Oslo, Vienna, Budapest, Prague, Bucharest, Warsaw, Shanghai, Beijing, Singapore, Kuala Lumpur, Seoul, Tokyo, Melbourne, Cape Town. Johannesburg, Boston, New York and Chicago.

Prior to establishing INSIGHT in 1991, Peter was the European Sales and Marketing Manager for ICI Dulux Paints.

For contact details, please see Chapter 33.

And it was all going so very well...

Have you ever found yourself in front of a new customer and, after 10 minutes of conversation, realized that you are speaking to the wrong person? It could be all sorts of things that are wrong – too junior, too new, too hung up about your price rather than your value. And worse, you're starting to think you know who the right person is, but try going behind your first contact now and they'll cut you off at the knees.

If nothing like that has ever happened to you then maybe it's because you plan your sales calls well, or maybe you're just lucky.... unlike Ken Reilly.

Ken Reilly is in the chemical business. The products he sells are far from the cheapest, but he knows they are the best. His customers are mostly manufacturers of high-quality goods, and most of them rate his products highly. Ken is new, and he's learning, but sometimes it's the hard way.

What makes Ken's products so good is the money they save the customer. They make the customer's process faster, they reduce wastage and they reduce harmful emissions. A dream sell, if you know how to go about it, meaning who to see and what to say.

Ken is calling on a new customer – a potential key account. He doesn't know the people at all, but he has managed to make an appointment with one of the buying team. He puts that down to his persuasive skills with secretaries and, of course, his natural charm.

He's led into a small office; the walls are bare, the carpet is frayed and the desk has been the site of a hundred spilt coffees – but that is not the real problem. The real problem is the buyer, a nice enough man, but the wrong man.

Ken has been talking for 10 minutes, and he's getting nowhere. The buyer is writing things down but, for all Ken can tell, it might be the man's shopping list, or a letter to his mother.

This is a junior buyer, a very junior buyer. He has been with the company for three months, knows next to nothing about the business, still less about manufacturing, and spends most of his time, or so it seems, meeting sales-people who leave him their brochures.

Ken realizes that all this buyer sees is an expensive product – 20 per cent higher than their existing suppliers. He also realizes that he should be talking to someone else, perhaps a more senior buyer who would understand the proposition, or maybe someone on the plant who needs his kind of help, but how can he go past his current contact? He can't just ask to see the boss.

The interview is coming to an end, and the buyer makes a suggestion.

'Why don't you look me up again, in six months, once I've got my feet under the table a little bit?'

Six months! Ken could be out of a job by then.

'Perhaps I could see someone on the plant, someone who might…' but Ken's voice tails off as the buyer gets to his feet.

'Oh no, they're very busy down there, and we can't have reps running about the place. I'll see you in six months.'

And that was final.

Part I

Definitions and purpose

1

The challenge

That Key Account Management is a significant challenge is something of which there is no doubt; if it were so very simple you would hardly be reading this book... So, what is it that makes it such a challenge? Let's begin by saying what it is not: it is not the theory. The theory of KAM (Key Account Management) is as straightforward as could be and, as has been pointed out to me on many occasions by delegates on training workshops, is for the most part plain common sense. The challenge comes in the practice, the practical application in the real world.

The real world is not a friendly place where answers taken from a textbook prove as effective and satisfying as they appeared on paper. For a start, when it comes to KAM, there are very few (if any) rules. This book is not a rulebook; it is a series of pieces of advice, of thought-provoking suggestions, of examples from the experience of others. Most of the changes that appear in this new and fourth edition are in the area of practical application, that being where the need for help is most pressing. Most importantly then, it doesn't aim to tell you what to do, and that's because it can't. Let me explain that comment.

Having said there are no rules, let's state one of the very few that I am happy to insist upon:

> The nature of your KAM practice must start, not with the nature of you, but with the nature of your customers.

And that's the first challenge: your customers are different from other people's, and so must your application of KAM be different. If you are a pharmaceutical company selling to the National Health Service in the UK, then the nature of your KAM will be very different from the way it might look if you were a food manufacturer selling to Tesco. And it's not the difference between a pharmaceutical and a food company that is of most significance here, it's the difference between the NHS and Tesco.

So much is perhaps obvious, but let's go further, but this time stay in the same 'market chain'. If you sell to Tesco and Sainsbury's, the nature of your KAM will be different from how it might look if you sold a step higher up the chain, to Unilever and Proctor & Gamble. Indeed, if you sold to those latter two customers, there would be a world of difference in your application between one compared to the other, as Unilever and P&G are two very different animals.

Rule number 1: You make the rules

What this means is that any rules to be set for KAM must be set by yourselves, not by an outsider who has no intimate knowledge of the nature of your customers. It also means that they must be set by those who do indeed have an intimate knowledge of the customers, which usually means those with direct and regular contact – the sales professionals, the marketing team (it is to be hoped), the logistics folk, the customer service team. The people with least to say in the making of those rules, I would suggest, are the members of the board. Such an idea is usually welcomed by the sales team, but sends shivers of fear and doubt through the minds of senior executives – and that's a challenge.

So, there are no rules other than those you set for yourselves, so be prepared to edit and modify as you read. Now lets add the second challenge, and that is the existence of some very tough choices. How about, for starters: how many key accounts should we have, and who are they? Obvious questions, but how often have I been asked to train people in the practical application of KAM only to find that these choices have not yet been made? Too often.

There was the phone call from a new client who, in answer to my question – 'How many key accounts do you have?' – came smartly back with the answer: 'Seventy-five'. OK, there are no rules, but I have yet to meet a company that can honestly convince me that they can manage 75 key accounts. Worse was to follow, as when I asked how many key account managers there were in the company, the answer was (and I hope I don't make anyone feel bad about this): 'Three'. That's 25 each, which is plain absurd, not to say impossible. In truth, this client had no key accounts – how could they when they aimed to spread their resources so thinly? I asked a few more questions: 'How did that label "key account" help them in allocating resources, time, and money?' – it didn't – 'How did they behave differently with those 75 customers compared with all the others?' – they weren't sure that they did – and most importantly of all, 'How did those 75 customers see their own business enhanced as a result of this label?' – and that was just the problem: they were telling my new client that they didn't see any advantage to them in the relationship…

I can't tell you how many key accounts you should have, but I do know that most people start the journey with ambitions that end up being cut in half once the realities set in. The total of the fingers of two hands is not a bad top limit in most cases. And if you are at the start of this particular journey, then isn't it going to be better to practise KAM with a very few, and do it well, than to attempt it with many and make a mediocre stab at it? I will share with you my views on 'being mediocre' in a later chapter…

What about who they are? Try asking your board that question and don't be surprised if the answers are less than crystal clear. Sometimes the directors don't know. Sometimes they ask their PAs for the report on that issue. Too often they get into an argument, because the director responsible for marketing sees the world differently from the director in charge of logistics, who differs again from the director in charge of R&D, and as for the director in charge of sales… Each function in a company might have its own view of who the most important customers are, and act accordingly – and that's a challenge.

'It's the big ones' – give me a thousand pounds for every time I've heard that as the answer and I'll stop writing books tomorrow. Maybe size matters, but are there not things that might be more important? We will answer this question in Chapter 3, but for the moment be assured that there are, and plenty.

On to the next challenge: as well as no rules and some tough choices, there are some big obstacles. The main obstacle to the successful implementation of KAM is one that is common to almost all, and it's not the customer, and it's not the competition: it's the supplier's own existing organization. Most companies are set up as they are for good reason: its worked, in the past. If KAM is a new venture for your company, don't expect the structure to be right as it is. Even if you have practised KAM for some time it is likely that you have unearthed many an internal issue, many a frustration, many an example of complacency or inertia – two major enemies of successful KAM (for the whole list see Chapter 25). And you thought KAM was just a different way of selling? It is that of course, but also so much more; it's a different way of organizing your whole approach to customers – and guess what, that's a challenge.

STRATEGY OR TACTICS?

Perhaps I'm depressing you with all this talk of obstacles and challenges, but there is good news ahead; indeed I hope that the majority of what is to come is good news inasmuch as it will help you to overcome those obstacles and to meet those challenges. The first piece of good news is that you are bright people, the people reading this book that is. Your choice of reading material is ample evidence of that, as is your interest in this so vital area, and so I can jump straight in to the first 'model', or figure (see Figure 1.1) that I will use to explain the task of KAM. It considers the types of salespeople who might be involved in the task, and I pick on salespeople because, while I will make clear the cross-functional team-selling nature of KAM, salespeople remain some of the most important elements of those teams.

KAM is about more than hard work...

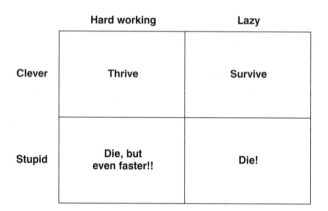

Figure 1.1   *Salespeople*

There are four types of salespeople. First are the hardworking types and the lazy types, and they feature on the horizontal axis of Figure 1.1. Then there are the clever ones and the 'not so clever ones', placed on the vertical axis. We know what happens to each of the combinations of types: the hard-working and clever sales professionals are going to get on – they will thrive. As for the lazy but clever ones, they will at least survive, and sometimes do a whole lot better than that. Being stupid and lazy is clearly a combination with no future, but it is not the worst – that is to be found in the stupid but hardworking sales professional, the sort who upset more customers in a day than anyone else, simply through their sterling efforts.

I could have labelled these axis in a different way, replacing the words on the vertical with 'sales strategy', good at the top, poor at the bottom, and those on the horizontal with 'sales tactics' or perhaps 'selling skills', good to the left and poor to the right, and leave the outcomes as they stand. With regard to selling, what we might mean by 'sales tactics' or 'selling skills' are the nitty-gritty of the task: the ability to ask questions, to make presentations, to handle negotiations, to manage the one-to-one interpersonal relationships. By strategy we mean the big issues: are you in front of the right customer in the first place, and in front of the right people in that customer; have you come with the right team, and are you having the right conversations that will lead you to the right propositions, and can you manage your own company's resources to bring those propositions to reality?

KAM must concern itself much more with those strategic questions than with the tactics of selling. Being 'clever' is a vital requirement, and that doesn't come from rules, and especially not from any rules imposed from the outside. Being 'clever' results from asking the right questions, doing the necessary analysis, and so determining the appropriate strategy.

None of this is easy, and I won't deny the hard work involved, but the purpose of this book is to help you with this challenge, step by step.

2

Why Key Account Management: aggressive or defensive?

THE JOURNEY

I have heard KAM described as a business strategy, and at other times I have heard it described as an inevitability. If the former sounds a positive – let's call it an aggressive – approach, then the latter might appear rather fatalistic, or defensive. In truth, most applications that I have encountered encompass both the aggressive and the defensive, and this is in fact all to the good, as we will see.

KAM is a journey, with all the uncertainties that exist at the outset of such, and with a fair share of surprises to be encountered along the way. It is unlikely to be a short or speedy journey, and there will be inevitable setbacks, and welcome surges forward – both experiences requiring a steady hand to manage appropriately. It may even be that the precise destination is not known at the outset; in this sense KAM might be considered as a journey of exploration.

In this chapter we will list what are perhaps the 10 most common reasons for businesses to head out on their own KAM journeys. I don't expect that they will all apply to your own circumstances, but I do hope that at least two or three will hit your mark. This is the first instance of you needing to edit and modify, and come to your own conclusion.

Being clear about the reason for your journey is important, even if you cannot be certain about the final destination, as it is in the nature of your reasons that we will find the likely nature of your rewards.

THE REASONS

Here then are those '10 most typical' reasons:

1. Customer consolidation – power and professionalism.

2. Global / regional customers demanding a uniform approach and service.

3. Increasingly complex decision-making processes.

4. New purchasing practices.

5. The supplier's own complexity – selling through multiple business units.

6. The growth opportunity requires prioritization of resources.

7. Products alone (neither yours nor your competitors) no longer provide a source of competitive advantage; relationships matter.

8. The desire to sell solutions.

9. The desire to make a positive impact on the customer's business strategy through truly customer-focused value propositions.

10. The pursuit of abnormal returns for abnormal efforts.

If you were an FMCG (fast-moving consumer goods) supplier in the early 1980s it didn't take a genius to see that the number of supermarket chains was falling fast, through acquisition (point 1 above), and that concentrating more resources on to those who were doing the acquiring, and growing fastest, was a good idea – and so KAM was born.

If your customer tells you that from now on you must deliver the same products at the same prices with the same services wherever the customer operates (point 2 above), then you will probably start to coordinate your sales teams around the region / world to ensure that this happens – and so KAM is born.

As customers grow in size, so they often grow in complexity. Selling to the likes of a Pfizer, a Wal-Mart or a BP is a challenging pursuit. Decisions get made behind closed doors, through committees, by functions far beyond the purchasing department, at locations hundreds of miles away from your normal points of contact (point 3 above); new responses must be developed to these increasingly complex decision-making processes – and so KAM is born.

If the purchasing professionals you meet are using new sources of information to make your life difficult, or are demanding the likes of open book trading (point 4 above), then perhaps some new responses are required, responses that arm you against these new pressures, or allow you to accommodate them with confidence – and so KAM is born.

If buyers tell you that, starting next month, they will no longer entertain four different sales representatives calling on them from your company, each with their different story (point 5 above), then you may start thinking about how you can get your act together better, perhaps considering which representative can best represent the interests of all – and so KAM is born.

Being defensive...?

Knowing your motivation...

So, KAM is the result of pressures from outside; the supplier is made to do it. There is good and bad news in this. The good news is that such external pressure tends to make things happen. The bad news is that nobody really wants to do it!

If that were it, then the rest of the story might become rather depressing, but fortunately we have at least five more reasons (to be cheerful?).

Being aggressive?

Reasons 6 through 10 express a rather more aggressive set of motivations: setting out on the KAM journey because it will do something for us, give us an edge, give us competitive advantage.

Some markets are still blessed with sufficient growth opportunities (point 6 above) to demand that you prioritize your resources and chase those that will be the best for you – and so KAM is born.

Point 7 (above) may sound like a defensive one, but in truth it is not; it simply recognizes that success today calls for more than good products: too many suppliers – meaning your competitors – have those in as great an abundance as you. What marks out the winner is the developing the greatest knowledge of the customer and building the most secure position, and doing that calls for the best relationships – and so KAM is born. (This point will be elaborated on more fully through Chapters 5, 6 and 7.)

If you have not yet been urged by your bosses to sell 'solutions' (point 8 above) rather than 'products', then I can only assume you have been 'away somewhere' these last few years. Selling solutions has become one of the necessary claims of any chairman's statement or CEO's address, though too few recognize that it is this aim, perhaps more than any other, that demands a KAM approach. To truly sell a solution you must first understand the customer's problem – so much is clear – but then there is more. If you are to win at the 'solution-selling game' then you must aim to understand the customer's problem *better than they understand it themselves.* You may even have to understand it well before they know they even have it! I will go even further: you will need to understand the customer's business, and their market, better than they understand it themselves.

The 'Holy Grail' of KAM...

Have I gone too far? Is this the realms of fantasy that you were worried about when you picked up this book? Not at all – this is the nature and task and aim of KAM. Consider it this way: do you think it possible that a team of people who work for the supplier (and let's make it a cross-functional team, all of whom are involved with the customer), if they choose to pool their knowledge and resources, should be able to understand the customer, their needs, their market and their business, better than any one individual *inside* the customer? And what if that individual *inside* the customer is the buyer? We are already a good way towards our objective, and yes, KAM is born.

I have elaborated on this point more than the others because in a way this is what we might call the 'Holy Grail' of KAM – the ultimate achievement – because it is from such a position that all the best rewards of KAM will flow. Which takes me to the final two 'reasons to practise KAM' on our list of 10.

You want to be more than a supplier: you want to be a key supplier, perhaps even a strategic supplier; and to achieve this you have to go one better than delivering good products on time and in full. You have to make an impact on the customer's business (point 9 above). If you can achieve this, through truly customer-focused value propositions that are communicated to the right people using the right language, and if you can secure the appropriate reward for those efforts, then I think you know what I am about to say – KAM is born.

I have said that there are no rules of KAM (Chapter 1) other than those you decide for yourself, but surely the last of our 10 reasons for KAM (point 10 above) must be a universal rule; that if you are to exert abnormal effort with your customer (and KAM will certainly involve that if we compare it to 'traditional' selling) then you must expect an abnormal return.

Being aggressive *and* defensive

It may seem to you that reasons 6 through 10 are the better ones. It always sounds better to be aggressive rather than defensive, but herein lies one of the challenges of KAM, one of the internal challenges. Such optimistic and proactive reasons are not always enough to force the changes that are required within a supplier's organization to make KAM work successfully. It is sad, though realistic, to observe that where KAM has been implemented fastest, and most effectively, it has usually been as the result of some shock to the system, a challenge from outside – one of our reasons 1 through 5.

What we see then is a need for a combination of both types of reason: the kick up the backside that will get things moving, and the promise of a reward through your efforts.

YOUR OWN JOURNEY

Know where you are headed...

What are your two or three most compelling reasons, and do they represent a defensive or an aggressive approach to KAM? If your reasons fall on the defensive side, then at least take comfort in the fact that you can use those external pressures to drive the internal changes required to make things happen. You might like to assess the level of urgency required, and so arm yourself with the case for your internal campaign (see Chapters 25 and 26 for more on this). If your reasons are more aggressive, then aim to be clear about the nature of the reward you seek for your efforts – only, don't expect the organization to change overnight just because you think it's a great opportunity!

Then ask: is our challenge local, national, regional or global? The stakes increase as you rise up the scale, as does the scale of the challenge. Don't give yourself a bigger task than is necessary, so aim to be honest about the scope of this customer. For the particular challenges of global account management, which is something a good deal more than KAM with time zones, see Chapter 33.

The final action needed to help define the nature of your journey is to identify the nature of the opportunity. We have been discussing 'reasons for KAM', and whether defensive or aggressive each one of those reasons suggests an opportunity, but let's be more specific. Do you have an opportunity to win new customers? That's one type of KAM journey. Do you have an opportunity to grow your business with existing customers? That's another kind of journey. Or do you see your main activities devoted to defending business already won? That's another KAM journey again. Of course, all three opportunities might exist in the same business, with different customer groups or market segments, and this is one of the reasons (as we will see in Chapter 28) why the selection of key accounts is subsidiary to the selection of markets and segments – the nature of the task will be so very different in these different circumstances. There is no rule against practising all three types, but there is very definitely a rule about not taking on the three tasks in the same way!

THE REWARDS

Having discussed the opportunity, that leads us inevitably to the reward. Rewards come in many ways, and salespeople in particular can be guilty of limiting their horizons in this matter. For them, it's all about volume – that is, if they are what we might call 'traditional' salespeople. It's hardly their fault of course, driven as they are by managers with short-term goals, and rewarded by packages tied to the simplest of measures – volume, volume and volume. For some, the horizons have been broadened by the addition of profitability targets, which brings into the reward equation the question of price and margin. This is good, and a step in the right direction, but the key account manager must go further. How about the following rewards of KAM:

- helping your business to better allocate its resources – in pursuit of greater effectiveness (perhaps even lower costs?) and enhanced profitability;
- building customer relationships designed to secure greater loyalty and longevity, perhaps through the attainment of key supplier status;
- helping you develop new capabilities through the experience of working with challenging customers;
- helping you to understand the true nature of the customer's market, and so their challenges, their ambitions and their needs (and perhaps, with an eye to the 'Holy Grail' of KAM, understanding this better than the customers do themselves);
- helping you win competitive advantage through new value propositions, and not just for the key accounts that take you to these new ideas, but for all the customers in your target market segments;
- helping your business to manage its future through the management of its most important long-term investments – its most important customers.

It is at this point that we must make an important observation: the key account managers are not just sales professionals (Chapter 27 will explore the question of whether they even need to be that); _they are business managers_. And not only should they regard their customer as a business, with its own profit and loss account, and its own cross-functional business team, but also as a vital spark in the engine of the greater business.

Making sure that KAM is good for you...

We have one client who uses KAM for a very singular purpose. Their business relies on continual technical innovation, which is expensive, and often the benefits are short lived.

If they are not careful, these two factors can act as internal brakes: the choice to do nothing can be strangely tempting, with disastrous results in the longer term.

They have chosen to identify their key accounts as those customers that will not only force them to innovate but will support them in their efforts. In practice this usually means customers who will promise to take our client's innovations on board before they are actually begun!

It is always a good idea to innovate alongside customers, but this approach has an added benefit: the customer can be used as a kind of battering ram to break down internal inertia and complacency.

At the start of this chapter I said that many refer to KAM as a business strategy, and so it may be – but take care not to fall into the trap of seeing it as an end itself. There is too much effort (and pain!) involved in the KAM journey for there to have been no better purpose than being able to say that you made it. Some people feel that the joy of travel is in the anticipation and not the arrival, and so that may be – only don't expect to impress your CEO with such sentiments!

APPLICATION EXERCISE

- What are the three most significant reasons for practising KAM in your business?
- Are these internal drivers (from your own organization) or external drivers (from the customer)?
- Do these reasons and drivers represent a 'defensive' or an 'aggressive' approach to the market opportunity?
- What will be the implication of this on your style of, and approach to, KAM?
- Is your challenge principally:
  - Local?
  - National?
  - Regional?
  - Global?
- What will be the implication of this on the nature of the obstacles and requirements?
- Is your opportunity principally:
  - Winning new customers?
  - Growth with existing customers?
  - Defending existing business?
- What will be the implication of this on the nature of your KAM task?

3

What is a key account?
An investment

Perhaps you have key accounts already. So how have they come by that name?

- Are they just the big ones?
- Are they the ones growing the fastest?
- Are they the ones that shout the loudest?
- Are they the ones you mustn't lose?
- Are they the 'jam tomorrow' customers, the ones that offer future profit?
- Are they the ones you want your staff to focus on – to look after the very best?
- Are they the ones where extra effort will bring extra returns?
- Are they the ones that challenge you and improve you?
- Are they the most successful players in their own markets?
- Are they the ones that will bring you kudos with others?
- Are they the ones that will take your business where you want it to go?
- Are they the ones you would most like to 'steal' from your competition?
- Are they the ones that are financially secure (and will pay their bills on time)?

This is a far from exhaustive list (Chapter 24 will discuss some means of compiling your own list as part of the key account selection process), and better definitions almost certainly exist, with greater relevance to your own circumstances and aspirations. It is for you to choose the definition, based on the dynamics of your own industry, your own customers and your own business.

It is unlikely that you will come up with a single issue definition (though the case with which we closed the last chapter came close), and indeed there are great dangers in doing so. Consider the dangerous limitations of some of these possible definitions:

- The ones growing fastest – the business world is awash with 'rapid rise and big crash' stories.
- The ones that shout the loudest – every industry has its loud mouths; does that make them any more important?
- The ones you mustn't lose – and you'll do anything to keep them, even if it kills you.
- Jam tomorrow is not to be dismissed – but from where will today's profits come?
- The ones your staff will focus on – and so do they ignore the rest?
- Stealing from the competition is always fun – but how do you think they are eyeing up your current portfolio?
- The financially secure ones are a safe bet – but how safe can you afford to be?

And of course, I leave the most dangerous of them all to last – it's the big ones.

THE PERILS OF 'SIZEISM'

Consider why your largest customers are the largest – it's all down to the past. It is history that has got them to where they are, and as they say in the advertisements for investment products: 'past performance should not be taken as a guarantee of future potential.' Of far greater importance is to be able to answer the following question: Will they be big in the future – what is the future potential of this customer?

Big is not always best

Selecting key accounts on the basis of their size alone is a dangerous course to pursue. The trap of what we might call 'sizeism' is unfortunately one into which it is all too easy to fall. It is the simplest method of selection of all, so simple that armed with nothing but your sales statistics I would be able to show you your key accounts, and without knowing a single other thing about you, or them – and that should worry you sick.

Picking the winners

I recall how my first sales director took great delight one annual sales conference in telling us how many of our former top-10 customers (by sales volume), from a list only five years old, had dropped out of that list, and in some cases no longer even existed as businesses. This was said neither out of spite nor out of despair on his part, but simply as a clear message to us that times were changing fast in our industry. And then he went on to remind us of those customers we had defined as key accounts five years before, some of them mere striplings at the time, and to point out how our business prospered with each, and how some of them were likely to top the top-10 list at next year's conference. In a fast-changing market, as ours most certainly was, he saw his job as picking the winners – and he had an excellent record.

As well as tying your future to the past, there are other dangers of sizeism (and I make no apology for discussing them at length – this is a problem to be faced head-on). Base your assessments on size alone and it won't be long before your big customers know it, and start demanding the kind of 'attentions' that their size so clearly warrants.

Focus on size, chase size, champion size, and you'll end up with big customers, perhaps at the cost of those medium or small customers who may bring all sorts of benefits (not least of all their margins), or may even be your future. If you had been a supplier to the telecommunications industry before the advent of the mobile phone revolution, and were casting around for customers to call 'key' and using size as your criterion, it is very unlikely that you would have given a second thought to Nokia, one of Finland's larger players in the paper industry.

Build your business around the largest customers and you grow dependent upon them – someone has to fill those factories that you built.

Of course, if you have a business that benefits from economies of scale then big orders from big customers will be very important, but even then, does that make such a customer a key account, or just a big account? This is a distinction that we will develop more fully in Chapters 24 and 25, dealing with account 'classification' and 'distinction'; for now, suffice it to say that the best way to handle such providers of scale may be just to milk them.

And what if you sell into a market where the customers just are big? How can you be serious as a food manufacturer, or a household goods manufacturer, selling into the consumer market if you don't work with the likes of Tesco or Wal-Mart? Ask yourself the question: Are these customers important because they are big, and send us big orders, or are they important because they give us access to those consumers that we target? There is a world of difference.

Perhaps you might claim at least one advantage of sizeism (though I should stress that this hope is on a par with the process of manufacturing silk purses from the ears of domesticated hogs): everyone in the business can see who are the big ones, and understand why you put them on a pedestal – the joy of alignment. But even here there is danger. Look deeper into the eyes of your people from R&D, manufacturing, logistics, finance and customer service, and you might see a range of common concerns: 'they're *too* big, they bully us, you salespeople let them get away with murder, they must be losing us money...' Don't expect too much enthusiasm and team spirit in a cross-functional account team made up from such beliefs.

In Chapter 30 we will look at the vital question of customer profitability, and see how it is all too easy for the largest customers to be the least profitable. No great surprise, you say, surely that is only to be expected? If so (and it doesn't have to be the case by any means), should you be going out of your way to devote even more of your business's valuable resources, not to mention your time, to such accounts?

Can a customer be too big? How would you feel (or sleep at nights) if one customer accounted for more than half of your business? Surely this would make it 'key', but must you get yourself into such a position? I know of several very successful (and highly profitable) companies that lay down rules about such things. The rule that always makes me smile is the one that will not allow any customer to represent more than 15 per cent of their turnover. It makes me smile because I always remember that supplier telling me the shock they dealt to Tesco when they turned down an offer of more business – it would have taken this customer to over 20 per cent. Both sides understood the reasons, and I'm even more pleased to say that the relationship thrives to this day – at a carefully managed and pleasantly profitable 15 per cent.

Size is part of the equation, of course it is, but try to come to it a little later in the assessment. If five other factors determine the customer to be a key account, and it also happens to be your largest customer, then no problem, but starting with size as the first selection criterion does tend to close (or at least blinker) your eyes to all other factors.

This, and other chapters, will I hope serve as an effective curative for what can be a dangerous and business-threatening case of myopia. Of course, just how long-sighted you choose to be, or can be, before the effects of 'wild-blue-yondering' take over, depends on your own market and business circumstances. For some, a year ahead might look like forever, while for others a 10-year plan is quite feasible. Aim to look behind the normal horizons, to stretch the timescales that you traditionally work within. Aim to regard your key accounts, not only as valuable assets today, but also as investments for the future.

THE INVESTMENT

When asked for a one-word definition of a key account, I have no hesitation with offering this one: a key account is an 'investment', of your time, of your colleagues' time, of your resources, of your assets, and all because you see a good return from that investment.

Choosing or being chosen – who makes the first move?

The UK in the 1970s and the 1980s witnessed an enormous growth in the DIY market. If the Englishman's home was his castle, then the moat was dug on Bank Holiday Monday, and the drawbridge came from B&Q. Throughout these growth years, there were big manufacturers of DIY products – the likes of Dulux and Black & Decker – claiming to have built this DIY boom. But, at the same time, there were big retailers like B&Q, Texas, Homebase and Do-It-All, each making just the same claim. There is no question, after the event, that these retailers were the key accounts of those suppliers, but who chose whom?

The truth is that many successful suppliers rode on the back of a retailing revolution – the growth of the out-of-town DIY superstore – and no shame in that, but those who hitched the ride most successfully were those who invested their efforts into these new retailers. Others, who fell by the wayside, failed to make the distinction between the winners and the losers, and failed to make the necessary investment in new ways of working, preferring to stick with those customers who had 'done them proud' in the past – the high-street specialists, the department stores and the supermarkets. Unfortunately for them, these customers were in serious decline, at least in the DIY market, and large amounts of money (subsidies, not investments) were wasted in trying to prop up a fast collapsing edifice. And why? Because they were still big, and had recently been the biggest.

This was the market that I cut my sales teeth on, and of which my first sales director (he of the sales conferences) proved such a good crystal-ball reader. He backed the emerging DIY superstores in preference to the future of our then largest customers (supermarkets, high-street specialists and department stores), despite the fact that those were the very customers with which he had built his own career.

His judgement was based on how he saw the dynamics of the retail market changing. He understood what the department stores and supermarkets were really saying to us, and to all their suppliers. What they said was: 'If you want to keep our business, you need to cut your prices.' What they meant, in the 'subtext' beneath their words, was: 'We don't see our future in DIY.' We backed those retailers who did.

He understood our customers' markets at least as well as they did, and often better, and by achieving that Holy Grail of KAM secured and sustained a level of brand leadership that others would have killed for. He also taught me some of my most valuable lessons in KAM. He once said to me that the single biggest asset for any sales director was to have a degree in horse racing, and the same might be said of a key account manager.

DOES EVERYBODY KNOW?

Knowing, whether it be by the instinct of an old hand or the statistical prowess of a market analyst, is one thing; making sure that everyone else is in agreement with you is quite another. Internal wrangling over such matters is one of the fastest and surest ways to ensure failure. Most importantly of all, agreement on which list of customers represents your key accounts must be clear at the very top of the organization.

I was once asked to convince a management board who were unhappy with the standard of their Key Account Management that they should provide their KA managers with some training. It should be said that they didn't think their folk were all that good, and I was given 30 minutes to convince them that training might help, and would be better than their favoured strategy – firing all the managers and starting again with a new team.

So I asked them a few questions. First I asked them to write down who they thought were their key accounts. There were seven directors in the room and guess what – seven different lists. Having seen them fail that test, I moved on to question number two: Could they define what a key account might look like? Again, seven different answers: the ones that keep the factory running, said the director in charge of production; the ones with the most predictable order patterns, said the director responsible for logistics; the biggest, said the sales director; but the finance director had the most heart-stopping answer of them all: 'Our key accounts are our largest, and least delinquent debtors…' After a little reflection on the nature of their conversation, they were beginning to see why KAM was failing in their business.

You make the rules, but make sure that your definitions are agreed at the very top

APPLICATION EXERCISE

- How would you define and describe a 'key account' appropriately for your own business and market circumstances?
- What would represent an 'exceptional return' on your investment in such a customer?
- Who in your organization needs to know and understand this definition?
- Who in your organization will be required to make changes to their activities, or to their attitudes and behaviours, in order to react positively to this definition?

4

What is Key Account Management?

WHAT'S IN A WORD?

Some people object to the word 'account': 'surely it should be key *customer*', they say; 'calling them accounts makes it sound like we're a bank.'

I justify the use of the word on one ground only, and that is that it represents the customer as an investment made by the supplier in its own future.

Key Account Management is about managing those investments, which is something rather different from selling. Put simply: *Key Account Management is about managing the future.*

MANAGING THE FUTURE

This is never easy, though in principle it's all quite straightforward. Figure 4.1 shows the three things that you have to balance if you are to be successful in this pursuit: your objectives, your resources and the market opportunity.

- The *business objectives* are concerned with where you are trying to get to – the sort of business you want to have in the future.
- The *market opportunity* is a consideration of the forces that will help and hinder. Among the latter are, of course, your competitors. Among the former are those customers that will best help you get to where you want to be.

Business objectives

Market opportunity

Business resources

Figure 4.1 *Managing the future*

- The *business resources* are those things that will support, or constrain, your progress – your capabilities, production, R&D, logistics, money and, not least, your people.

The closer we get to the future, the more our certainties are challenged

So, a very simple model, on a sheet of paper; the task itself is not so easy. First of all, the model is not static; one of this trinity is continually changing, and doing so without your control – the market opportunity. Just as you settle on your objectives and get your resources lined up, off it goes again. Second, and this is one of life's challenges, the closer we get to the future, the less it seems to be as we expected and the more our certainties are challenged. Third, and this is the real killer, we too often start out with the wrong one of the three.

WHERE TO START?

Objectives?

Starting with objectives is of course the easiest approach, and might seem logical, but too many 'hockey-stick graphs' (see Figure 4.2) in business plans project sudden and spectacular growth after long periods of no growth or even decline. When you see such graphs ask two questions: What has changed with the market opportunity, and how are you using your resources differently to take advantage of this? If the answers are nothing and we're not, then ignore the projections for growth – why should they happen just because someone writes them down?

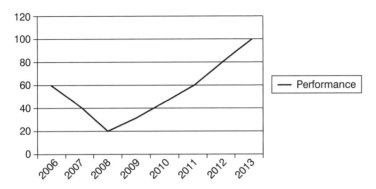

Figure 4.2   *The hockey-stick graph*

Resources?

Sounds sensible, but here's a thought for you. Your current resources are probably ideal for the opportunity of about two years ago. So why start with what you've got today? This can only restrict your view even before you start your journey.

Market opportunity?

Of course, but it's not so easy. You are already plunged into the market, already responding to today's demands. Stepping back and viewing the future is not easy, but it is vital. More than that, it is one of the key purposes and one of the most valuable benefits of the KAM approach.

THE IMPORTANCE OF BALANCE

Balance is everything. In the real world resources tend to lag behind the market opportunity, while the objectives surge ahead of it. Is that how it is in your business? It is in most, so don't feel too bad about it, but what can be done to improve things?

Is it about persuading the bosses to be more free with the cash for resources? Here's an observation that I have found to be true more often than not, and stands in support of those penny-pinching bosses: most businesses have adequate resources for the task, it's just that they don't have them deployed in the right places. While this might support their penny-pinching, it certainly doesn't support their management skills or judgement!

Is it about persuading them to relax their 'stretch targets'? You will need to be silver-tongued indeed for this one!

There is an easier way, and that, perhaps not surprisingly, is the practice of Key Account Management. KAM aims to deploy your resources more effectively, by focusing more of them onto that small number of customers we call key accounts. It deploys them in such a way to ensure that you learn about the *real* opportunities in the customer and in the market, by penetrating deeper into the customer's business, by getting a true understanding of their ambitions, challenges and needs, by aiming to understand their business and their market better than they do themselves. KAM aims to ensure that this understanding is communicated back into your own business, so that cross-functional teams can develop truly customer-focused value propositions. It aims to ensure that after all that effort, you get your just reward, by understanding your true value.

It's a demanding task, but if done well, we start to enjoy the 'virtuous circle' of managing the future through KAM, where improved knowledge of the opportunity allows better deployment of the resources, which results in yet better understanding of the opportunity... and so it goes on (see Figure 4.3).

Figure 4.3 *Getting the right balance: the virtuous circle*

Getting this balance right is important for all sorts of other reasons. Putting the wrong resources in front of the customer will have all sorts of bad outcomes: if the resource is too much, then profitability is going to suffer (only you probably won't know it, as most businesses don't measure such things), and if it's too little, you risk letting the customer down – and we know where that leads.

Being realistic about objectives is important, and realism will come from the true understanding of our virtuous circle. Indeed, realism is a vital tenet of KAM, as opposed to the bragging and exaggeration too often found in traditional sales forecasts!

Realism shouldn't be seen as any lack of vigour or ambition. Wild hopes may seem brave, but they can be the source of a kind of stress that pulls you and your business apart at the seams. George Soros, the international financier, said that when he was hopeful he didn't sleep at nights – it was worrying that made him feel secure!

Finally, it is only in the context of this balance that you can properly define your key accounts. Let's say you are a manufacturer of a food product.

Chasing the big guys...

If your business objective is to achieve dominant market share, with a standardized, low-cost product (*objectives*), then you must find customers that will accept standardization and will provide the volume required (*market opportunity*). If you have the production capacity, and enjoy the economies of scale derived from large orders (*business resources*), then you might find a happy balance in identifying your key accounts as the major food supermarket chains. Change any of the elements in this analysis and you may need to change your key accounts.

Chasing the quality guys...

A business with restrictions on its scale of production (*business resources*), cannot take full advantage of the economies that come with large orders. Indeed, they become a burden, and the business may choose to avoid the larger customers. And if economies of scale don't apply, then why restrict yourself to low-value sales to the largest buyers? If there are customers that demand greater added value (*market opportunity*), perhaps you can secure a premium price and greater profits by acting as a quality producer (*objectives*). Such a supplier might regard specialist or up-market food retailers as its key accounts.

Chasing the small guys...

Looking at another example and taking a different starting point, let's say you are in the biotech industry and you aspire to a reputation for leading-edge technology, gaining competitive advantage from a highly differentiated product rather than volume and market share (*objectives*). Let's also say that there are customers in your market that require complex, high-tech, bespoke solutions to very specific problems (*market opportunity*). If you have an R&D department well placed to work on a wide range of different projects and product applications (*business resources*), then your key accounts need not be huge; they will be defined more by the value of the projects involved, financially, and in how they enhance your reputation.

GUESSING, OR MAKING THE FUTURE?

John Maynard Keynes was in the business of predicting the future, like any economist, but he was honest enough to express his doubts; there were only two certainties, he said: death and taxes.

If KAM is about managing the future, how certain do we need to be about what is in store, and how brave should our predictions be? Can we go even further, to suppose that we might even take a part in making the future happen?

Let's just compare two philosophies of 'making-it-happen': two extremes. We might label them the *'Viking'* and the *'gently does it'*.

Viking...

The 'Viking' philosophy...

This one argues that you should row onto the enemy shore, disembark your troops and burn your boats. That way, making things work is your only option. Success in such circumstances is bold, daring and the stuff of legend. Failure is brutal and unsung.

...or gently does it?

The 'gently does it' philosophy...?

This one argues that you should hold offshore, viewing the enemy through long-range binoculars, looking for signs of weakness, hoping that they might fall into a hole of their own digging, and then creep ashore to take their place. Success is met by praise of your great wisdom and tactical genius. Failure brands you a coward.

How fast do we expect the future to arrive?

Don't expect KAM to be a quick fix. The essence of KAM, as we will see, is in building relationships, and this takes time. If your sales objectives are short term and call for big volume increases then you might be better placed seeking these from what we might call 'opportunistic customers' (see Chapter 24) rather than key accounts. There is an essential conflict between building relationships based on trust and pressuring the customer for short-term sales volume.

Sales growth targets are part of the real world, but don't expect to satisfy them solely through KAM, and certainly don't compromise your future security by 'abusing' your KA relationships.

SANITY CHECKS

In Chapter 2 we identified three particular opportunities or objectives that might determine the nature of your KAM journey:

- winning new customers;
- growing the business with existing customers;
- defending existing customers and business.

Let's consider each of these objectives in the light of the model for managing the future (Figure 4.1), looking to see whether we can achieve a proper balance. I regard this as a kind of sanity check to our aspirations.

Winning new customers

- *The market opportunity.* Are your competitors failing any of these target customers? Have you segmented the market to identify the customers with the best combination of attractiveness and accessibility? Have you identified the customers where your value proposition will be of most interest?
- *Your resources.* Do you have a unique value proposition good enough to break down the barriers to entry? Do you have the necessary 'hunter' skills to open the doors? ('Hunters' will be fully described in Chapter 7.) Is your support team deployed in the right manner to seize the opportunities?

Growing the business with existing customers

- *The market opportunity.* Do you know what percentage of their business the customer will grant to any one supplier? Do they have plans for new products or services? Do you understand their ambitions and their worries with regard to those new products or services.
- *Your resources.* Do you have the necessary 'farmer' skills to develop new opportunities? ('Farmers' will be fully described in Chapter 7.) Are you able to penetrate their decision-making processes? Is your support team deployed in the right manner to identify new opportunities and project manage the responses?

Defending existing customers and business

- *The market opportunity.* Will your customers remain loyal to 'key suppliers'? Is it possible to sustain competitive advantage against new entrants? Will your competitors aim to break down the barriers to entry through new business propositions?
- *Your resources.* Can you build barriers to entry, through relationships and through tailored solutions? Is your support team sufficiently 'locked-in' with the customer?

And you?

Take a moment to consider the balance, or imbalance, of objectives, resources and opportunity in your own circumstances. To what sort of 'making-it-happen' philosophy do you adhere? Do the sanity checks find you sane, or dysfunctional? And where should you be putting your effort in order to improve your chances of managing the future as you wish it to happen. (I don't want to prejudice your answer, but for most people extra effort spent on the 'virtuous circle' pays dividends, which is why, of course, KAM is so important.)

A WORKING DEFINITION

I say 'working' because the idea of KAM as 'managing the future' is only that: an idea. For the day-to-day task we will want something a little more tangible, a little more robust. It is of course for you to determine your own definition of KAM in this regard, but I have given below two examples – one very simple, the other a little more detailed – that have been used with success by others. I don't recommend them as a template, and still less as a set of rules, only as an example of the kind of thing that you might aim to work towards.

We start with the simple definition – KAM is:

- developing the nature of the customer relationship in order to enhance understanding and to identify the true opportunity;
- aligning the business resources to act on that enhanced understanding, in order to secure competitive advantage and to enhance profitability.

Or, for a more detailed exposition – KAM is:

- a long-term investment of resources into a small number of customers that offer an exceptional return for that investment;
- the management of cross-functional business teams, with clearly defined goals, roles and obligations;
- the desire to understand the customers' business, and their challenges, better than the customers do themselves;
- the development of truly customer-focused value propositions, designed to achieve competitive advantage and key supplier status;
- the creation of formal written plans for each key account, to be shared across the whole business;
- using customer profitability as the final measure of success.

What KAM is not

I'm so keen to avoid pushing any particular definition on to you, that it may be more useful (and I will feel less guilty) to list those things that, by this point in the book, it is becoming obvious what *KAM is not*:

- KAM is not short-term. The implementation of KAM is unlikely to bring any immediate improvement to the bottom line, though it must be able to show what kind of improvements will be made, and to a realistic timescale.
- KAM is not a sales initiative. Any attempt to implement KAM by sales professionals working alone is almost certainly doomed to failure. It is a cross-business and cross-functional business process.
- KAM is not for loners. Teamwork is everything, and the qualities of leadership come at a premium.
- KAM is not a tactical response to customer pressure. If you feel the need to fight with your customers, look for another approach – KAM must be a collaborative activity between supplier and customer.
- KAM cannot be implemented with large numbers of customers.

Some things to avoid

THE KAM MODEL

There is such variation in the KAM task that to condense it into a single model is probably unwise, but I have been asked so many times to do this, that I offer the following as a 'best attempt' (and I hope that the peculiarity of your own circumstances don't lead you to add: 'at a bad job').

Figure 4.4 shows four elements to the KAM task. The elements are not wholly distinct from each other, and they are not necessarily sequential. They split into two pairs: one pair representing the investment side of KAM, the other representing the reward – the return on that investment. The analysis of the customer and their market is a major task, and a significant investment of time and effort, but on its own it doesn't guarantee any reward. Similarly, building a relationship with the customer is a significant investment, perhaps of several people's time, but on its own it brings no reward.

The rewards of KAM come from the selectivity of your analysis and relationship management: with whom you choose to do it. And they come from the results of that hard work – the value propositions that you create.

The rest of this book will take us through these elements, not in any rigid order, sometimes leaping from one to another and back again, just as it will be in real life.

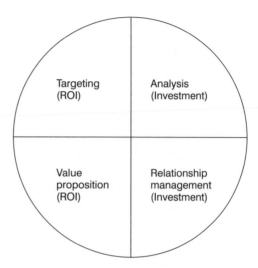

Figure 4.4   *The KAM model*

APPLICATION EXERCISE

- Assess the balance between objectives, resources and market opportunity in your own business:
  - Where are the 'misfits' or 'inconsistencies'?
  - What actions are required to remove these 'misfits' or 'inconsistencies'?
- How would you define 'Key Account Management' appropriately for your own business, market and customer context?
- What would represent an 'exceptional return' on your investment in KAM:
  - for an individual customer;
  - for your business?
- Who in your organization needs to know and understand this definition?
  - Where are the priorities to ensure understanding?
- Who in your organization will be required to make changes to their activities, or to their attitudes and behaviours, in order to react positively to this definition?
  - Where are the priorities for change to occur?
  - How will you begin the change process?
- Which parts of the 'KAM Model' will you need to focus most attention on:
  - targeting;
  - analysis;
  - relationship management;
  - value proposition?
- Given that particular focus, will you be largely in the 'investment' phase, or the 'return on investment' phase of the KAM journey?
- What are the implications of that for your business?

Part II

Analysis: opportunity and value

5

Knowing the market, knowing your value

THE OPPORTUNITY CHAIN

Hindsight is a wonderful thing, making us all out to be the best of strategic thinkers and tacticians, but its greatest benefit, if we are wise (rather than just 'smart') is that it helps us to learn. In Europe we can all look back and see why those agrochemical companies who tried to persuade us to love, and buy, genetically modified foodstuffs failed, and spectacularly. They had great technology, they had a history of success in North America, and they had a caseload of benefits for the farmers who might buy their seeds. But then came the problems, beyond the farmers. Focusing on the benefits of greater crop yield and lower pesticide use, as they did, they all too easily failed to look further down the chain, through to the wholesalers and the food producers, and on to the retailers and the consumers, which was where of course (hindsight permitting) their problems lay.

Fired up by the press, environmental groups and in some cases the government, consumers were soon showing their wariness of such 'Frankenstein foods', and retailers were quick to seize on a point of competitive advantage by declaring that their shelves were free from such things. And the seed suppliers, all the way back up the chain? All this opposition took them by surprise, and wrecked their plans to the point that they as good as gave up.

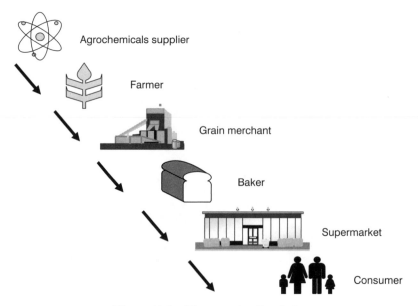

Figure 5.1   *The opportunity chain*

Understanding the market beyond the customer is vital

We all work in a chain – the one we have been discussing is shown in Figure 5.1 – some of us closer to the end user than these seed suppliers, some of us yet further away. The reason I call them 'opportunity chains' is that we have to analyse their dynamics to see where the true opportunities lie, for our proposition, for our value and for our reward.

Looking for the hotspots

What we must look for are what we will call the 'hotspots', of which there are two principal types:

- the hotspots where the decision is made to buy or not buy;
- the hotspots where our value impacts.

In the case we have been discussing, and simplifying things a little, we might say that the decision hotspot happened 'down the chain' somewhere between the consumer and the retailer, while the value hotspot was 'up the chain' with the farmer, as shown in Figure 5.2.

And here we come to the nub of the problem – when these two hotspots are separated, and by such distance in the chain, then it is very likely that the value of the offer will be eroded by the time it reaches the point of decision to buy. In this case, it had more than eroded; it had become negative value.

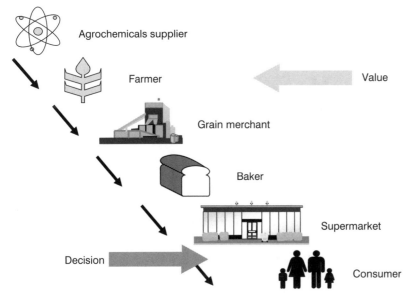

Figure 5.2 *The hotspots in the opportunity chain*

So, what is the moral of this tale? Is it that we must always aim to work at the far end of the chain, with the end user? Not at all, and just as well, as many of us simply don't have that opportunity. The moral is in fact one of the vital tenets of Key Account Management:

It's the hotspots that matter

Aim to identify the hotspots, and so understand the nature of your own value.

If the hotspots are with the end user or consumer, then that must be where you focus your attention; this is the case in the world of FMCG (fast-moving consumer goods), but in many B2B (business to business) circumstances the hotspots will be higher up the chain.

The following analytical exercise is one well worth doing for the opportunity chain that you occupy with your own key account:

- Draw out the players in the 'opportunity chain', through to the end user:
  - Note the main lines in the logistics supply chain (the flow of product).
  - Note the lines of influence on the final decision.
  - Are we biased towards the supply chain or the lines of influence?
- Where is the value created by our offer:
  - inside the customer, or beyond?
- Where are the key decisions, regarding our offer, taken:
  - inside the customer, or beyond?

- Is there a separation between these two 'hotspots', and if so:
  - what is the impact on our value?
  - What can be done to protect our value?
- Where in the chain do we currently have good understanding, and good contacts?
  - Where in this chain do we need to develop better understanding and better contacts?
  - At what points in the chain do we need to 'sell', and where will we need to 'influence'?

Value inside the customer is good ...value beyond may be even better...

A phrase appears in this exercise that needs explaining further: 'inside the customer, or beyond?' Figure 5.3 illustrates some of the differences between value inside or beyond the customer. It is to be hoped that your product or service gives both kinds, but let me see if I can make you feel just a little guilty for a moment. Which of these two types of value is the more important if you are seeking to develop a long-term relationship with the customer, and wish to be viewed as a key, or strategic supplier? And which of these types of value do you spend most of your time focused on, and put under pressure for, in your discussions with the customer? It is quite common for the answers to the first of these questions to be 'beyond', and the answer to the second to be 'inside'. If that is so, then it is usually for two reasons: because it is easier to measure the value 'inside' and because the people you meet with in the customer (the buyers) focus their attentions there. This is not to say that value 'beyond' cannot be measured, nor that we shouldn't seek out those in the customer that do care about such value (see Chapter 6) – indeed, it is precisely to achieve these two things that we practise Key Account Management.

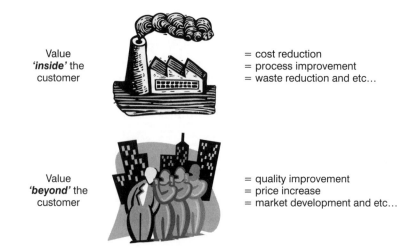

Value **'inside'** the customer

= cost reduction
= process improvement
= waste reduction and etc...

Value **'beyond'** the customer

= quality improvement
= price increase
= market development and etc...

Figure 5.3 *Value inside, or beyond the customer?*

The team investment

Two important considerations become evident at this point. The first is that you can hardly do this kind of analysis on your own – you will need the assistance of colleagues from other departments and functions within your own company, and you will need the assistance of the customer. We begin to see why KAM is described as a team activity. The second consideration is that this kind of analysis takes time and effort, and cannot be done for every customer. Here we see an example of the kind of thing that distinguishes a key account from the rest; the amount of analysis that you are prepared to 'invest'.

Acting on the analysis

And after the analysis, we come to the all-important question: what are you able to do about it? One of the reasons for calling a customer a key account is that you are stating your intention to behave differently – to understand them better, to understand your own position better, and to enhance your own value and reward.

If we return to the case of the supplier of genetically modified seeds, what would you do? There are two broad choices if you find yourself working in a chain where the two hotspots are separated: change where the decision is made (great if you can, but this is seldom easy, and in the case we are describing, given the dominance of retailers in the market, almost impossible), or change the nature of your value.

Rather than looking at yield, you might look to issues such as product quality, or freshness, or product appearance, or extended shelf life, or improved availability, or extended seasons, or health advantages, or absence of pesticides... in other words, value that might impact on the retailer or the consumer. Knowing exactly where to look only comes from knowing the dynamics and the trends of the market, which is why you hear me repeating so often the assertion that KAM is so much more than 'selling'.

A combination of consumers demanding 'greener' products and supermarkets seeking competitive advantage by offering products free of anything that could be construed as 'harmful' has led retailers to seek better evidence for the greenness and cleanness of their suppliers' offers, often through the provision of what are called 'food passports' (a record of where the product came from, how it was grown, how it was treated, and how it was processed and transported). A seed supplier wishing to help their customer, the farmer, must understand the pressures farmers are under as a result of such trends, perhaps developing seeds that require lower pesticide application or that leave less residue. Perhaps they might try to influence the consumer's understanding of what 'harmful' means – after all, pesticides help ensure disease-free food. Perhaps they can seek to agree standards with the food industry, including the supermarkets. And this is all a great deal more than 'selling'.

Case studies

As this is such a vital issue for KAM, it will be worth considering a few more examples. The following case studies explain and explore the need for opportunity chain analysis, each with its own 'angle' on the task.

Knowing what you sell – paper, or packaging solutions?

A company sells different types and grades of paper used in the packaging industry. The immediate customer is the 'converter': the company that takes the paper and other products and turns them into finished packaging, whether it be a humble food carton or a glossy box for an upmarket perfume. Figure 5.4 shows the different markets into which the converter sells – the opportunity chain for the paper supplier.

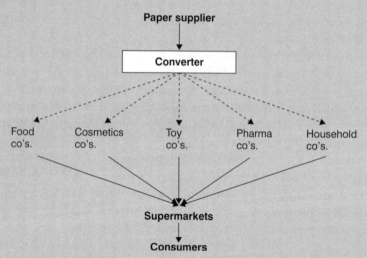

Figure 5.4 *The packaging chain*

I once worked with a paper supplier that denied they had any need to 'independently' understand the market beyond the converter, as the converter would tell them all they needed to know, case by case. If they had meant that they aimed to understand the markets 'in partnership' with the converter, then I would have been happy, but unfortunately they meant that they would simply do as they were told.

This was of course a buyers' paradise, for the buyers chose to tell only what they saw as useful in the negotiation. 'Our market is driven by cost,' they said, citing the household goods customers as their example. So much was true, but what they didn't say was the range of other values that mattered to other customers: the food companies requiring high standards of hygiene, the perfume and cosmetic manufacturers concerned principally with image, the toy producers looking for safety above all else, the garden chemicals companies eager to see longevity and durability.

So costs were driven downwards, and the supplier was steadily commoditized. When the buyers had the company lying prostrate on the floor, they delivered their next set of demands: 'We need paper that will improve hygiene levels, allow products to "glow in the dark", be non-toxic, and super tear-resistant...'

So the supplier works on those new values but, from their position as a commoditized and downtrodden supplier of paper, they never quite managed to achieve their just rewards as a supplier of packaging solutions, and all because they didn't think they needed to 'independently' understand their customer's markets.

Clever idea, poor reward...

It's fairly easy to have clever ideas, and to come up with novel solutions to problems, but so much harder to get the reward you deserve. The last case considered the plight of a paper supplier; let's turn to the problems of their customer: the manufacturer of those cardboard cartons.

The carton supplier was approached by a soup manufacturer looking for an alternative packaging solution to the standard tin – they wanted a cardboard tub.

The packaging supplier knew little of their client's challenges, and worse, rather than making enquiries proceeded to make some assumptions on their behalf. Cartons were not as good as tins or bottles: they were less durable, more likely to be damaged in transit, liable to leak, and would have a markedly shorter shelf life. The client could only be looking for a low-cost solution and so the carton supplier cut their costs and margins to oblige.

...fresh out of value

They won the contract and celebrated, only to find, when they saw the customer's product on the supermarket shelf, what an opportunity they had missed. In the supermarket, where a tin of soup might sell for £0.60, a carton of soup might sell for four times as much at £2.40. Why? Because soup in a carton is 'fresh' soup, 'up-market' soup, 'added-value' soup, 'gourmet soup', and it is all down to the new packaging that enables the supplier to communicate these positions.

The supplier underrated their own importance and value because they didn't understand what the customer was really looking for. In this case they could see their error because the result appeared on a very public supermarket shelf. How often have you committed this sin and never been any the wiser?

Is the customer always the one who pays the bill?

Let's turn in this last case to a happier outcome. A company supplies reusable plastic trays and crates for the delivery of fruit and vegetables to super-markets. While this is a standard item now, in the past there were various methods of getting the tomatoes to the shop floor, mostly involving cardboard boxes that might collapse at vital moments, and that had to be disposed of, with all the problems that might entail. So the plastic tray or crate was a great new idea – saving money, reducing damage and wastage, and significantly more environmentally friendly.

> The company might have approached the fruit and vegetable suppliers, the people who were going to use the trays and crates, and the people who would therefore receive the supplier's invoices, but there were problems there. For one thing, there were hundreds of these suppliers, and for another, they tended to be traditional and conservative – unlikely to change to this new method of handling their products. So the tray and crate supplier took a different tack, knowing the nature of their value as a result of their analysis of the opportunity chain.
>
> They regarded the supermarkets as their key accounts, even though they would receive no payment from them. The supermarkets had plenty to gain from their product – less damage, greater hygiene, easier backdoor and shopfloor handling, and no problem of disposal. If the supermarkets accepted their proposal then they would instruct their own suppliers to make use of these trays and crates, making the sale for the supplier so much easier.

Internal chains

So far we have considered chains as being made up of separate commercial entities – the customer, the customer's customer, and so on through to the end user – but we might also encounter 'opportunity chains' that exist within the customer itself: the supply chain.

Figure 5.5 illustrates one such, that of a hospital and the departments concerned with sourcing, managing and using surgical instruments. A particular supplier of surgical instruments, in pursuit of competitive advantage in a market that has become focused on price and where it is hard to argue any kind of 'value' to the buyers, is launching a new product – the 'procedure pack'. This new item aims to do the customer's thinking for them, delivering a complete pack of all the items required for any particular operation, or 'procedure'. It has several advantages over the old method of selling instruments as individual items, not least the question of safety at the point of use – there being no risk of the surgeons finding themselves without an important instrument at a vital moment.

Figure 5.5 *The hospital 'supply chain'*

The supplier presents the idea to the buyer, who rejects it. All the buyer sees are premium priced products, gathered together in a box instead of sold individually. It is clear to the supplier that their value 'hotspots' are to be found 'beyond' the buyer, with those who physically move or manage or use the instruments, but that the decision-making 'hotspot' is resolutely stuck in the hands of a 'gate-keeping' buyer – the same problem encountered in our very first example, that of the seed supplier. This supplier is up to the challenge however, and sets about fully understanding the nature of their value beyond the buyer, as shown in Figure 5.6.

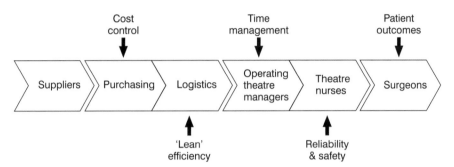

Value is in the eye of the beholder

Figure 5.6   *The nature of value in the supply chain*

Now comes the choice; which value to pick on? In theory, the intensity of the supplier's value increases as we move to the right-hand side of the chain – saving lives is 'more valuable' than smoothing the path of the logistics people. But this is 'in theory'. What if there have been no incidents 'in practice' suggesting any kind of problem with the old method of sourcing? What does this theory mean in any case to a buyer expected to save money from a shrinking budget and who is focused on financial measures of performance?

The supplier chooses to focus on the value brought to the operating theatre managers – the procedure pack saves them time, often as much as 40 minutes per operation. Now time can be turned into money, and so a value proposition can be put to the buyers in their own language. What the supplier is doing, of course, is bringing those two hotspots (value and decision) closer together. And better still, in the hands of a skilled account manager, it will not be the sales person that argues the case, but the operating theatre manager, appealing to their own buyer to source this new 'valuable solution', armed of course with the necessary information by the supplier.

That the procedure pack has become the norm in this particular market is evidence of the success of the approach, but that success should not lead us to underestimate the effort involved. This was not something that could have been achieved by a sales professional working alone. This called for a cross-functional supplier team, and for an investment of that team's time in analysing the opportunity chain and the nature of their own value inside that chain. It called, in short, for Key Account Management.

COMPLEX NETWORKS

The examples discussed so far have all described the opportunity chain as a straight line, but the truth of the real world is often more complex than this relative simplicity. Often we find ourselves working inside networks (not to say spiderwebs) of competing influences and decision makers. This added complexity doesn't alter the principle of opportunity chain analysis, but is certainly does raise the nature of the challenge, and in so doing argues yet more strongly for the importance of conducting such analysis.

Figure 5.7 illustrates (in a much simplified and somewhat stylized form, it should be stressed) one such complex network, that of the National Health Service in the UK.

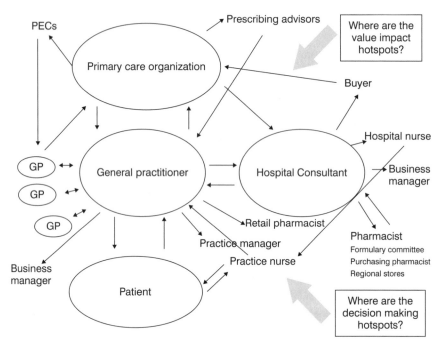

Figure 5.7 *The NHS network in the UK (much simplified and abbreviated)*

This is the situation facing any pharmaceutical supplier, and it is increasingly true that it will be to those suppliers that best understand this complexity, and best navigate their way through its ever-changing form, that the victories will go. Account management has become a vital strategy for many pharmaceutical companies (replacing the traditional approach of large field sales teams focused on 'call rates' and 'coverage') precisely because the complexity of these networks has not only increased, but has also become a real barrier to entry.

Sales professionals operating alone in such a market can no longer hope to gain access to the right people, and even if they do manage to get through the doorway, they are hardly likely to be able to argue the right case, or deliver the appropriate value proposition. Account management has developed here in a form unique to its circumstance (remember that golden rule form the very first chapter?), something that we might call 'network management'. There is no one entity that on its own determines the future success or otherwise of the supplier; it is down to a network of entities, some of which hardly know the impact they have on others.

Managing a complex opportunity network

Our last example in this chapter considers the case of a paint supplier, not one concerned with decorative paint such as we use in our homes, but one that supplies the kind of paint used to repair damaged cars, often called 'refinish paint'. Its traditional view of the market chain, and so its 'traditional opportunity', is shown in Figure 5.8.

Managing complex networks – the route to competitive advantage

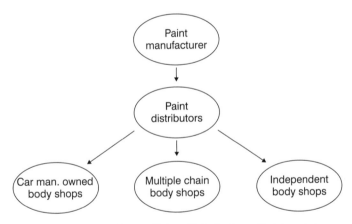

Figure 5.8 *The 'traditional' chain for refinish paint*

The paint is sold through distributors to three kinds of body shop, and it is fairly clear who the key accounts will be in this set up – the all-powerful distributors. All-powerful, and also in control of the main opportunities, managing their paint suppliers as simple providers of products while they (the distributors) come up with the value-added solutions, and the added-value rewards. This was the picture before the supplier started to analyse the opportunity chain more deeply.

Figure 5.9 shows the addition of a key group of people, the end users, motorists like ourselves, car hire firms, and the like. But this is still not the full story. For that, we have to consider the dynamics of this chain in real life.

Just consider what you do if you are unlucky enough to damage your car and need to get it repainted. Your first port of call isn't even on this map: it's the insurance company – an 'external' player, but one that will affect the paint supplier's future prospects significantly.

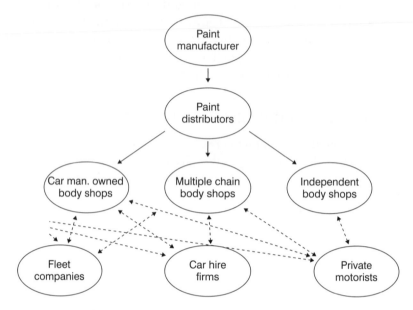

Figure 5.9   *Adding the end users to the chain*

If the insurance company sends the motorist to a body shop that stocks the supplier's products then fine, but if not…? In the past, the answer to this issue (always known, but rarely acted on) was to have large sales teams chasing the widest possible distribution, and so hoping the company will win more often than it loses by the insurance company's actions.

Such an approach was expensive, and failed to act on the true dynamics of the chain. So, what to do? Perhaps the insurance companies could be influenced in their decisions?

Before coming to any fast conclusion we should complete the picture of the network (or market map, as many describe it), by adding the insurance companies, and also the final 'external' player – the motor car manufacturer. This is shown in Figure 5.10.

We all know that car manufacturers no longer make their money just selling cars (and that too many fail to make *any* money by selling cars); they look increasingly for their profits from the repair of cars, servicing of cars, the spare parts and so on. It is vital for them that when we crash our car we actually take it to one of their own managed or franchised body shops.

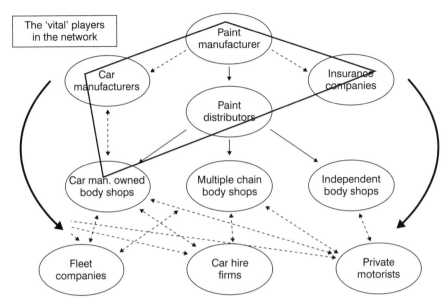

Figure 5.10   *The full 'opportunity network'*

Warranties have been the traditional mechanism for ensuring this, but could there be another solution?

Now we have the full picture, we can consider the kind of 'solution' the paint supplier might bring to the needs of this complex network. First, they concentrate on those that they see as the 'vital players' in the network. And how do they come to this particular grouping? It is based on their analysis of the 'hotspots' – the value, and the decision-making hotspots.

Then, the supplier approaches the motor manufacturer: 'In return for you stocking our product in all your controlled body shops, we have a means of bringing more customers to those body shops,' they say.

They also approach the insurance company: 'In return for you sending your clients to the body shops we recommend, you will be paid a commission,' they say. A key part of this proposition is that this commission will be paid, not by the paint supplier, but by the motor manufacturer.

They also approach the distributor: 'Please keep delivering the product,' they say.

So who is the key account now? Is it any one entity, or is it in fact the network? If it is, then we are looking at the task of Key Network Management, and a challenge well beyond the capacity of any sales professional acting alone.

A final thought

This has been a long chapter, with several examples, each aiming to stress the same basic point: understand the true nature of your customer's market, and so understand the true nature of your own value. But, on some very rare occasions, we might even go one step further, aiming to break the mould of that market and to establish a whole new dynamic in the opportunity chain.

Not for sales alone…

This is what happens when new technologies replace old ones (digital cameras, for instance, or mobile phone technology), when new business models oust old and fusty ones (budget airlines, for instance, or internet shopping). If you have the opportunity to break the mould of your own opportunity chain, then please don't leave it to the sales force. Here, more than in any of the examples used so far, we see the need for a truly cross-functional team, wedding sales with marketing, R&D with manufacturing, and senior management with those that carry out the work at ground level. In other words, Key Account Management.

APPLICATION EXERCISE

Select a market segment, and a key account within that segment:

- Draw out the 'opportunity chain' through to the end user:
    - Start with the logistics supply chain.
    - Include the lines of influence.
- Where is the value created by your offer?
    - Inside the customer or beyond?
- Where are the key decisions (the ones that affect your future) taken?
    - Inside the customer or beyond?
- Is there any 'misfit' between these points of value and decision?
    - If so, do you need to change the nature of your value proposition?
    - Are you able to change the nature of the decision-making process?
- Where in this chain do we currently have good understanding, and good contacts?
    - Where in this chain do we need to develop better understanding and better contacts?
    - Is this about selling, influencing, or understanding?
- Who from your team will be best placed to develop this?

6

Knowing the people,
knowing your value

THE 'OPPORTUNITY SNAIL'

The last chapter urged key account managers to invest time in looking beyond the entities with which the traditional sales professionals spend their time – the immediate customers. This chapter urges them to look beyond the *people* that the traditional sales professional will spend most of their time with – the buyers.

It is no great surprise that, without an active plan to do otherwise, customer contacts tend to settle down to a few regular meetings with the same faces. Most commonly these are faces within the purchasing department. The feeling of comfort and stability that this can bring is dangerously illusory: when the face changes so can your fortune. Genuine security is usually the result of deep relationships with as broad a range of contacts as possible.

Even while the face remains the same, the supplier is in danger of missing out on the real opportunities. Working with a gatekeeper buyer (what I heard someone once call the 'abominable no-man') can be a very limiting experience. We saw in the last chapter, with the cases of the paper supplier or of the carton supplier or the surgical instruments supplier, how the buyer in each case was not exactly eager to recognize the supplier's true value.

If we consider the way that ideas and decisions are generated in the customer's organization, we might begin to see the way to uncovering real opportunities, whether for new business or to add value to existing arrangements.

Let's consider, as an example, the way that a particular customer goes about deciding to launch a new product, one to which another company hopes to be a supplier. The customer is an FMCG (fast-moving consumer goods) company, the manufacturer of a number of leading food and confectionery brands, a company like Unilever, Nestlé or Mars. Our supplier in this example supplies food flavours, high-specification products of significant value to the customer. The supplier's principal contact is with the purchasing department, but is this where the real opportunities lie?

Figure 6.1 shows an example of what we will call the 'opportunity snail', as it exists in this customer. The snail represents the typical route that a new idea takes as it develops on its journey from 'wouldn't it be great?' through to a product launch. In our FMCG company, the initiator might typically be the marketing department, the centre of the snail, with a hundred bright ideas a year.

Figure 6.1 *The opportunity 'snail'*

Each of these ideas proceeds through a series of checks and developments, often called 'stage gates'. These include: market research, to see if the market is interested in the product; R&D, to see if it can be made; manufacturing, to see if full-scale production is viable; purchasing, to source the raw materials; back to manufacturing to make the materials; and then on to sales and distribution to get it into the market. This snail is of course something of a simplification, as in reality there would be a complex series of loops, and loops within loops, but in its simplified form it serves an important purpose, illustrating the serious problem of making contact with the customer only at the outer edge.

The limitations of 'the mediocre interface'

Figure 6.2 shows such a circumstance, the 'mediocrity' of a single interface – sales professional to purchasing professional. I refer to this as a mediocre interface because it is so very clearly not good enough. It may suit normal times, the handling of repeat orders for an established product, but how will it fare with the challenge of a new opportunity or a new obstacle? We should not be satisfied with being mediocre of course; it is hardly an aspiration to be encouraged (who, after all, ever remembers Alexandra the Mediocre?).

Figure 6.2 *The 'mediocre interface' – sales: purchasing*

Here are just some of the limitations of this interface. What will the buyer be interested in? Price, price, terms, and perhaps price (though see the chapters in Part IV for an account of a more varied purchasing repertoire). Is this the area where the supplier has the most to offer? If so, then be happy with this interface, but the very fact of your reading this book makes me suspect this is not your own situation. Worse, chances are that others, further inside the snail, have already made the real decisions on suppliers; specifications are already set and there is little you can do as a supplier to improve your chances other than talking money. Buyers are often the last to know about new initiatives in their company (though again, see the chapters in Part IV for a different view of the 'modern buyer'), often for reasons of security as much as anything else – talking to suppliers is about the fastest way to let your competitors know what you are up to! This means that you are given two weeks to come up with an offer, where two months would have been tight.

PENETRATING THE SNAIL

Contact with the R&D department could bring a significant advantage. Here you would be talking technical capability, and perhaps this is your real strength? And better still, you are now involved with 'potential products' where decisions are not yet made and there is still an opportunity to influence specifications. Of course, the 'potential products' discussed in the R&D department might not see the light of day, and some would say that these discussions are then a waste of time, and even argue the virtues of the single sales–purchasing interface; that you only discuss real products there, with real orders being imminent. On occasions such a criticism may be right, but this simply highlights the skill required in managing a key account – where and when to invest your time and energy.

Of course, the buyer might not allow you immediate access to the R&D people; it may take some time and skill to penetrate the customer's decision-making process. (Some specific techniques for such a penetration are discussed in Chapters 8 and 9; for the moment we are concerned simply with why such penetration is a good idea.)   **Getting beyond the buyer**

Should we penetrate further into the snail, beyond R&D, right back to the marketing department? Inevitably there are pros and cons to doing this, and we are back to that essential skill of the key account manager – knowing where and when to invest your time and energy.

- Some possible reasons in favour of penetrating to the centre:
    - You can discover the real hopes and ambitions of the customer.
    - Early contact allows you to set the criteria so that you are the only viable choice, and price is a very minor issue once the buyer becomes involved.
    - Perhaps you have a particular capability that will help your customer speed development of their new product, or improve its

chance of success after launch. If so, and if you can demonstrate this to the marketing people (who, in the FMCG environment we are discussing, typically suffer plenty of internal obstacles that can often kill over 90 per cent of new ideas, and then suffer very high failure rates post-launch) then surely you are on route to being considered a key supplier.

- Some possible reasons against penetrating to the centre:
  - What does the buyer, or your R&D contacts, make of you talking to marketing? For some this would be tantamount to dealing with the enemy! The key account manager must always be aware of the 'political' realities within the customer (see Chapter 30 for more on this requirement).
  - If so many of their ideas 'go nowhere', couldn't this close involvement with marketing lead you horribly astray, perhaps even take you into projects that could pull your own organization apart at the seams?
  - You have nothing to offer them: your proposition has no positive impact on their issues.
  - This will take a particular capability (familiarity with the ways of marketing in FMCG) – do you have it?
  - This all takes time – do you have it?

Let's just take that those last two possible points 'against' penetrating to the centre: lack of capability, and lack of time. If we are discussing a key account, then one of the tasks of the key account manager is to assess the capabilities and the time required for success with the customer – the level of investment required – and then to go about building those capabilities and making that time available. If the organization will not permit such development, then perhaps this is not a key account, or perhaps the organization is not really willing to practise KAM, with all its implications.

Some obstacles to penetration

There are three big ones:

- The buyer won't let you – don't forget that you may be challenging their power and their desire to control information.
- The sales professional won't go beyond the buyer – it may not be in their job description, it may not be within their capabilities, it may not be in their budget (what if the buyer is on their sales territory but the R&D department is in another country?).
- The R&D people (sticking with that particular example) don't want to see a salesperson.

The need for a key account team

Can a sales professional do this alone? Are you really sure? Let me just ask you this again...

Don't try to go it alone

The more complex the snail, and the more it involves people in specialist functions, then the less likely it is that sales professionals can do this on their own. Figure 6.3 shows a possible three-person team and their penetration of the opportunity snail.

Figure 6.3 *The key account team approach*

Even if the sales professionals can do it alone, even if they do have such a broad set of skills, perhaps it is still best that they don't:

- Penetrating beyond the buyer is never easy, but if it is someone other than the salesperson doing the penetrating, then that can sometimes ease the way.
- Can the sales professional really be credible in so many different guises?
- Wouldn't specialists prefer to speak with someone who 'speaks their language'? If you were selling to a customer in France, and couldn't speak French, that would be a problem, and you would find someone who could speak French (I hope, rather than taking the 'learn French in two weeks' tapes out of the library).

- You'll be amazed at what a real expert can uncover when speaking with their opposite number.
- Where were the sales professionals going to find all this time to do all this penetrating?
- Do you really want to put your future with a key account into the hands of one individual? People get sick, people leave, people get promoted…

Disciplines of penetration

There are of course some issues about such multi-contact relationships, issues that will be explored in detail in Chapter 7, but let's just note one for the moment. The more people you involve with the customer, the greater the chance for confusion of messages, and especially so if those people are not talking to each other. Penetrating snails is not about throwing people at the customer, like mud against a wall hoping some of it will stick. Penetration should be carefully managed, and strict disciplines of what is being said to the customer must be observed across the penetrating team.

How often has a salesperson dropped an R&D or manufacturing colleague into hot water by promising timelines that cannot be met? How often have those technical or operational people dropped the salesperson into just as much hot water by giving things away for free, things that the salesperson had been negotiating hard to sell? It's a cliché I know, but a key account team must always sing from the same hymn sheet.

Involving the boss

There is also the question of seniority and status to be considered. Perhaps the sales professional has a relationship with the buyer, but the supplier wishes for a relationship also with the buying director. Who might be better placed to make that contact – the sales professional (needing to go above the buyer's head), or the sales professional's manager (who can match status with status)? There is no absolute answer of course, but the question should always be asked, and key account managers should come fitted with special 'ego-suppressing' devices in their brains to avoid the 'I can do everything' syndrome, when someone else can do it better.

A supplier of printed leaflets and adhesive labels to the pharmaceutical industry (the leaflets and labels that appear in and on pill bottles and packets) had a great idea. Like all great ideas it came from an observed problem. Pharmaceutical companies would like to say a lot of things on those leaflets labels; indeed, they are obliged by law to say plenty already, but the problem is space. And there is another problem – there is a legal obligation for the pills to be sold with the right leaflets and labels, to ensure that the patient uses those pills correctly, and printed-paper leaflets in particular just have a way of becoming separated. Even if they make it to the patient's home correctly attached, they have a knack (almost a mission) of getting into the wrong bottles and boxes once the pills are in the bathroom cabinet.

The great idea was something called the concertina label, to be affixed to the small space on the lid of a pill bottle, but then capable of being unfolded to allow all the information required. Plus, once stuck, it stays stuck.

Unfortunately the buyer of labels in the first pharmaceutical company approached with the new product saw only a more expensive label, and said 'no thanks'. Yet more unfortunately for the supplier with the great idea, this rejection was repeated in each and every pharmaceutical company. So, it was obviously not such a great idea, they concluded, and thought about dropping it from their range.

Fortunately (and I trust you don't hope to rely on such good fortune in your own business) one of their salespeople happened to bump into the marketing director at one of the larger pharmaceutical companies – perhaps they got lost in the maze of corridors, but whatever the reason for being there, they struck gold. The concertina label was the answer to the marketing director's prayers, and its extra cost was an irrelevance when compared to the costs of not solving the labelling problem, and an even bigger irrelevance in the grand scheme of pharmaceutical company marketing budgets. The label buyer was instructed to source it, no questions asked, and a new sales strategy was born.

PUTTING 'CHAINS' AND 'SNAILS' TOGETHER

The aims of this chapter must be combined with those of the last – to understand our true value we must understand the customer and their market, but to do anything about that understanding, to get the reward we deserve, then we must also understand the customer's organization, their people and their decision-making processes.

Chains and snails are two pieces of analysis that must be worked on together. It is through their combination that we will begin to approach that Holy Grail of KAM spoken of in earlier chapters – to be able to say that you understand, as a key account team, the customer's business, the customer's market and the customer's organization, better than they do themselves.

From that starting point, things will go from good to better. Such a supplier will be able to help their customer in ways that a more reactive supplier cannot hope for. They can speed the process of new product development, they can enhance the success of new product launches, they can provide assistance with market research, they can discuss trends, they can advise, they can consult, they can argue, they can even disagree.

It may seem a strange note to close this chapter on, but the ability to say 'no' is not granted to all suppliers. It is a mark of a key supplier that they have this liberty, and it comes less from any balance of power positioning than from the nature of what they know.

A significant benefit of KAM is the way in which it enhances such knowledge, through the analytical part of the task. In the next few chapters, making up Part III of this book, we will be looking at how the management of the customer relationship aims to build on that knowledge, while adding another significant benefit of KAM: business security.

APPLICATION EXERCISE

Identify a key account, and a decision-making unit within that account:

- Draw out the customer's decision-making 'snail':
- How deep and broad is our current penetration of that 'snail'?
- What opportunities might a deeper or broader penetration highlight:
  - beyond the current contacts;
  - at different levels of seniority?
- What new entry and contact strategies might be required to take advantage of these opportunities?
- What problems might be caused within the customer's organization by expanding the points of contact?
  - So how should you proceed?
- What problems might be caused within our own organization by expanding the points of contact?
  - So how should you proceed?

Part III

Relationship management

7

From 'bow-ties' to 'diamonds'

Figure 7.1 recalls the KAM model introduced at the close of Chapter 4, reminding us that the task of relationship management is, along with the task of analysis, a significant investment on the part of the supplier.

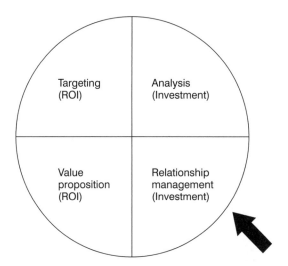

Figure 7.1   *The KAM model: the relationship management investment*

Building relationships takes time, it can eat up resources, and in itself it doesn't promise any particular return – even the best relationships do not *in themselves* promise additional orders, higher volumes, premium prices, better margins or any of the other sought-after rewards. There must be a purpose to the relationship, a desired outcome, or we are at risk of building it simply for the sake of the thing, which can so easily lead to an escalation in costs (rarely noted or measured) and a reduction in our chances of an effective return on the investment.

Being liked, or being respected?

Too often suppliers seem to regard the definition of a 'good relationship' as being synonymous with 'being liked'. We're all human, and it's nice to be liked, but it's a poor basis for the kind of competitive advantage you should be seeking, and in any case, is 'being liked' even necessary?

So, every relationship with a key account must be built with the ends in mind. Those ends should be clearly articulated in the key account plan, and so must the nature of the investment. Such clarity is important if we are to avoid wasting the time of many people on *both sides* of the relationship. Getting this right will result in something far more important than 'being liked', and that is 'being respected'.

Getting it right?

So what does getting it right mean? As suppliers and key accounts differ, so will the sought-after goals of the relationship, and so then must the nature of those relationships differ. There is no ideal model; rather, it is a question of choosing the right relationship for the right circumstance, and so there are endless possibilities, all of which could make an already long chapter painfully so.

I propose instead to examine four specific relationship models (we will call them the 'bow-tie', the 'one-on-many', the 'cotton-reel' and the 'diamond', as shown in Figure 7.3 later in this chapter), each one calling for a different level of resource from the supplier, each one aiming for a different level of breadth and depth with the customer. Any one of these four (and all the nuances in between) could be right for your own circumstances, which include the nature of the opportunity, the range of your ambitions and the receptivity of the customer.

If the opportunity is big and your ambitions are high, then may it not be that anything short of a deep relationship through the use of a KA team would be a mistake? Reduce the opportunity, and such a relationship could quickly become inappropriate. And while you make your choices, never forget a vital truth: you can't force any particular relationship onto a customer.

Knowing which to pick, knowing how to move between them, and knowing how to 'make it happen' with the customer is undoubtedly the 'art' of KAM.

THREE APPROACHES TO SELLING

Before turning to those models, let us go back a step and consider three different approaches to selling, and the kinds of customer relationship they engender. We will call these sales approaches: the 'milk-round', the 'hunter' and the 'farmer'.

The milk round

Go back no more than 10 to 20 years and this was the standard approach for many, particularly in an established and mature market with little prospect of change. Large teams of field-based sales representatives were armed with weekly journey plans – clover-leaf or whatever – and trained to seek ever more efficient ways to service a territory where all customers are considered equal. And when I say large teams, I mean large, managed by layers of sales management from area to regional to national.

Relationships with customers were necessarily 'shallow' as the representatives were encouraged to move on swiftly to their next call – the magic six-a-day being the classic requirement. Deploying any kind of account team was rarely considered as it could only slow work down and damage the sought-after efficiency.

In a time when customers were many, and mostly small, such an approach worked; and where we still find such circumstances today we still find examples of the milk round, pharmaceutical companies selling to general practitioners being one of the better known.

It is however a rather 'self-fulfilling' philosophy of selling. If all customers are regarded as equal and given the same allocation of time and attention, then the clues that might distinguish greater potential in one over another can easily be missed. Making good investment decisions calls for good knowledge, and that was never the prime objective of the milk round. Moreover, few management teams were willing to hand the choices of where to invest to the sales professionals in the field, preferring to manage through strict call-rate and coverage targets.

When customers were equal

The milk-round approach is in rapid, perhaps terminal, decline. The nature of the customer base has changed for most, while technology has brought greater efficiencies to selling than a journey plan ever could. The killer blow has been their cost, but even then some have found it difficult to move away from the approach: large field sales teams with multiple layers of management are certainly expensive, but they also come with an awful lot of inertia.

From the KAM point of view, it is a decline not to be mourned. Too often such regimes only served to 'dumb-down' the sales professionals, while KAM aims to raise their status to that of a business manager.

The hunter

The hunter sees the target, applies a pair of blinkers to the eyes, and goes in for the kill. It's fast, aggressive, and often very effective.

Relationships with customers are to a clear purpose – to make the sale. Key decision makers are targeted and fast-acting propositions are rehearsed. The hunter-killer sales professional might call in colleagues if they are vital to the kill, but in the main the hunter prefers to operate alone.

Any supplier in a fast-growing market will be very grateful for hunters, and so will suppliers launching new products (especially if they have short life cycles). Any supplier wanting to penetrate a new market, stealing customers from the competition, will seek hunters for the sales team in preference to all others.

Are they right to be so thankful, and so single minded? We will address this question a little later; for the moment, let's continue with the characterization of the hunter.

Youth is often apparent in such sellers, or at least hunger. Give a hunter a clear target and motivation in the form of a well-designed reward package and it can be a simple case of 'lighting blue touch paper...'

When the laws regulating the provision of telephone services started to be relaxed across Europe, companies like Mercury and MCI Worldcom made rapid inroads into the territory of established giants such as British Telecom and Belgacom. Customers were hunted with a ruthless energy that left the incumbents standing – and some big commissions were earned. But then BT started to win those customers back ('thousands of customers coming back every week' read the adverts – an intriguing mixture of candour and boastfulness), illustrating one of the potential downsides of the hunter approach – poor levels of customer retention.

The farmer

The farmer aims to develop the customer's potential over time. Investment is the name of the game, marshalling resources in pursuit of long-term rewards. Never happy with the status quo, the farmer always wants to improve the business, and will stick with the current client in that pursuit, in preference to chasing business elsewhere.

With customer retention as a prime goal, relationships tend towards the broad and the deep, and the farmer will always call on the help of colleagues whose expertise can 'add value'.

I don't have to go any further for it to be clear that I am describing a Key Account Management approach, but that is not to suppose that farmers are always given the support they need. Bosses often saddle them with unrealistically short-term targets. Those same bosses (who perhaps grew up in a hunter environment and were hunters themselves) might prefer measures of efficiency over measures of effectiveness, and so manage accordingly. Their staff might be rewarded through inappropriate packages stressing volume and short-term wins, a package more suited to the hunter. Finally, they are expected to farm far too many customers. In other words, farmers often find themselves stuck in hunter-dominated environments, and so they struggle.

Are farmers better than hunters?

It is probably fair to say that the majority of sales professionals tend towards a hunter mentality, or philosophy. It is also true to say that where businesses are recruiting for KAM positions, they are increasingly on the lookout for farmer capabilities. In some cases this has even led to the situation where non-salespeople are preferred as KA managers (an idea we will explore further in Chapter 28), arming them with hunter-killer sales professionals as members of their KA team.

So, at first glance it may seem that the farmer is to be preferred to the hunter for the KAM task, while the hunters are better suited to the smaller customers, or to the penetration of new customers. Indeed, some businesses will divide their sales resource into two: a hunter team tasked with winning new customers, and a farmer team tasked to develop those same customers after a suitable handover. One might at first glance prefer the farmer, but a more studied examination will soon find that there is a role for both approaches in the KAM task.

It is a very rare sales professional that is 100 per cent hunter, 0 per cent farmer, or vice versa. Equally, very few are split 50:50 across the two approaches. Most KA managers (like most sales professionals) are then a mix of the two, which is perhaps just as well, as there are certainly pros and cons of each approach, and there are certainly times to farm and times to hunt.

Let's consider some of those pros and cons (and I fully recognize that this is a rather stereotypical picture, so feel free to soften the edges with your own assessment).

Hunters: the pros and the cons

The good things about hunters are: they're fast, independent and resilient; they target key decision makers; they're focused on results and quick to change if circumstances change; and they're easy to motivate.

The less good things about hunters (in the KAM environment) might be: they prefer to work alone and so make poor team players; they're reluctant to involve others in *their* customer; they might ignore 'secondary' decision makers; they're short-term – 'investment' is of little consequence to a hunter focused on this month's commission who may not plan to be on the team next year; they go for the easy kill (consider how a lioness chooses her prey); and they might be guilty of 'abandoning' the customer.

This point about 'abandoning' the customer requires a little explanation, and is illustrated in Figure 7.3. The hunter stalks the customer, coaxing them into wanting more contact, and then pounces, to make the sale. Having got the contract, the hunter leaves, to hunt elsewhere, just at the moment when the customer's need for contact goes up (post-sale worries, questions, problems, and etc). The farmer would aim to fill the gap, as of course will the clever hunter, perhaps by bringing in a colleague.

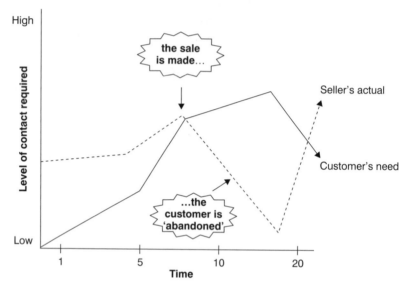

Figure 7.2 *Abandoning the customer*

Farmers: the pros and the cons

The good things about farmers are: they're in it for the long haul, they have patience; they value a team approach; they invest time in analysis and relation-ships; they penetrate snails; they think strategically and 'politically' (see Chapter 30 for more on the idea of the 'political entrepreneur'); they plan ahead.

The less good things about farmers might be: they may suffer from analysis paralysis; there is a danger that it's always 'jam tomorrow'; they can become so committed to the long-term plan that they miss the short-term opportunities, or worse, blind themselves to change. There is a danger that the farmer, as viewed by the hunter, can appear slow, plodding, and lacking in energy and imagination (just as the hunter, viewed by the farmer, can appear slick and facile). The smart farmers will realize this, and aim to manage their style accordingly.

THE KAM JOURNEY

Some tasks are eminently predictable and call for a uniform set of skills and capabilities. KAM is not one of those tasks. There will be times when the qualities of the hunter are to be sought, and others when the farmer must come to the fore, and yet other times when approaches yet to be described will be required. This is best understood if we remember the description of KAM in Chapter 2, that of a journey.

Most salespeople, at some stage in their career, have had to draw up journey plans: where will you be on Thursday at 10 am, have you got your regulation six calls in the day, and did you drive the most efficient route? Such is the prosaic journey plan of the milk round, but KAM is a different kind of journey – a journey of relationships.

Figure 7.3 illustrates the possible path of one such journey, along with the four relationship models introduced at the start of this chapter. The foundation of this model is in the relative 'strategic intent' of both supplier and customer: that is to say, the extent to which each side sees value to be gained from putting more effort into the relationship. The higher the strategic intent, or the greater the envisaged reward, so the greater the application of effort. What we mean by 'effort' in this regard might be characterized in two ways. First, an increase in the points of contact (or what some refer to as 'touch-points') between supplier and customer, moving from a simple 1:1 relationship through to a more complex team-on-team based relationship. Second, the nature of that relationship will build from one based on short-term 'transactions' – doing deals – towards

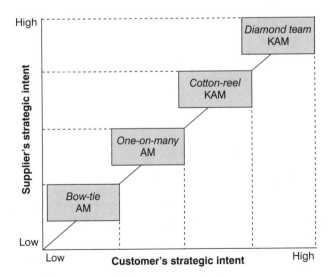

Figure 7.3 *The KAM journey*
Adapted from a model first developed by AF Millman, and KJ Wilson (1994)

one of genuine 'collaboration' – working together towards joint objectives and aspirations.

The four models (the 'bow-tie', the 'one-on-many', the 'cotton-reel', and the 'diamond') describe the particular nature of the relationship at four different stages in the journey. At this point we should make some very important observations about the nature of this journey and its attendant models of relationship.

The need for management, over time

Account manager, or relationship manager?

Progress along the path shown does not happen of its own accord. Progress must be sought, consciously and by both sides, and managed with great care and diplomacy. Some businesses have seen this element of the KAM task as so pre-eminently important that they have called those responsible their relationship managers, rather than key account managers.

The timescales involved in moving from one 'stage' through to the next can be long, and often longer than senior managers care to wait. We are not speaking of weeks or months, but rather quarters and even years. Not only must the KA manager be a diplomat, but also a counsel of patience.

The need for mutuality

Progress requires both sides to share the same strategic intent. As has been said before, no particular model of relationship can be forced onto a customer, and in this sense the model you get can only be the model you deserve (see Chapter 10 and 'the ugly story').

This will often call for great patience from the supplier; it is not unusual for their strategic intent to be some way ahead of the customer's. If this is so then they must learn to bide their time, and work on the customer's beliefs and attitudes, coaxing them to progress on a mutual basis. To do anything else will only lead to frustration, and that can be damaging to both parties, even terminal.

Avoiding frustration

Figure 7.4 illustrates the peril of stepping outside the boundaries of mutual progression, and slipping in to one of two 'frustration zones': the supplier's, or the customer's. If the supplier attempts to forge a relationship based on a strategic intent that outpaces that of the customer, then it is unlikely to secure any of the gains for which it hopes. At best, the supplier is frustrated. Worse, the supplier will be wasting the customer's time, and their own. Not only can this be hugely damaging to profitability, but it can also result in the rejection of the supplier's advances, and even in the rejection of the whole KAM approach by a supplier too depressed and disillusioned to carry it on.

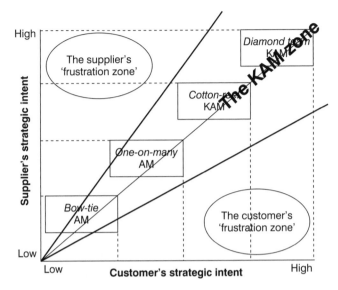

Figure 7.4 *The frustration zones*
Adapted from a model first developed by AF Millman, and KJ Wilson (1994)

If the supplier's intent lags behind the customer's, then they cannot be surprised if that supplier should look elsewhere, for someone who will give the time and attention required for the fulfilment of their hopes.

Getting the right match

It would be easy to suppose that the customer will be most demanding at the early stages of the relationship, a sort of 'show us what you're made of' phase. Easy, but quite wrong! The expectations placed on suppliers increase as the customer's strategic intent increases. This should be understood and looked out for; complacency is a great killer of mature relationships (one only has to understand marriage to know the truth of that!).

Base your relationship on the expectations of the customer, while also aiming to coax those expectations in a direction that will be to your own advantage. No easy task, but one familiar enough (if I may be old-fashioned enough to use the phrase) to anyone who has courted, or been courted. First, you eye each other up, then you might like to know a little bit more about the other, perhaps you try to meet their friends, then you introduce them to your own friends, and then, presuming your strategic intent is high enough, you introduce them to your family…

A little old-fashioned courtship…

To put it a little more prosaically, at the outset of the relationship the customer may want little more than a product at a price. As things develop they may look for more, with expectations of their supplier as a problem

73

solver, and that requires the supplier to think harder, to know the customer's needs better, to speak with more people, and perhaps also to involve others from their own side. If that goes well, then the customer's expectations may rise again, looking for the supplier's help not simply as a supplier, but as a genuine business partner, and that will call up another type of relationship again.

Reading the signs is crucial to getting it right. I have heard a customer say that a supplier was fired because all they had was good products. I have also heard a customer say that a supplier was fired because they had ideas beyond their station.

Knowing when to stop

You don't have to proceed beyond the point that satisfies your intentions and those of the customer. Knowing when to stop is as much the art of KAM as being able to take the relationship to the 'diamond KAM' stage. 'Diamond KAM' is not for every key account, and should not be regarded as 'better' than 'bow-tie KAM', or 'one-on-many KAM' or 'cotton-reel KAM' unless the circumstances and the opportunity and the mutuality of intentions demand it.

It isn't a race

The idea of KAM as a journey should not be taken to imply that there is a race; it is not about who can get their customer to the end of the path the quickest. If there is any sense of competition at all among account managers, then it is: who did the best job at forging the right relationship for the circumstances?

If we remember that relationship management is about managing an investment, then the praise should go to those who secure the best returns on those investments, and the best returns will result from avoiding those damaging 'frustration zones' discussed earlier.

There may also be a time for taking the relationship backwards down the path described. This is often a much harder task than building upwards; people get used to high levels and frequency of contact, and a certain inertia can be experienced once complex team-on-team relationships have been formed. Again, if moving backwards is the right thing to do given the circumstances and the opportunity, then such a move should not be considered a failure, but rather a success – the appropriate management of the investment.

CHARTING THE COURSE

We have spoken about 'bow-ties' and 'one-on-many' and 'cotton-reels' and 'diamonds', as if their natures were crystal clear, and as that is probably not the case (for which my apologies) it is high time we turned to describing them and what they entail. The models are not intended as templates to be copied slavishly, but as indicators of what things might look like through the journey. The key account manager is charting a course, and it is always helpful to know what the scenery might look like as you pass it by.

Each model is marked by its own 'typical' characteristics. Each has its own strengths and weaknesses. Each has its own opportunities, and own health warnings. Each demands its own skills and capabilities, and each its own management style. That being so, a few generalizations about what to expect as the 'steps are climbed' might be useful.

Progressing upwards through the four relationship models could see an increase/improvement in each or any of the following 'issues':

- the complexity of the decision-making process (on both sides);
- the value (volume, money, share, etc) of those decisions;
- the level of interdependency between supplier and customer ('lock-in');
- the level of risk, for both parties (the stakes being higher);
- the effective management of risk (through collaborative processes);
- the value to the customer of the supplier's proposition;
- the supplier's competitive advantage;
- the supplier reward.

A note on the figures

Figures 7.5 through to 7.9 illustrate the models, using as their example a fairly typical B2B circumstance, a manufacturing company selling to another manufacturing company. This is of course only an example, and the functions and departments and job titles used are not intended as any form of template or instruction. Nor do the numbers of contacts between supplier and customer suggest any ideal state – you must of course determine what is right for you in your own circumstance.

A note on the use of the word 'key'

You will notice that the sections dealing with the 'bow-tie' and the 'one-on-many' models are both headed 'account management'; the word 'key' is omitted. This is deliberate, indicating a view (my own) that neither of these two relationships is really appropriate to what we might call 'true' Key Account Management, where a team-sell is involved.

What's in a word?

They are instead steps along the way, and worry should set in fast if they are considered to be end points in the journey. If they really are considered to be the appropriate end points, then you must ask whether this customer is truly a key account, or whether your business is practising Key Account Management in truth, or in name only.

We could debate for a long time whether this point is fairly made of the 'one-on-many' model.

'Bow-tie' account management

Figure 7.5 illustrates what is perhaps the most common supplier/customer relationship of them all – the bow-tie relationship.

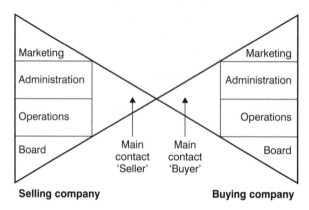

Figure 7.5 *Bow-tie account management*
Adapted from McDonald, Millman and Rogers (1996)

Some 'typical' characteristics of the 'bow-tie' relationship

- The principal contact is between two people – usually the salesperson and the buyer.
- The relationship may be competitive, with each seeking to gain advantage; at worst, it may be confrontational.
- The buyer may see any attempt to gain access to other contacts as a threat to their own position and power.
- The seller may regard any attempted involvement by others from their own company as unwelcome interference.
- Both seller and buyer regard the relationship as one that gives them a high degree of 'control'.
- Price discussions probably dominate.
- The supplier focuses on increased volume.
- The sales professional is trained in transactional skills such as negotiation.
- The focus is on short-term and transactional dealings.
- Buyers may use performance criteria that are not shared with the supplier.
- The customer is still assessing alternative suppliers.
- Disputes can lead to long-term breaks in supply.

This is perhaps the archetypal hunter model, with all its strengths and weaknesses as already discussed. Perhaps its biggest attraction for the seller is the sense of control that they have, matched with the sense of achievement when it all goes well. And this hints at its biggest danger, the danger of staying there. Why move on when you are in control, with no distractions from badly informed colleagues, and getting all the praise for success? Add to this, the buyer is happy, for they are just as much in control (only we know that they are more in control really!).

Control...

We should add a final 'truth' about sales professionals. Too often they have a low regard for their non-sales colleague's capabilities to deal with 'their' customer. I once heard a salesperson say: 'I know what you are trying to make me do Peter, but the only time I have ever lost a customer was when I involved someone from head office.' Was it true, or a case of a seriously swollen ego?

I would readily concede that involving colleagues takes time, and often it will be quicker to just 'do it yourself', but this view can consign you to a lifetime of doing it yourself. Perhaps there is a time to make an investment of time in getting others to be just as smart as you are already?

Some downsides

Why move on? Consider some of the potential downsides of this relationship:

- Because they are not penetrating the snail (see Chapter 6), sellers may be unaware of the true decision-making process, and so be unable to influence it as they would wish.
- The sellers are probably ignorant of their true value, through lack of knowledge of their impact on the customer's business and market.
- The supplier is playing into the hands of buyers who wish to restrict information as a basis of increasing their power. This is particularly true for those who sell to the grocery retail trade, a market where restricting the suppliers' knowledge has long been a favoured means of managing large and powerful suppliers.
- Expertise on both sides is seriously underutilized.
- The seller and the buyer are expected to be all-round experts – an unlikely scenario.
- Messages from other functions are mistranslated (and littered with 'Chinese whispers').
- Projects and activities are held up by the sales/purchasing bottleneck.
- There is over-reliance on one relationship, and if it breaks (buyers retire, salespeople move on) the whole thing must start again; the future is permanently at risk.
- Salespeople can become 'kingpins' who cannot be promoted for fear of losing the business – a sad end to a promising career.

...but at a price

Of course there are some advantages to this kind of relationship; it's simple, relatively low cost, and controllable; and if you are certain that it gets you what you want, then there may be no need to go beyond it. But take care: be sure that your certainty is not just complacency.

What is my best advice to anyone managing a genuine key account through this relationship?

- Aim to know more by getting to speak with more people.
- Get beyond the buyer – but always with their approval.
- Learn to let go – curb your ego and get your colleagues involved.

'One-on-many' account management

Figure 7.6 illustrates what many would consider as advanced selling (some might even dignify it by the title of 'strategic selling'). This is where the sales professional breaks out of the restrictions imposed by the 1:1 bow-tie, and establishes direct contact with a range of other people in the customer.

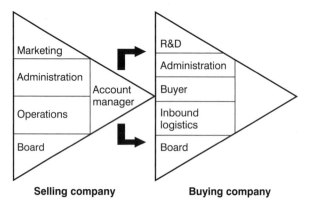

Figure 7.6 *One-on-many account management*

Some 'typical' characteristics of the 'one-on-many' relationship

- The seller broadens their base of contacts – this may be a reconnaissance, to look for further opportunities, or a recognition of a less transactional relationship.
- If this is with the buyer's permission, or encouragement, then this is indicative of an increase in the customer's strategic intent, recognizing the supplier's need to understand more about the customer's circumstances and needs, or to manage interactions with a broader range of functions.

- If this is without the buyer's permission, then *caveat vendor* (seller beware) must be the strong warning – buyers have a way of getting you back for such cheek.
- The seller continues to work alone, either through lack of resources in their own business, or through a deliberate desire to maintain control.
- Price will probably still dominate discussions, but the buyer will perhaps be more open to discussions around 'cost in use', in view of the seller's greater knowledge.
- Sellers may start to be aware of performance criteria beyond the purchasing department.
- The seller may be able to develop aspects of 'lock-in', beyond the buyer; however, by restricting the buyer's subsequent freedom to look elsewhere this might in turn make the buyer's reluctant to allow such contacts – *caveat vendor* again.
- Disputes can sometimes be moderated by people beyond the seller–buyer interface.

Perhaps we could think of this model as that of the clever hunter. The sellers are clearly attempting to penetrate the snail (see Chapter 6), and will be enhancing their knowledge. But we should note that this enhancement might often stay inside their own heads, as it is not necessarily shared with their colleagues.

...great research...

If the intention of this approach is a kind of reconnaissance on the part of the seller, to see where opportunities may lie, and to see where value can be added, then this is a thoroughly commendable advance on the bow-tie. The challenge then becomes: what if you spot new opportunities and new means of adding value; can you do anything about it on your own? And if the result of asking that question is to involve others from your own business, so moving the relationship on to the next stage of the KAM journey, then again, this will be thoroughly commendable.

Unfortunately, it is too often the case that there is no intention, or possibility, of involving others, and that the sales professional is expected to be like Superman or Superwoman, representing the supplier on an impossibly wide range of issues. If that is so, then all this enhanced knowledge is likely to go to waste. Seeing this model as the endgame carries a risk of consigning your KAM to a sub-optimal approach – it isn't in fact about being Superman or Superwoman, it's about being mediocre.

...but not the endgame

So what is my best advice to anyone managing a genuine key account through this relationship?

- Aim to make this a staging post, not the endgame.
- If it *is* the endgame, reclassify the customer as something other than a key account (see Chapter 24 for the options).

● Use the knowledge you gain to make better use of your resources (the matching process we discussed in Chapter 4, in the section on 'Managing the future').

'Cotton-reel' Key Account Management

Figure 7.7 illustrates the point at which the solo sales professional steps over the line from account manager to 'key' account manager, through the utilization of others in their business. We step from being a sales professional to a business manager, from a hunter (straight, or clever) to a farmer.

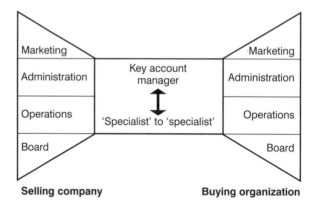

Figure 7.7 *Cotton-reel Key Account Management*

Some 'typical' characteristics of the 'cotton-reel' relationship

● Direct contacts between supplier and customer functions are established through the auspices of the KA manager, pairing 'specialists' or 'experts' with each other.
● This might be done in order to facilitate greater mutual understanding, or to implement shared projects.
● There is an increase in time briefing and coaching colleagues.
● Internal communications also increase (it is to be hoped!) – with a potential burden of excess information or bureaucracy if this is not managed appropriately.
● There is improvement in customer awareness and customer focus within the supplier's organization.
● Knowledge begins to translate into action.
● There are increasing opportunities for 'lock-in' through genuinely customer-focused value propositions that might speak more about value than price or cost.

- Increased trust and openness develop with the customer; disputes become things to be resolved through the involvement of the appropriate people (but see next point).
- It is however at this stage, with the introduction of new people on both sides, that the greatest chance for 'mishaps' occurs; new people can do and say a great number of wrong things. Great care must be taken, but you will be wise to expect occasional setbacks all the same.

The role of the KA manager as coach becomes apparent at this stage (for more on this see Chapter 28). The best way to avoid 'mishaps' is to spend time, and plenty of it, briefing and coaching those newly involved. First visits will almost certainly be 'in tandem', and perhaps later visits also – the briefings and the coaching will continue in any case.

Coaching, coaching and coaching

Some of this coaching may have to deal with what a sales professional would see as very basic issues; how to present yourself to, and work with, a customer. A recent survey of buyers in the UK, asking what they disliked most about the suppliers who came to see them, ranked facial jewellery at number two on their list. That surprised me too, but don't expect your colleagues to know the etiquette, or for that matter to have the same confidence that you do, in working with the customer. This applies to senior members of your team as much as junior – I have known many a head of IT or R&D go to the customer quaking at the prospect of what might be going to happen to them.

Of course, none of these pairings are instituted without the buyers' consent, and ideally, their active involvement. If they are not directly involved in the meetings that follow, then make sure they are sent full briefings.

Hard work, but well worth the effort

For the KA manager this is without question the 'hard-work' stage. Diamond teams may appear more involved, but they are designed (or should be) to have a strong streak of self-management. Cotton-reels are only the start of diamonds, and the workload on the KA manager is consequently high. Great care should be taken not to overload KA managers by expecting them to manage too many customers at this stage of the journey. What constitutes too many? For me, if the customer is at this stage, and the intention is to move on to a true diamond team relationship, then one is quite enough.

As well as being the hard-work stage, this is also the true investment stage. You are beginning to commit resources, but it is unlikely that any return benefits will flow for a while. People can get impatient, particularly senior management, and some may start to say that KAM is not bearing fruit, or is not worth the effort. The temptations to go back to the relative comforts of the 'bow-tie' or the 'one-on-many' are many and strong. I can only counsel that you resist!

Parallel cotton-reels

In some cases the pairings we are describing may happen individually, in others, the picture may resemble that shown in Figure 7.8 – a series of parallel cotton-reels. This is a diamond team in the making (see the next section below). We might ask then, what is the difference between a diamond team and a set of parallel cotton-reels? Is a diamond team just a fat cotton-reel? Is a cotton-reel just a thin diamond team?

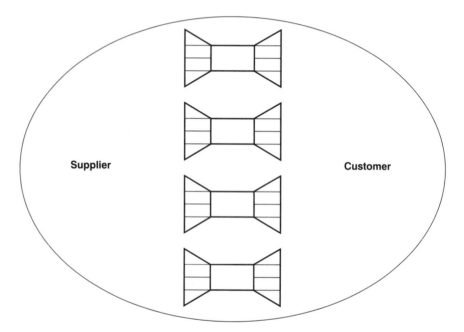

Figure 7.8 *Parallel cotton-reels*

I have heard it argued that cotton-reels might be transitory, while diamond teams are permanent. Often true, but I wouldn't want to make it a rule. In the world of KAM, where the art is to observe change and act upon it through the management of the relationship, diamonds are most certainly *not* forever.

A better distinction is to say that a diamond team is just that, a team, working in concert, whereas the parallel cotton-reels may be isolated from each other. This is of course precisely one of the dangers of this stage, and the KA manager must resolve either to proceed towards the control and discipline of a genuine team, or live with the workload (and the frequent frustrations) of juggling so many balls at once.

> A key account manager was struggling to make this stage work. The biggest frustration was the limitation that each of the newly introduced people put on themselves. Each one showed great reluctance to be involved any further than achieving their own narrow objectives, which were often less than the KA manager hoped from them. They were certainly not in any sense part of a team with bigger ambitions.
>
> During a coaching session, on being asked why they had such reluctance, it became clear that fear lay at the bottom of things. 'When I visit the customer,' they said, 'I get in and out as quickly as possible.' 'Why is that?' asked the KA manager. 'Well,' came the reply, 'what if I was to meet someone important, and they asked me something difficult?'
>
> Easy to laugh, or to be cynical about the capabilities of non-sales professionals, but if you are to make this stage work, or wish to build beyond it, then such fears must be thoroughly overcome.

"But we might meet someone important..."

'Diamond team' Key Account Management

Figure 7.9 illustrates the step beyond parallel cotton-reels, where the individuals on the supplier side have formed a genuine team, and work in concert with their opposite numbers who, ideally though not always, also see themselves as a team. Remember, the figure is just an example and there is no requirement for you to mimic the functions involved or the numbers involved – diamond teams can comprise three people, or they can run to hundreds.

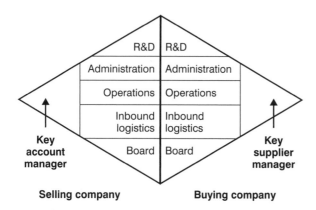

Figure 7.9 *Diamond team Key Account Management*
Adapted from McDonald, Millman and Rogers (1996)

Some typical characteristics of the 'diamond team' relationship

- The individuals involved are aware of their role within a team, and operate accordingly.
- Each member has clarity on their own goals, roles and obligations to the team.
- Contacts are secured at all levels, from operational to senior management.
- The KA manager's role is principally one of coordination; managers may even choose to step aside from the day-to-day sales activities, delegating those instead to a sales professional within the diamond team.
- It is very likely that key supplier status is awarded – few customers will allow such involvement by suppliers with any other than key suppliers.
- The customer mirrors the KA manager with a key supplier manager whose focus is on developing the supplier's capabilities rather than challenging them.
- Relationships are based on trust – they have to be for such a relationship to function.
- The supplier's security of tenure is high, though they must take care not to become complacent.
- Access to people is facilitated and information is shared, perhaps through shared communication networks (viz intranets).
- Supplier and customer staff may be trained together, focusing on collaborative teamwork rather than transactional skills (viz negotiation).
- It is possible that both sides have developed shared business plans.
- The customer gets the supplier's new ideas first; they may also have an expectation for some measure of exclusivity.
- Continuous improvement is expected from those suppliers.
- Clear 'vendor ratings' and 'performance measures' are discussed and agreed.
- 'Value' is the watchword, sought through integrated business processes (value inside), and/or through a focus on the customer's markets (value beyond).
- Collaboration speeds the pace of joint activities; new product development can be hugely enhanced through such teams.
- Longer-term contracts are likely to be more common, including agreements on pricing, which is usually more stable and less transactional; it may even be that the higher levels of trust in this relationship allow for transparent pricing, costings, and margins, from both sides.
- 'Step-outs' are permitted: that is to say, disagreements are allowed. The supplier does not always have to say yes for the relationship to continue.

This is a long list, and taken as a whole such a description would be wildly optimistic; if all of these characteristics were to exist at once then you would have found the Holy Grail of KAM indeed! Regard them as a list of potential ambitions, or as a checklist against which you can judge to what extent you are still travelling towards a diamond team KAM relationship, or have arrived.

Compared with the earlier relationship models, perhaps the most important thing to say is that the diamond team brings you the best possible knowledge, gathers a cross-functional team (not all of whom have to be customer facing) capable of acting on that knowledge to create new propositions and, through the resultant competitive advantage gained, brings an unmatched level of security to the relationship.

Some issues with diamond teams

People working to 'tangential agendas'

One of the benefits of such teams is the way that collaboration speeds the pace of joint activities, but be warned: as things move more quickly, so the risk of saying or doing the wrong things also increases. We saw how KA managers had to take on the role of coach to facilitate the new contacts developed at the cotton-reel stage. Well, at the diamond team stage they must not only enhance those skills, to become 'super-coaches', but also take on the additional role of 'super-coordinators'.

That highly enthusiastic IT expert that you have brought in might take you down some unwanted paths if left uncoached and unmonitored, as might that young and confident R&D chemist – as indeed might the boss.

The tale of the CEO

The CEO of a multinational manufacturer was visiting one of their business unit's distributors – a key account. The business unit sold clear plastic sheeting used, among other things, to build all-round-viewing squash courts. The distributor suggested that having such a squash court on their premises would be a great sales aid, much better than the sales brochures. The CEO readily agreed – a free 'sample' would be installed. It was certainly an aid, but unfortunately the CEO had not been aware of two facts.

First, he didn't know that the cost ran into tens of thousands of pounds. Second, and in a sense worse, he didn't know that the distributor had been asking that selfsame question for some time, and had been given the selfsame answer by the KA manager: 'Sure, when you pay your bills on time, and stock our new ranges, and employ two new sales reps, and meet the following targets…'.

So, whose fault was it that a 'free squash court' was given away with nothing gained in return? The CEO should have known better, but the KA manager is equally, if not more, responsible for failing to brief the CEO. KA managers are responsible for all communications, transactions and activities between supplier and customer.

I recognize that it's not easy briefing the boss, but nobody said KAM was easy! it's actually one of the toughest challenges going, for reasons that are plain if we consider three truths about diamond teams:

● Few, if any, of the members work directly for the KA manager.
● Some may be senior to the KA manager.
● All (if they are worth their membership) are 'smarter' than the KA manager, with regard to their own speciality.

Quite a problem, and rest assured, full consideration will be given to the solutions, to be found in a combination of structural and leadership considerations (see Chapter 27), skills and capabilities (see Chapter 28) and processes (see Chapter 8, and in particular the 'contact matrix' and 'GROWs'), but for the moment we will elaborate further on the problem.

The worst of all outcomes...

Figure 7.10 illustrates what we might regard as the worst of all outcomes for a KA relationship, and much worse than all the limitations of a bow-tie. There is no team. Each point of contact is its own bow-tie, each working on its own agenda, each in danger of going off at some inappropriate tangent. We have just seen (in the tale of the CEO) the damage that can be caused by high-level departures from the script.

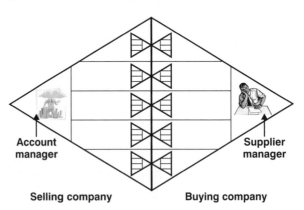

Figure 7.10 *The worst of all outcomes*
Adapted from McDonald, Millman and Rogers (1996)

It is not uncommon for this situation to exist with important customers that have not been properly managed (often through lack of authority rather than intention on the part of the KA manager) over a long period of time. Contacts have developed that were not even known about, let alone coordinated.

Watching the elephant dance

> I was once the after-dinner speaker at a sales conference of a large pharmaceutical company. The sales team (which ran to over 400) were sat at the regulation round tables, and I had decided to give them a little exercise by asking them to re-seat themselves at tables suitably labelled with the names of their accounts – in this case, the hospital trusts across the United Kingdom. Imagine my surprise to see them shyly shaking hands with their new table companions, the majority of them having not met each other before. They had been selling to the same customer for at least a year, and most of them for many years, and yet they didn't even know each others names.

The absence of an opposite number

What if there is no mirror image to the KA manager in the diamond team, no key supplier manager? They don't always exist, and their absence will certainly slow down progress towards a truly integrated team-on-team relationship. I know of at least one KA manager who, aware of this problem, worked hard to build his own main contact up into this position. There was no job title to formalize the arrangement, but more important, the contact behaved as the supplier wished, helping to build the supplier's capabilities, not simply to challenge them.

Must diamond teams always be multi-functional?

The example used – a manufacturer selling to a manufacturer – calls for a cross-functional team, but it is quite possible that a diamond team would be made up of salespeople, perhaps representing different regions or territories, or perhaps different business units, or being responsible for different product lines. A pharmaceutical company, for example, might deploy such a team, the sales professionals each representing different therapy areas, for a specific hospital trust. As ever with KAM, the team must suit the circumstance and the opportunity.

Bureaucracy, bureaucracy, and bureaucracy...

Diamond teams can be large, and their management can be daunting. The task of maintaining communications across such diverse groups can become a nightmare. Internal meetings can become so frequent that nobody has time to see the customer anymore. Perhaps I exaggerate, but the warning should be clear. The answer is simply not to allow things to develop in that way.

Take meetings for instance. Does the whole KA team have to gather for every meeting? Try to identify what we might call a 'core' team, perhaps of no more than three or four people, perhaps those with the most significant customer contacts and roles. This core team, kept within manageable bounds, should be more able to meet as often as required. The wider team – call them the surround team, or the supporting team – may meet far less frequently, and as a whole group perhaps only once a year, or in some cases not even that.

Recognize the true costs

Diamond teams don't come for free – but so often the real costs are not considered, or accounted for. People's time costs money, and the KA manager is spending that money by bringing people into the team. And don't expect to establish a diamond team while cutting travel budgets; these relationships require personal contact, particularly in the early days.

Does the KA manager not have a customer-facing role?

In extreme cases, they may not, but for 99 per cent of the cases of course they will – so why does the model (Figure 7.9) suggest otherwise?

The model is drawn to stress the extreme difference in the task between that of the sales professionals in a bow-tie relationship and KA managers in a diamond team. In the former case, they have to be great salespeople. In the latter, they have to be great business managers. In emphasizing this, the figure does appear to exclude the KA manager from customer contact, and that is perhaps a deficiency. Perhaps the picture shown in Figure 7.11 might serve the purpose better?

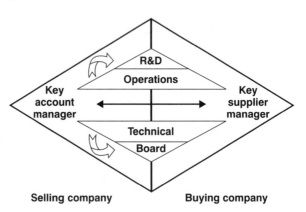

Figure 7.11   *The KA manager's customer contact*
Adapted from McDonald, Millman and Rogers (1996)

So why not show it this way in the first place? The main reason is the need to avoid any assumption on the KA managers' part that, once they have put their colleagues in touch with their opposite numbers, then they can go back to their old job of looking after the buyer. As has been said many times, the KA manager in a diamond team may be a salesperson by background, but will have to move well beyond being a salesperson in attitude and behaviour.

Yet even Figure 7.11 doesn't represent the full truth, which will have the KA manager involved with a number of those on the customer's side. Let's remember that it is a model that is attempting to represent a concept, not a specific 'map' of the relationship. If I can ask for your patience a little while longer, I promise a tool (The 'contact matrix', in Chapter 9) that will cure the problem once and for all.

Trust and partnership: real world, or myth?

These two words will figure large when aiming for diamond team relationships. You must decide what definition of each is sensible or realistic in your own circumstances. What is regarded as commendable honesty and openness in one business might well be seen as sheer stupidity in another.

> A supplier has found a solution to one of its key account's manufacturing problems. This isn't the cause for celebration that you might imagine, because the solution doesn't involve the customer buying the supplier's product; it involves a tweak to the customer's own manufacturing process that allows them to use a cheaper competitor material.
>
> So what does the supplier do: tell the customer or withhold the solution? The former is certainly collaborative, but is it foolhardy? The latter leaves open the awful prospect of being found out: 'so you knew but you didn't tell us'. I leave you to decide.

Heads you win, tails I lose?

Take care in particular with the word 'partnership'. Wait to hear it on the customer's lips first. Even then, take care. Perhaps your customer will use the lure of 'partnership' as a trap: 'Let's work in partnership,' they say, meaning: 'You give us your cost breakdowns, and then we'll take you to the cleaners…'

Is this being unduly cynical? Consider the final 'case study' in this chapter, and this time, it's entirely fictional.

> A pig and a chicken decide to go into partnership together – it was the chicken's idea. They decide to go into the catering business, specializing in traditional English breakfasts, and because it was the chicken's idea the chicken presents its ideas first.
>
> 'It's a great idea this partnership thing,' it clucks. 'I tell you what, why don't I supply the eggs, and you supply the bacon …'

The tale of the pig and the chicken

APPLICATION EXERCISE

Consider your own customer portfolio:

- For what type of customer would the *bow-tie* relationship be most appropriate?
- For what type of customer would the *diamond team* relationship be most appropriate?
  - For how many customers would something approaching the *diamond team* relationship be a practical consideration?
- Do you consider the *one-on-many* relationship to be a staging post, or the end game, for any of your key accounts?
- Who should be responsible for deciding where each customer relationship is to be pitched?
  - By what criteria will they determine the right level?

Consider your own key accounts:

- Where are your relationships at present?
- Where would you like them to be, and by when?
- What actions will be required to take them there?

Pick a live key account:

- Identify the membership of an 'ideal' *diamond team*.
  - Start by identifying the members of the decision-making 'snail'.
  - Who from your own team will be required to match up to these people?

8

Contact strategies

Remember Ken Reilly from the opening pages? He was calling on a key account and he had a good story to tell, but he was telling it to the wrong person. His contact strategy appeared to consist of 'sweet talking' secretaries.

The supplier has a daunting task when facing up to a key account: who to talk to in an organization that may positively blossom with departments, functions, sites and ever-changing job titles. The path to the real decision makers can seem like a maze, only most customers will not allow you the luxury of exploration; there are no second chances if you take the wrong turning.

And then the customer does you a favour, it seems, by making it easy for you, by supplying someone called a buyer. It gets better: perhaps your salesperson and their buyer get on like a house on fire – same hobbies, common backgrounds. Of course the salesperson has been well trained to work on those kind of leads, and soon relaxes into the comfort of familiar surroundings.

Alarm bells should already be ringing. Buyers may suggest that they are all-powerful, and may promise the prospect of a trial, a big order and a glowing future, but is it really in their hands? Except in the simplest of organizations, they are almost certainly only one part of a much larger jigsaw.

The buyer may only be the 'front man', held hostage by a variety of people in the organization, each with a different set of interests and influences. Perhaps the manufacturing department has laid down clear rules on what materials they need, and whom they should come from, and the buyer's teasing promises that they might consider a change of supplier are little more than warm air.

Yes, there is life beyond the buyer

91

The buyer may be no more than the puppet of those other interests, a rubber stamp, but how many would admit to such a position? This has ever been the supplier's dilemma: is the buyer the real focus of power, or should that be sought elsewhere – and if so, how, without antagonizing the buyer?

This chapter aims to provide a series of tools that can be used in pursuing the answers to that question, and others to come. They will help us to analyse the customer's decision-making processes, and identify the key players in that most mysterious of entities – the DMU (decision-making unit). This will in turn enable us to plan the most appropriate contact strategy, using the most appropriate relationship model (see Chapter 7).

THE CUSTOMER'S DECISION-MAKING PROCESS

Let's begin with how customers decide, in the most general sense, what to buy. (This will get a good deal more complex soon enough, but let's keep it simple for now.) A typical buying decision will go through three broad stages:

- realizing that a need exists;
- looking at the options;
- clearing up concerns, and making the final choice.

The supplier must work through that process, operating on three broad levels:

- selling to the business need decision-making process (Parts IV, V and VI of this book will deal with this aspect in some detail);
- selling to the personal need decision-making process (see Chapter 9);
- selling to the organizational decision-making process.

This matching process is represented in Table 8.1. All three levels must be worked on in parallel, which is a significant challenge when dealing with a complex decision in a complex organization. Unfortunately, such complexity tends to lead people towards attempted 'short cuts'.

New and enthusiastic but inexperienced people, particularly those from a technical or scientific background, often forget that customers are human. They discount the personal needs and head straight for the features and the benefits. By only considering one of the three selling levels, they very often lose the sale.

Older, more experienced people often have the personal side of the job sewn up. They know the individual quirks and oddities of the people they have dealt with for years, yet they too can lose the sale by thinking that this is all that matters, forgetting the need to sell on the other levels. This is a

Table 8.1 *Matching the decision-making process*

	Selling to the business needs	Selling to the personal needs	Selling to the organization
A need exists	Questioning strategies	Assessing styles	Who has the need?
Looking at the options	Presenting solutions	Matching styles	Who makes the decision? (The DMU)
Clearing up concerns, and final decision	Negotiation	Building rapport	Helping the DMU to decide

condition that some describe as having 'gone native'. At its worst, people start to think that they are being a nuisance by asking their customers to change – and then it is time for a change themselves.

The level too often ignored by so many, new or old, is the customer's organizational decision-making process, contained within the DMU.

THE CUSTOMER'S DMU (DECISION-MAKING UNIT)

Most decisions, or at least the important ones, are made by decision-making units. In some companies, these may be quite formal – project teams, sourcing teams or the procurement committee. In others, they may be so informal as to be unidentifiable; but they are there all the same, working by inference, by nods of the head and the raising of eyebrows. There are three broad types:

- authoritarian DMUs;
- consensus DMUs;
- consultative DMUs.

The authoritarian DMU

A single person – perhaps the boss, typically the owner of a smaller business – will take the decision and impose it on their colleagues and staff, sometimes even against the better judgement of the latter.

For the seller this is the easiest DMU to influence, if you can identify that individual, gain access to them, and take with you the right message, while all the time taking pains to meet their personal needs. It may be easiest to make the sale – but what about maintaining the business after that first order? It may be that the boss's decision upset others in the organization, and you may be part of the cause, having ignored their views and taken the easy road to the boss. For the unwary, short-term success may be followed by a concerted campaign against them. The wise salesperson will target the key decision maker, but be sure to keep the rest involved.

The consensus DMU

This involves some kind of 'democracy'. Perhaps all members of the DMU must agree, or maybe it is a case of a majority vote. Typically, consensus DMUs might be found in cooperatives, institutions, the government and civil service, and voluntary groups.

For the sellers this is much harder work, as they must ensure that they meet and persuade at least a majority of members, if not all.

Such decisions are often taken in private, with no supplier access to the 'committee'. The problem here is that you don't always know the mechanism and criteria for their decision. You get the order, but if you don't know why, maintaining or developing that business might be difficult. You lose the order, and if you don't know why, then you will be no further forward the next time around.

The temptation is to put it down to fortune, whichever way the decision went, but the wise salesperson will spend some time looking for the reasons, and learning from them.

The consultative DMU

Here there is an appointed decision maker – very often the commercial buyer – who will make a decision based on the views of the key influencers in the DMU. They will consult with those people and decide accordingly.

For sellers this can be the toughest one to crack – they need to know so much:

- Who is the appointed decision maker?
- Who do they consult with?
- Who do they listen to more?
- Which views carry more weight?

THE ANALYTICAL TOOLS IN THE DMU TOOLKIT

It is when faced with such a range of questions that we need to turn to our DMU Toolkit. Figure 8.1 shows a range of tools, eight labelled as 'analytical tools' and two labelled as 'action tools', that can be used to develop our contact strategy.

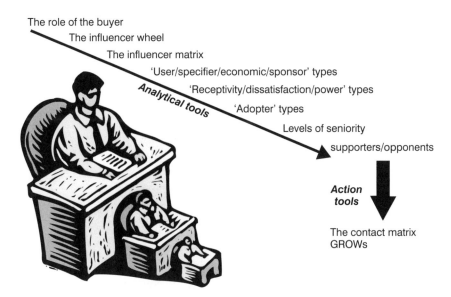

The role of the buyer
The influencer wheel
The influencer matrix
'User/specifier/economic/sponsor' types
Analytical tools
'Receptivity/dissatisfaction/power' types
'Adopter' types
Levels of seniority
supporters/opponents

Action tools

The contact matrix
GROWs

Figure 8.1 *The DMU toolkit*

We will work through the analytical tools in this section, and conclude the chapter with a discussion of the two all-important action tools: the contact matrix and GROWs.

It should be stressed that there is no need to use all of the analytical tools on any particular occasion – each one suits a different circumstance, and some will be used more often than others. You may choose to ignore some altogether if they do not match your own world. As ever with KAM, it is for you to choose.

The role of the buyer

For all our ambitions to see beyond the buyers, we must not ignore them. More than that, the ideal way to get to people beyond the buyer is *through* the buyer, with their help and encouragement. We must then begin our understanding of the DMU by establishing the role of the buyer within it.

First establish the role of the buyer in relation to the rest of the DMU

Figure 8.2 shows four potential roles, or types of involvement, based on the level of interest that buyers show in your activities and propositions, and their level of involvement in the decision-making process.

The 'lead' buyer

With both high interest and involvement, expect this buyer to take a leading role. It is very likely that the decision under question will have a direct impact on their own measures of performance, which means that the

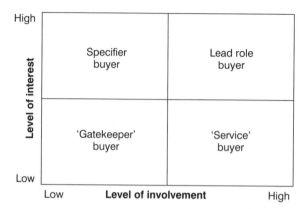

Figure 8.2 *The role of the buyer*

supplier is about to become a champion, or a sinner. Such buyers may take a positive role in introducing you to others in their organization that can contribute to a positive outcome – a true ally then in your ambitions to penetrate the snail.

The 'specifier' buyer

Very often this position suggests that the decision is to be made elsewhere and that the buyer has been called in to contribute professional expertise, helping to set guidelines for others to work by. This is very much the kind of situation where the suppliers need to get themselves in front of that group of people deeper inside the snail (see Chapter 6). Seek this buyer's advice on how to do that, volunteer the input of your colleagues, and keep the buyer informed of what goes on – a good supplier can become the eyes and ears of a buyer in such circumstances.

The 'service' buyer

We might call this the 'reluctant' buyer – performing their role on behalf of someone else, but seeing no real benefit or advantage to themselves. This can be hard going for the supplier, faced with a buyer who doesn't really care. The wise supplier might find ways of volunteering their services to take on some of the buyer's role, but will also take care to demonstrate their ability to be trusted with such involvement.

The 'gatekeeper' buyer

Why should a buyer who has no interest in your propositions, and no real involvement in the decision, still refuse you access to others? Surely they will be pleased to let you go past them? Such a buyer, contrary to the folklore of sellers, may actually be doing a good job, protecting their organization from the 'interference' of over-zealous salespeople.

The problem for suppliers is clear – they just don't know what is going on behind the scenes. They have then a choice: make the buyer more interested, through propositions that are relevant to their own interests, or aim to get past them, with the buyer's permission of course. The latter option requires persistence while avoiding becoming a nuisance, and a good approach may be to suggest that there are others in the supplier's organization better placed to do this – in other words, it isn't the salesperson trying to bypass the buyer.

The influencer wheel

Having determined that there *are* others involved in the decision beyond the buyer (a DMU), then the next step is to list them. Figure 8.3 shows a simple way to do this, as a pie-chart, the graphic nature of the listing having the advantage of being a 'foundation' tool, on to which we will add the information to be culled from the succeeding tools. We can already add, for instance, the characterization of the buyer's role from the analysis shown in Figure 8.2.

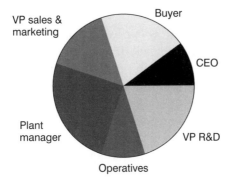

Figure 8.3 *The influencer wheel*

Some suggest an organization chart for such a list, and if you can get your hands on one that is up to date (which they rarely are!) then this is of course a good start, but it is only a start. If the members of the decision-making unit are conveniently all within a distinct organization then all is well and good, but life is not always that neat.

The influencer matrix

If we recall the challenge of the consultative DMU (above), we will see the benefits of the tool shown in Figure 8.4. The supplier needs to know: who is the key (or appointed) decision maker, with whom will that person consult, and which of those views will carry the greater weight? In other words, who influences whom?

THIS PERSON...	IS INFLUENCED BY...						
	John Smith	Sue Rogers	Terry Paine	Alex Holland	Steph Higgins	Barry Munroe	Alice Hill
John Smith		**		**			
Sue Rogers					***		*
Terry Paine							
Alex Holland		**	*				
Steph Higgins		*					
Barry Munroe	*****	**	**				
Alice Hill		**					

Figure 8.4   *The influencer matrix*

This tool is in fact a practical exposition of the concept introduced in Chapter 6, the 'opportunity snail'. By entering the members of that snail down the side and along the top of this grid, we can now map out who influences whom, and by how much (using the asterisks). It goes one better than the snail, which suggested a straight line progression of decision making, by allowing us to consider the real-world complexity of interacting multiple influencers.

Many of the 'who influences whom' questions will be answered by the realities of hierarchy and seniority, but it is just as important to consider the role of personal chemistry, inter-departmental rivalries, and politics. The aim is to seek what are called 'positive influence pathways', or in plain English, the best route to particular targets. In the example shown in Figure 8.4 it is clear that John Smith makes a big impression on Barry Monroe, and if Barry Monroe is your ultimate target, then spending time with John Smith will be a sound investment.

People who wield significant influence, as does John Smith, tend to attract the alert supplier's attentions, and chances are that plenty of time is already spent with this individual, but what about Sue Rogers? She doesn't pack such a punch with any one individual, but she appears to carry some weight with a broad range of people. Is it worth spending more time with the likes of Sue Rogers?

Completing the matrix

Where will all this knowledge come from, to make it possible to complete such analysis, and isn't it all terribly subjective? The answer to the first part of that question is, from any and all of those who have contact with the customer. The answer to the second part is, yes of course, but if it is the pooled views and observations of the team, and not the solo view of the KA manager, then it has its own value regardless of that subjectivity: it is a vehicle for stimulating debate and discussion, and the sharing and the arguing of views about that all important subject: the customer.

User/specifier/economic/sponsor

These terms will be familiar to anyone who has attended Miller–Heiman sales training, or read one of their many splendid books (see the section on 'Further reading' in the final chapter). Most decision-making units can be seen to contain people making up the four 'types of involvement' illustrated in Figure 8.5. These 'types of involvement' might exist as separate people, or an individual might have multiple reasons for being involved.

Why are they 'involved'?

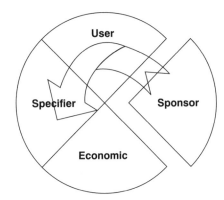

Figure 8.5   *User/specifier/economic/sponsor*
(Influence through 'type of involvement')

The sponsor

The 'sponsor' (also often called the 'coach') is someone who wishes you to succeed, for whatever reason, and will help you in your task through the provision of information, advice and support. They may be junior or senior, and they might not even be one of the active decision makers – they just have to wish you well!

A key contribution from good sponsors can be the way that they ease your path through the complexity of the customer's organization, perhaps pointing out to you the specifiers, the users and those with the economic interest.

The user

Users are people who make use of the product or service (yours or a competitor's), either actively by physical use, or by receipt of its benefits. It is quite likely that they will have strong views on what they want, and on the problems they encounter, and herein lies their importance. The customer's true needs (as opposed to what the buyer tells you) are often to be found by speaking with the users, often, and quite literally, those on the shop floor.

The problem for the supplier is that users are not always the easiest people to make contact with, and especially by a salesperson who the buyer chooses to keep at arm's length. Here is where to make full use of colleagues, whether technical service engineers, customer service staff, merchandisers, or anyone else who has good reason to make contact.

The specifier

The specifier is the person who lays down the target outcomes and other criteria for the decision. These are the 'brass-tacks' of the decision, and vital to know, but very often they might be set by someone who is at least one step removed from the physical use, and so the reality of the need. We have all been frustrated by such 'theoretical' influencers, people determined to have it their way even though the rest of the organization is crying out for something quite different.

The economic

And so we come to the money interest, the person most interested in, or most influenced by, the financial issues. They are often seen as the most important person in the DMU, and it is certainly true that they can be an ultimate roadblock – however good the case made elsewhere, they may decide it just cannot be afforded – but that is not to say that this is where the sale should be made.

Understanding these roles has some very significant advantages to the supplier seeking to navigate a path through a complex DMU:

- Focusing on the nature of someone's involvement in the decision, through these 'types', can bring far greater clarity than focusing on job titles.
- It helps identify an order of contacts – who first, and who last. A born 'hunter' (see Chapter 7) might go straight for the economic interest, the

jugular you might say, while the 'farmer' (see Chapter 7) might choose to understand their true value by speaking with users and specifiers *before* taking on the 'why are you so expensive?' challenge. The arrow in Figure 8.5 gives away my own preference in these matters.

● It helps you to consider who from the supplier team might be best placed to work with the different people in the customer's DMU.

Receptivity, dissatisfaction, or power?

You may be able to characterize individual members of a DMU by one of the three attitudes illustrated in Figure 8.6: people who are receptive to your ideas, people who are dissatisfied with the current situation, and people who wish to have power (or control) over the decision.

Why are they 'interested'?

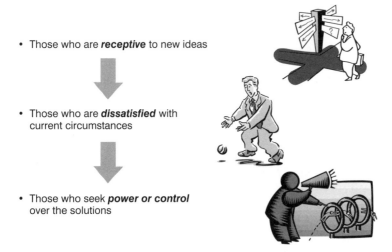

• Those who are **receptive** to new ideas

• Those who are **dissatisfied** with current circumstances

• Those who seek **power or control** over the solutions

Figure 8.6   *Receptive/dissatisified/power (Influence through 'attitude')*

We all like people who are receptive to our ideas, but are they the most important to us? We are all drawn towards people who want power and control, but are they the most important to us? Surely it's the people with the dissatisfaction that are the real key? These are the people with the problems, and problems mean needs, and needs mean solutions, and solutions mean value.

The value of the receptive folk is that they will lead us to the people with the dissatisfaction.

And what of those wanting power and control? They perhaps have the authority to decide, may be senior, and may control the purse strings, and so we by no means ignore them. Better than that, we prepare ourselves for them through our true understanding of the people with the dissatisfaction, and so the true value of our solutions.

Adopter types

People take up new ideas at different rates. Some people like anything new; we might call them 'innovators'. Others might be last in line for change; we might call them 'laggards'. Figure 8.7 illustrates the spectrum of attitudes between these two extremes.

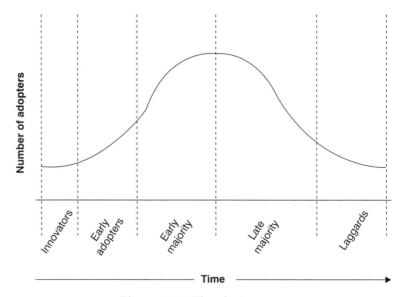

Figure 8.7   *The adopter curve*

This is a model much used by marketing folk as a means of segmenting markets, targeting effort, and tailoring messages. It is equally applicable for the purpose of targeting effort across different members of a DMU, and tailoring the messages in each case.

At the left-hand end of the spectrum, the innovators and early adopters are relatively easy to sell to. They like novelty and the words 'leading edge', 'risk', 'trial', and 'you're the first' are music to their ears.

At the right-hand end, the 'late majority' and the 'laggards' are much harder. They want evidence and proof. They want to see a track record of success and to know that somebody else has ironed out all the problems.

In the centre, the 'early majority' represent the people who come knocking on your door in floods once the idea or product is fairly well established.

Navigating the right path

Who would start their persuasion task with the laggards? They do have one benefit to the supplier – they will give them an exhaustive list of the obstacles to come and the hurdles to be jumped. As an exercise in market research, speaking to laggards has its place.

How about the innovators? Easy to sell to, certain to say yes… but won't they be just the same when your competitor comes knocking? The real problem with innovators is what everyone else in the spectrum thinks about them: nutters, crazies, weirdoes, suckers for anything new, and geeks. Not the best platform on which to base your sales approach to the next in line. Sell to innovators by all means, but don't expect them to be the most persuasive influence within their own DMU.

Aim to build your case with the good solid early majority, with a bit of help from the early adopters. And make sure you do this by using the right language, and by putting the right people in front of them. People buy most readily from people like themselves – don't send your own laggards to stimulate the customer's innovators, and take care when putting your most enthusiastic innovators in front of the customer's 'good solid' early majority.

To use this model in practice will certainly call on the KA manager's skills as a coach, as we discussed in Chapter 7 when speaking of the cotton-reel and the diamond team relationship models.

Levels of seniority

Don't get stuck at too junior a level, but also don't cause resentment in the ranks by only attending to the bosses. Figure 8.8 suggests (admittedly rather simplified) the roles taken by different levels of seniority in the customer's organization, so suggesting the nature of the contact and relationship you might be seeking with each.

Are we at the right level?

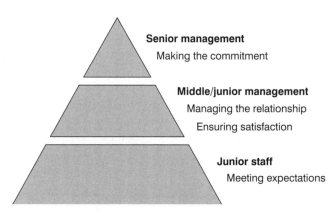

Figure 8.8 *Levels of seniority*

Junior staff have to stick to the rules, while breaking the rules is what makes senior managers senior. Junior staff have targets to meet, while senior managers set those targets. Junior staff are focused on today, while senior management (it is to be hoped) are focused on far beyond tomorrow. Obvious stuff perhaps, but too often suppliers end up having the wrong conversations at the different levels, and all too often because they rely on one person to handle them all – that Superman or Superwoman of a Super-rep working in the one-on-many relationship model (see Chapter 7).

An interesting exercise can be to note down some comparisons of the wants and needs of these different levels ('wants' are desires, 'needs' are necessities). What do the junior contacts want and need, compared with the middle managers, compared with the bosses? Do they correspond or do they conflict? What does this tell you about the nature of the customer's organization? Does it suggest that your propositions might be better suited to one level than another?

Making it to the top

One of the marks of a key supplier, and of a mature key account diamond team relationship, is that contacts are made at the very top of the customer's organization. It is no surprise then that many a salesperson dreams of finding themselves talking with the customer's CEO – some might even loiter around receptions' lobbies at ludicrously early hours of the day in just such a hope... Perhaps there is a better way of establishing those contacts: get your own CEO involved. If this is a genuine key account then they should be interested enough.

You don't need to be a 'lobby-loiterer'...

Supporters and opponents

Books on business are often filled with four-box matrices, and this one has its fair share, but this next is one of my own favourites. Figure 8.9 aims to plot the members of the customer's DMU based on two considerations:

- Do they support your proposition on a business level?
- Do they have trust and confidence in you as a supplier?

Some interesting things happen when you get a KA team to plot the people in this way. Sometimes they find themselves in violent disagreement, and so the tool has worked on one level – a vehicle to stimulate debate. Sometimes they find that all the names go into the 'supporter' box, and yet they have less than 20per cent of the customer's business. So are they fooling themselves, or are they ignoring a whole chunk of people?

Avoiding people who neither like your company nor go along with your proposition (opponents) is a very human thing to do, but as a key account team you cannot afford this particular human frailty. Opponents are

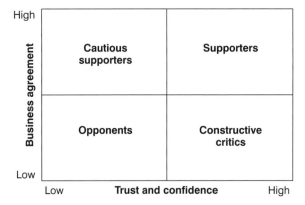

Figure 8.9 *Supporters and opponents*

particularly susceptible to what we might call the 'fester-factor'; at best they sulk and gripe (a peculiarly infectious behaviour when it is rife deep inside a customer), while at worst they may be actively campaigning against you, energetically boosting your competitors (your opponent may very likely be your competitor's coach). Such people cannot be ignored.

Aim to discover why they have such low trust and confidence in you: is it history, is it personal chemistry, is it misunderstanding? Then aim to do something about it. Don't try to move opponents upwards in the matrix before you have moved them rightwards: people who don't trust you won't listen to the very finest of propositions (a truth that you may need to spend some coaching time discussing with the technical and scientific members of your key account team).

A great exercise for an account team debate

Cautious supporters are a potential risk – they are effectively waiting for a better option to come along, from a 'better-looking' competitor. Again, aim to understand their reservations and act to remove them.

Constructive critics can tell you where you are going wrong, which is something that we should be eager to hear, even though they don't agree with our propositions.

In short, aim to cover all four groups of people (and it is usual for all four to exist even in the best of relationships), perhaps by deploying your team in a way most likely to effect the movements rightward and upward that you need.

USING THE TOOLS IN PRACTICE

We have examined a range of analytical tools and should stress once more that they form a toolkit to be dipped into as suits the particular circumstance.

Some work well in concert with others, some might be best used as individual pieces of analysis.

I want to close this section by looking at two last examples that are in their different ways a synthesis of much of the analysis we have considered.

Who sits around the table?

The first is a synthesis is a very general sense of the interactions within a DMU, conceived as a series of round tables around which different people sit. Figure 8.10 shows a central table around which a small number of decision makers sit. They are important, but it is not enough to focus on them alone. A larger table has sitting around it those that we call influencers, the nature of their influence being any mixture of the kinds we have been considering throughout this chapter. A third table has a yet larger group of people sitting around its edge – the implementers.

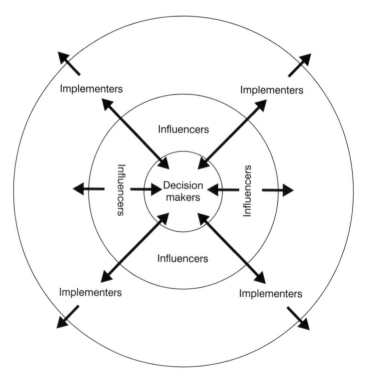

Figure 8.10 *Who sits around the table?*
(with thanks to Steve Lobb)

The arrows remind us that the flow of influences and decisions goes both ways, and it is for the supplier to determine which of those lines they wish to work along, which to develop, and perhaps even which to attempt to remove.

What I like about this tool is the way it gets used by a team. Draw it up on a flipchart, issue everyone in the team with pads of that wonderfully half-sticky yellow paper, and ask them to write the names of all their contacts and affix them to the flipchart. Stand back and cue the debate...

Another great tool for team discussions...

Putting the tools together

The second example shows how one KA team combined three of these analytical tools into a hugely valuable composite analysis, from which they have been able to develop a very successful contact strategy. This is shown in Figure 8.11.

...and perhaps one to put in the KA plan?

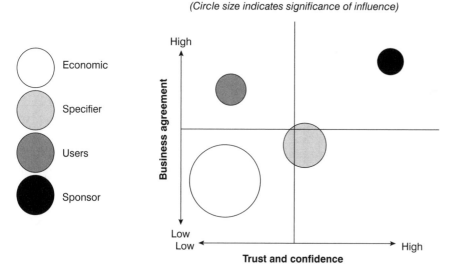

(Circle size indicates significance of influence)

Figure 8.11 *Putting the tools together*

The team combined:

- the opponent/supporter matrix;
- the user/specifier/economic/sponsor analysis;
- the information from the influencer matrix.

In this case, the economic buyer is clearly a big problem, and there must be a strategy to improve that person's feelings of trust in the supplier – achieved through something of a 'charm offensive' by senior management (after much discussion it was recognized that the economic buyer's low level of trust was due to a long period of inattention by the supplier to an individual clearly motivated by status and recognition).

There are allies within the customer's DMU, although the team recognized that they had been putting too much faith in a sponsor who loved them but was not particularly well regarded.

The users were very positive about the product they received, but had felt let down by a poor delivery track record – the KA manager quickly secured the help of the logistics people on the team to assess the cause and implement a highly promoted improvement plan.

The specifier was in need of a boost to their confidence in the product, and this was achieved by sending them some detailed reports on its efficacy, drawn up by the supplier's technical service team working alongside the users.

A repeat analysis was conducted after six months, with the gratifying sight of the circles moving steadily rightward and upward.

THE ACTION TOOLS IN THE DMU TOOLKIT

It has been stressed that the analytical tools in the toolkit (Figure 8.1) are 'optional', depending on the circumstance. They lead us towards the two 'action tools' – the contact matrix and GROWs (Figure 8.1) – which are so important, so valuable and so fundamental to the practice of KAM that I would like to suggest you regard them as mandatory. I did say back in Chapter 1 that there were very few rules of KAM, but here we come face-to-face with one of them.

Let me go further. Any KA plan that lacks these two tools is in my view deficient. Any KA plan that is made up *only* of these two tools is a good deal more than half a KA plan.

The contact matrix

The contact matrix is what makes the difference between a 'sales plan' and a 'key account plan'

The pure essence of any practical KAM strategy, and any workable KA plan, has to be: *who works with whom, and for what purpose*. In Chapter 7 we looked at the introduction of colleagues to the customer, whether working through individual 'cotton-reel' models, or as a combined 'diamond team'. Those models were either conceptual or idealized, and I promised a tool that would bring them to a practical and real-world life. That tool is the contact matrix, shown in Figure 8.12.

The significance of this simple tool – listing the supplier team along the top and the customer team down the side, and indicating the contacts by some method of XXXs – becomes apparent if we remind ourselves of some of the challenges of diamond teams:

	Account manager	Your team member	Your team member	Your team member	Your team member	Your team member
Buying director	XXX					
Their team member	[XX]		XXX	X		[XX]
Their team member		XXX			X	
Their team member	X			[XXX]		[X]
Their team member						
Their team member	X					[XXX]

Figure 8.12 *The contact matrix*

- Very few if any of the members of a diamond team work directly for the KA manager.
- Many of the members may be senior to the KA manager.
- All of them, in their specialist capacity, are 'smarter' than the KA manager.

The danger of people following independent agendas was well discussed, and the contact matrix, alongside its attendant GROWs, is the means of avoiding those problems.

Most CRM (customer relationship management) IT systems should have a capability of creating a contact matrix, but I confess I prefer to keep it as a separate document, perhaps using an Excel spreadsheet, that is available not only to everyone in the team, but also those who sit around the team, and that is referred to regularly, and certainly at every formal meeting of the KA team.

If an Excel spreadsheet is used, the 'comment' facility allows you to add all sorts of information to the matrix, perhaps recording the DMU analysis (as shown in Figure 8.13), and the all-important GROWs (which we will come to in just a moment).

What it tells us

The example in Figure 8.12 should shout a few things out loud:

- There is one member of the customer team that nobody sees. This is not uncommon in a complex situation where everyone thinks that 'someone else is handling that one'. The contact matrix brings such mis-assumptions to light.

- Four people are in contact with one member of the customer's team. Again, not uncommon in a situation where contacts have developed over long periods of time, but is the poor soul being swamped by the supplier, or worse, are the team members speaking at cross purposes. The contact matrix alerts us to such issues.

- If the number of crosses is used to indicate the importance of a particular contact, and if symbols or colours are used to indicate whether those contacts are 'good or bad' (the bad contacts in the example are shown by the crosses within boxes), then there should quickly be some more alarms sounding. First, action needs to be taken with the two 'triple-cross' contacts that are showing as poor. Second, a coaching session is long overdue with the team member who has three points of contact, all bad.

The ever-changing scene

When working with a complex customer, there may be several DMUs in operation – perhaps separate business units, or locations, or buying processes – and it may become too confusing to try to capture all of this on the one contact matrix. Separate matrices are fine, provided you don't lose the big picture – perhaps a grand summary, or 'master matrix' will remain useful.

The contact matrix is not a static tool, people come and go, and those changes must be captured by regular reviews. Keep it simple, and the reviews will not be a burden; over-complicate the tool and it will fast become a bureaucratic nightmare. Above all else, adapt this tool to suit your own circumstances.

The GROWs

Of all the tools of KAM, perhaps this one is the most valuable?

The matrix shows the fact of a contact, but what of the purpose of those contacts? They will be many and varied of course: to gather information, to promote your solutions, to secure an order, to solve a problem, to implement a project, to enhance your credibility, to remove a competitor, and so they go on.

With such scope and variety, it is vital that everybody involved with the customer knows their own purpose, the purpose of others, and any links or boundaries between those purposes. Without such definition, all the potential perils and pitfalls of the cotton-reel and diamond relationships highlighted in Chapter 7 can, and probably will, beset you.

So we add to the contact matrix our second 'action tool' – the GROW:

- G = Goal – *the overall purpose of the contact.*
- R = Role – *the activities to be carried out in pursuit of that goal.*
- O = Obligation – *the responsibilities of the team member to the team.*
- W = Work plan – *the details of dates and actions.*

Each contact should have an attached GROW, as shown in Figure 8.13.

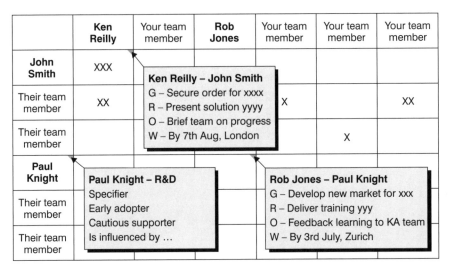

	Ken Reilly	Your team member	Rob Jones	Your team member	Your team member	Your team member
John Smith	XXX					
Their team member	XX			X		XX
Their team member					X	
Paul Knight						
Their team member						
Their team member						

Ken Reilly – John Smith
G – Secure order for xxxx
R – Present solution yyyy
O – Brief team on progress
W – By 7th Aug, London

Paul Knight – R&D
Specifier
Early adopter
Cautious supporter
Is influenced by …

Rob Jones – Paul Knight
G – Develop new market for xxx
R – Deliver training yyy
O – Feedback learning to KA team
W – By 3rd July, Zurich

Figure 8.13   *The contact matrix with GROWs (and DMU information)*

Who should write the GROWs?

Certainly not the KA manager, however tempting it may be. The purpose of the contact matrix and GROWs is to establish a team approach, within which are the different elements of expertise and specialism. To do this, aim to follow a few golden rules:

- Specialists will often know better than the KA manager what they can contribute to the team and the customer.
- It is the KA manager's job to extract that contribution, through discussion with the team member and through coaching.
- People will be more motivated to contribute if they feel they have had a hand in deciding their contribution.
- People, particularly those that don't work for the KA manager, and may be senior to the manager, rarely respond well to being 'told' what to do.

- As the KA manager, you want the members of your team to develop a level of self-management, to be achieved through the simple discipline of GROWs regularly discussed and updated.

What is the timescale of a GROW?

Experience shows that making GROWs too short term can lead to problems. If people have to renew them every two weeks, then they won't get renewed after the first occasion. The real answer to this question depends of course on the nature of the task, but in any case, aim to make the 'GRO' portion as long term as possible, leaving the 'W' for the short-term actions.

APPLICATION EXERCISE

Identify a live key account:

- Work through each of the analytical tools described in this chapter:
    - the 'DMU' type;
    - the role of the buyer;
    - the influencer wheel;
    - the influencer matrix;
    - the 'user/specifier/economic/sponsor' types;
    - the 'receptivity/dissatisfaction/power' types;
    - the 'adopter' types;
    - the levels of seniority;
    - the supporters/opponents analysis;
    - the 'who sits round the table' analysis.
- Which of these analytical did you find the most useful?
- Who else from your team will need to make an input into these tools?
- Based on this analysis, draw up a first draft contact matrix.
- Write your own GROW.
- How will you ensure that the contact matrix is populated by a full set of GROWs?

9

The human factor

The high levels of analytical and planning skills required for KAM have led some to liken it to a kind of mathematical process. While there can be some merit in such a view it does run the danger of forgetting that, beneath all the analysis and all the process, we are dealing with people, human beings with all their foibles and weaknesses.

In Chapter 8 we described a three-pronged sales approach for working through the customer's decision-making process; selling to their business needs, their personal needs, and their organizational needs. Chapter 8 considered the organizational needs and the realm of the DMU. Much of the rest of this book (Parts IV, V and VI) will deal with the mechanisms for matching the customer's business needs. This chapter will look at how we might aim to match their personal needs.

Make sure that everyone on the team realises how important this is

We are talking here of interpersonal skills, and when it comes to the question of what training might be required for the members of a KA team, this always figures high on the list, particularly if the team is newly formed, composed of members with little experience of customer contact, and approaches life with a strong scientific or technical bias. It should also figure high on the KA manager's list of topics for coaching.

This chapter will take a deliberately broad sweep at the subject, to establish some of the concepts that you should aim to have instilled in your team, but then I will leave it there, not attempting to discuss or instruct you about the particular skills required; those will be best tackled through formal training and regular coaching.

LOGIC OR EMOTION?

Perhaps the hardest lesson for non-salespeople to learn (and, for that matter, a few sales people as well) is that the customer does not always make decisions for logical, let alone rational, reasons. Harvard Business School tells us that their research shows as much as 80 per cent of decisions taken in business are taken for 'emotional' reasons.

'80% of decisions taken in business are taken for "emotional" reasons' (Harvard Business School)

Consider a buyer looking to buy a steel-making plant. This is a massive task. The decision will run over months, maybe years. The decision will involve large teams of people from the buyer's own organization and from various potential suppliers. Even once a decision is made, there will be a lengthy process of determining specific needs and tailoring the supplier's offer. All in all, the buyer might expect to be dealing with the chosen supplier over a number of years. In such a circumstance, how far will the buyer proceed with a potential supplier that they cannot trust, that they feel uncomfortable working with, and just plain 'don't like'?

Research has shown that when customers change suppliers, while it might be expected that the key reasons were things like finding better products or prices elsewhere, the real reasons lie in more human issues. Figure 9.1 shows that the biggest killer is 'indifference' – a supplier that just doesn't seem to care. Think of your own purchasing decisions as a consumer: do you return to shops that don't seem to know you are there?

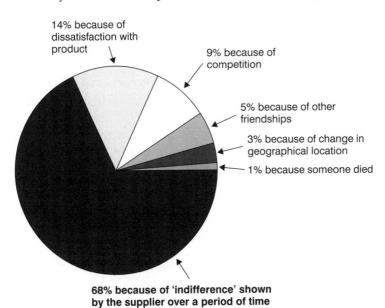

Figure 9.1 *Why customers change suppliers*

Consider a buying decision. Two companies are offering the same product, a commodity. Their specifications are identical, as are their prices. There is no previous history of supply with either company. How does the customer decide?

- How were they treated during the sale?
- Who do they trust?
- Who do they like?

Consider another buying decision. Two companies are offering high-tech solutions to a complex problem. They both have the right technical capabilities. The buyer knows that a successful supplier will have to work with a wide range of people, identifying with their individual needs and sometimes arbitrating between different views and opinions. How do they decide with which supplier to work?

- What skills of tact and diplomacy did the supplier display?
- How might the supplier handle conflict?
- Will they understand the human factors?

Two different decisions but deep down the same issues: are they 'people' people?

BUILDING RAPPORT

Building rapport is one of the keys to good interpersonal skills – the ability to identify the other person's personal motivations and then to work within those bounds.

There are dozens (perhaps even hundreds) of models that break the complexity of human motivations down into bite-size chunks and then suggest some behaviours on the seller/persuader's part that will help them to develop the desired rapport. Many are excellent, some are tawdry, and provided you avoid the latter it doesn't much matter which one you adopt. If there is already a language (for that is what these models are) used within your business, then stick with it. If not, the following might help:

- Being persuasive is much less about the logic of your case and far more about the way in which it is argued.
- What the customer believes is more important than what you know to be the facts.

- The best persuaders recognize the importance of the client's personal motivations.
- The best persuaders aim to persuade not through telling but through involving.
- The best persuaders speak little and listen a lot.
- The best persuaders recognize that they will only be listened to once they have earned the right to be listened to – shown that they are honest and trustworthy (being the 'expert' comes a long way down the list after those two).
- Speaking like a silver-tongued angel will come to nothing if you fail to empathize with the listener's issues.
- To be persuasive in a 1:1 situation it is important to get the chemistry right.

Getting the chemistry right

Excepting all those marriages made up of complete opposites (the happy Mr and Mrs Jack Spratts of this world), the most common route to rapport through the right chemistry is the matching of like outlooks and like attitudes. People driven by ambition usually get along best with like-minded souls – those that just want to get through life unruffled are likely to frustrate them, or just leave them cold. Similarly, those that thrive in the company of others will seek out similarly sociable animals.

Figure 9.2 describes three particular personal motivations, or chemical elements. The model suggests that we all make our decisions in life as a result of all three of these motivations, but that each individual has a unique chemical mix.

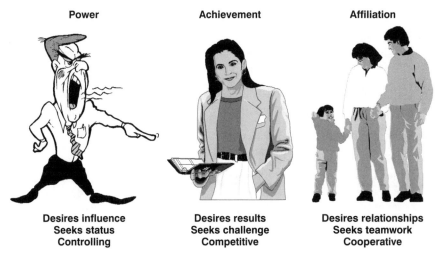

| Power | Achievement | Affiliation |

Desires influence
Seeks status
Controlling

Desires results
Seeks challenge
Competitive

Desires relationships
Seeks teamwork
Cooperative

Figure 9.2 *Personal motivations*

Most people, it is suggested, will have one of these three as their 'lead' motivation, and any attempt by a 'persuader' to build rapport will need to take that lead motivation on board.

- The power motivation is about a desire for control, for getting things your way, being in charge, making sure things are in good order.
- The achiever motivation is about seeking challenges and wanting success, beating targets, being competitive, perhaps with others, perhaps with yourself.
- The affiliator motivation is about recognizing the value and importance of relationships, of teamwork and of cooperation.

Learning to observe

With good training it is possible to learn how to observe these motivations in others, from the words they use, the nature of their environment, the way they work with others, their use of time, their behaviour in meetings, and plenty more besides. Table 9.1 summarizes some of the more typical 'clues' to a person's personal motivation.

Table 9.1 *Spotting the motivations*

	Spotting the 'achiever' motivation	Spotting the 'affiliator' motivation	Spotting the 'power' motivation
The words they use:	'It' (ie the task)	'Us' and 'we'	'I' and 'me'
The way they involve others:	Focus on experts	Broad – valuing a team	Limited
The attitude to relationships:	Fine if they move things forward	Valued in themselves	For me to control
The nature of their demands:	'What's the bottom line?'	'How will we benefit?'	'What's in it for me?'
Their use of time:	Faster – 'don't slow me down'	Slower – 'don't rush me'	My pace…
How they handle meetings/agendas:	'Let's cut to the chase…'	What's our agenda?'	Here's my agenda…'
Their environment:	Organized	Personalized	Dominating
Their clothes:	Making a statement?	Conforming?	Making a statement?

It must be stressed that each individual observation in this summary, when taken in isolation, may tell us nothing about the individual. Someone sitting behind a large desk isn't necessarily motivated by 'power'; they may be borrowing someone's office for the day, they might even hate the desk! No one thing labels a person as 'power', 'achiever' or 'affiliator'; it is a jigsaw puzzle of observations over time that may build towards a picture.

Continue to observe, continue to question your assessments, resist the temptation to pigeonhole anyone as an 'absolute anything', and above all, discuss your thoughts with your colleagues. Use the language in coaching sessions and aim to establish it as the team's way of discussing the individuals in the customer's DMU.

Learning to match

That same training that will help you with your observation skills will then help you to identify those behaviours most likely to build rapport. The idea of matching is important.

If you are working with an 'achiever' then it will be wise to be organized, on time, to come with a plan, to focus on results (good and bad), keep records, show progress, and *maybe* suggest a working lunch (or even better, working breakfast).

With an 'affiliator' you might bring colleagues, recognize the importance of the introductions and the 'small-talk', discuss the opinions of others, express your own feelings, and show that nobody is in too much of a hurry.

Such matching is important, but not absolute; matching the power motivation head on might not always bring the best results! This one requires a little more subtlety, perhaps positioning yourself as someone who will be an achiever 'on their behalf'. Be sure to ask their opinions, seek their advice, give them alternatives from which to choose, and if they have a position of status, find ways to recognize it.

Developing the skills

For all the comments in this chapter it is important for me not to suggest, through too many 'pat' examples, that this is something to be seen in black and white. In any case, you don't develop skills in this kind of area through reading books. If you know that you or your team need to improve their interpersonal skills then I strongly suggest that you look to training and coaching (see Chapters 28 and 33 for some suggestions) for your solutions.

A conscience prodder: **do you select your ILA managers based on chemistry, or geographic location?**

APPLICATION EXERCISE

Identify a live decision-making unit in one of your key accounts:

- Assess and describe each member using the achiever/affiliator/power definitions.
    - What clues helped you to make those descriptions?
- Imagine you are briefing a colleague who has to interact with three members of the customer's DMU, each one defined by a different one of these three motivations:
    - How would you brief them to behave in front of each person?
    - What are the most important 'do's'?
    - What are the most important 'don'ts'?
- How might you build this analysis into the contact matrix and GROWs?

10

The good, the bad, the sad and the ugly

This chapter shares five examples of real experience: two good, one bad, one sad and one ugly. They are all genuine cases, but for reasons that I hope are obvious some details have been changed.

It is usually easier to come up with the bad, sad and ugly stories than it is to come up with the good ones. This is not because there are more failures than successes, but because the failures always seem to have more that we can learn from – hence my ratio.

Having said that, the 'good stories' are very good, and will be kept till last. The 'bad' is bad because KAM was never considered in a circumstance that cried out for it. The 'sad' is sad because the supplier was trying hard to forge a true diamond relationship, but a few slips in discipline let them down. The 'ugly' is much worse than the bad and the sad put together – it is about an excess of zeal that nearly pulled the business apart.

THE BAD STORY

A while back, the international community came together to ban a particularly damaging product that had been identified as being a major contributor to global warming: CFCs.

**What happens
when you ignore
'chains' and 'snails'**

Surprisingly, this was particularly good news to one manufacturer of that product, or perhaps not so surprisingly – they had been looking ahead and had developed an alternative product, one that didn't have the same bad effects. Not only that, but for now at least, they were the only supplier with such an alternative.

The old product had been used in a range of applications, from refrigerants to air conditioning and aerosol sprays. The manufacturer had simple, but good, relationships with their customers in each of these markets; the bow-tie relationship (see Chapter 7) was the norm.

Based on their current sales of the old product, plus a significant growth forecast due to their new competitive advantage, the supplier proceeded to build three new manufacturing plants – this was going to be a big one, and on a global platform.

What they didn't do, at least any more than usual, was talk to their customers. Why should they? After all, the old product was banned, they had a replacement, and customers would have to beat a path to their door. All they needed to do was ask their existing contacts, the buyers, how much of the old product they bought (from the manufacturer and the competitors), and use this as a forecast for the new product. Simple, and a task easily accomplished through the existing bow-tie contacts.

Unfortunately things didn't go to plan. The buyers had seemed ready to accept the new product, even agreeing to the new premium prices that it carried, but the customers (that collection of people sitting beyond the buyer) resented the 'arrogance' of the supplier in supposing that they had no choice. They actively sought alternatives, and instructed their buyers accordingly.

There were no alternative suppliers of the new product, but there *were* alternative solutions to the problem presented by the CFC ban. Take the aerosol market (which accounted for over half of the manufacturer's sales projections): how many aerosols with propellant gases, banned or otherwise, do you see nowadays? It's all roll-ons or pump-action. Admittedly, they are often inferior in performance to the old aerosols, with a tendency to dribble down the elbow, but they *are* the choice of the market.

The supplier's new manufacturing plants were never filled to capacity, or anything like it, and a technically brilliant product landed up in the 'how do we dispose of this?' file.

Moral of the story?

A new product, no matter how good, will risk failure if the supplier doesn't talk with the market. The buyer alone is not the market. Indeed, the buyers had seemed happy that the supplier had an answer to their problem – the banning of an existing item. The 'market', or what in Chapter 5 we called the 'opportunity chain', included the customer's manufacturing people (who led the charge in resenting being told what they had to do), the R&D people (who had a dozen better ideas, as they always do), the sales and marketing people (who had no desire to see the price of their products increase), and then beyond that, the customers' customers. It was a situation crying out for a cross-functional team sell.

The supplier chose to go it alone. Their value was eroded through their lack of knowledge and understanding. There could have been alternative approaches, but how likely were they to be seen, or acted upon, given the 'hunter-killer' sales approach pursued?

In short, if we recall the model for managing the future discussed in Chapter 4 – Figure 4.3), there was a disastrous imbalance between the true market opportunity and the resources applied by the supplier – too big a manufacturing effort (three plants!), too small a sales and marketing effort. Where KAM might have helped, 'selling' was expected to be enough.

THE SAD STORY

A very capable supplier of ink had been developing a diamond team relationship with its number one customer, a manufacturer of office printers. The supplier had been developing their capability from being a simple 'supplier of products' towards a 'supplier of solutions', and high hopes were held for a newly formed contact between the two R&D functions, what both supplier and customer saw as the effective hub of a new business relationship.

Partnership is great, but it should never lead to complacency

At their very first meeting the customer briefed the young chemist sat before them on a new project – the most important they had to date, they said. The project was to develop what they called 'dry-fasteners', an additive that would make the ink dry faster on the page, and so help them with their number one goal: faster, smudge-free printing. If they succeeded, the supplier would gain significant competitive advantage, and so the young chemist reported back to the R&D boss, and a new project was set up. The project proceeded on target, and on time, and a significant sum of money was invested.

After 18 months of work the project was nearly complete when the customer rang to say 'it was all off'. To the supplier's great distress, it transpired that a paper manufacturer had approached the customer with a new type of paper, one that would help ordinary ink to dry faster.

The story gets worse, and sadder. The new paper worked just as well with much cheaper grades of ink, so not only did the project fold, but the supplier saw the low-grade ink manufacturers rubbing their hands…

The story gets worse, and sadder still. The new paper was only a temporary expedient. The real solution was to be a change to the printer itself – the addition of arms that held the printed paper while it dried – a solution that made it even easier for the printer manufacturer to consider cheaper ink suppliers.

Moral of the story?

Asking the customer is great. Doing what they tell you is great. Managing successful projects is great. But, if you are really to help the customer, you have to understand the dynamics of the market in which they operate. Were there other solutions to the 'faster, smudge-free printing' problem? Of course there were, and we have seen two of them. Should the supplier have known? Of course, but unfortunately they allowed the R&D contact to drive the whole show.

Figure 7. 10 (see Chapter 7) illustrated what we called the 'worst outcome' of a supposed diamond team, with individual bow-tie relationships taking on their own agenda. Is this what happened here? And where was the KA manager all of this time?

A sharp-witted KA manager, coordinating the team and looking for the broader picture, should have seen that the customer was asking them to develop a 'feature' (dry-fasteners in the ink), while what they should have been discussing was the problem (the aim of faster, smudge-free printing).

This particular R&D function responded quickly to the request for a feature – the technical spec was wonderfully clear – and went at it like a racehorse, blinkers applied. Indeed, the KA manager wasn't even informed until after the project had been set up. Not that the manager objected overly much, being busy enough with other things, like doing deals with the buyer.

THE UGLY STORY

Overkill and oversight – two sins to avoid

A manufacturer of a fast-selling consumer product, working in a very mature market, saw their salvation in KAM. Developing 'strategic partnerships' with their most important retail customers was to be the route to competitive advantage.

Nine key account managers were appointed for 15 key accounts, and were given broad new authority to act. Their first act was to gather about them key account teams, or KATs, representing the company's functions. *Everyone* was represented. With so many teams and so many members, and with so many meetings, a whole wing of the head office was refurbished as a suite of 'KAT rooms'. This was to be a high-profile 'initiative'.

Now the fun began. Teams met, and met, and met. Interminable meetings, badly run, with key account managers imposing their views on team members from functions they but poorly understood.

The more ambitious teams went out to meet the customer at the earliest opportunity, and seasoned buyers were pleased of the chance to lecture new faces on past failures. The teams came back eager to get to work on a huge range of corrective projects.

But this was KAM out of control, and sin was committed after sin:

- Teams didn't need representatives from *every* function. Many members were confused and then frustrated by the whole affair. The functions began to resent the whole idea.
- Customer service suffered as people met, rather than served.
- Keen but commercially naive people were put in front of customers who were only too quick to get commitments to all sorts of promises, most of which could not be kept.
- As in the Chinese Cultural Revolution, a 'thousand flowers' were encouraged to bloom. Most were badly conceived projects with little or no real customer commitment, doomed to expensive failure.
- Dominant egos were allowed to run riot and excess followed excess.
- After a while the customers began to tire of an excessive number of visits, meetings and wordy reports. The supplier was banned from a whole range of contacts, even those that might have been to mutual advantage.
- Before long, the words 'key account' brought a bad taste to the mouth and those things that *should* have been done were ignored under an excuse of world-weary cynicism.

Moral of the story?

KAM is not a 'sales initiative', nor a reckless revolution. It is a serious, cross-functional management process, requiring disciplined management. It takes planning, with clear objectives and outcomes, and a proper balance of resources against the market opportunity.

It was excessive zeal that killed KAM: a desire to do everything at once, at fever pitch, involving as many as possible, and all to the same mould and pattern. Even that *might* have succeeded, had the supplier's zeal been matched by the customer's. In Figure 7.4 (Chapter 7) we considered the 'frustration zones' of KAM that result from a mismatch of strategic intents – and this supplier found themselves firmly and squarely stuck in one such zone, or perhaps we might better call it a frustration mire.

HINDSIGHT, OR FORESIGHT?

OK, the telling of such bad, sad and ugly stories is all down to bucket-loads of hindsight. I make no apology for that; in fact I would go as far as saying that KA managers should be fully qualified in the art of hindsight – it teaches us a good deal.

They should have even better qualifications in that other great art – foresight. And the solution is at hand; one of the essential strengths of diamond team relationships is that they help to give us foresight, which brings me to the 'good' stories.

THE GOOD STORY

Diamond teams and foresight...

A customer decided to ask its supplier for consignment stock, having grown tired of depending on a less than scintillating OTIF (on time in full) performance. What it actually wanted was better OTIF, and consignment stock seemed to the buyer to be the easiest way to get it.

That could have been it, and if there had been a simple bow-tie relationship between supplier and customer it almost certainly would have been, but this supplier had a diamond team relationship, and those wider contacts began to alert the team to some pending problems.

First of all, there was no physical room on the customer's premises for such a consignment stock. Then it became clear that the client was shifting their production from a small number of standard lines to a far more bespoke offer that would require a wider range of raw materials, often in small or hard-to-forecast quantities. Added to this, there was a long-term plan to spin off much of the manufacturing activity to satellites. Saying yes to consignment stock was going to commit the supplier to three or four separate consignment stocks, each of hard-to-forecast and infrequently used materials.

With that in mind the supplier suggested an alternative. Why not use our contacts with your manufacturing logistics and marketing people to help us *both* prepare better forecasts? The result was the improved OTIF the buyer wanted, and a raft of additional benefits for the supplier in terms of yet greater knowledge.

Moral of the story?

Knowledge helps you make better choices, and true knowledge comes from a breadth of contacts. The most significant part of this success story is of course the fact that the individual contacts reported back their individual knowledge to the team – a *true* diamond team.

THE SECOND GOOD STORY

The supplier was in the packaging business, working with the food industry. They were organized into four business units, each specializing in their own product: corrugated card, plastic film, glass and metal cans. Each unit sold to the same customers, but in very different volumes. It seemed that what one business unit regarded as a key account, another might easily regard as a plain nuisance!

Most investments depend on a little luck. KAM is about making your own luck.

The customers saw the supplier as four separate entities, with no particular strengths carried over from one to another. The result was a patchwork quilt of relationships and a certain amount of frustration from buyers having to deal with so many different people and four rather different standards of service.

One of their larger customers bought cans from the supplier, but nothing else. They were perfectly happy with that supplier, indeed, they were considered a key supplier, but thought nothing of the other products on offer – glass, card and film were purchased from competitors.

The customer had a problem, not with the supplier, but with their own packing line in general. Hundreds of thousands of cans and bottles were filled each day and yet the whole line could come to a halt because of shortages of boxes or film at moments of peak volume. It was all down to the problems of forecasting for four different materials, each with its own lead times, and on a line that was pressed for space at the best of times.

The key account manager for the can supplier saw the problem, quite by chance when visiting the line, and a solution occurred to her. The supplier had access to the best forecasts available from this customer – cans were important, and as a key supplier they were kept well informed.

If they could use that information with their sister businesses, then perhaps a better flow of materials (bottles, card and film, as well as cans) might ensue? Moreover, if they could make coordinated deliveries of *all* materials, the customer's goods inward bays would be saved the chaos of peak periods and the materials would find their way to the line more speedily.

At the end of a long story, all of this was achieved – shared forecasts and coordinated deliveries from all four businesses. Deliveries were made in 'just in time' returnable 'pods' that contained the right mix of all four materials. The crowning glory of the idea was the redesign of the customer's packaging area, using these 'pods' as the basic building blocks. Key supplier status was achieved for *all* packaging materials, with a significant increase in the security of supply for all concerned.

Great stuff, but how did it happen? Well, first of all, not in anything like the time this description might have suggested. This was a three-year project.

The toughest challenge was getting the four businesses to work in unison, or even think of working in unison. The breakthrough, one year into the project, was getting an agreement that this was a key account for each of the businesses, despite the very different histories of supply. It took support from the top, it took the appointment of a cross-business key account manager, and it took a lot of communicating and educating.

This got the project to the halfway point, a semi-committed supplier with the semblance of a solution. Now came the task of engaging the customer. The supplier, it should be remembered, was only seen as a supplier of cans; the buyer of the cans had no responsibility for other materials and no great interest in the workings of the company's own production line. Their job was to get cans, and they did it well, within those narrow confines.

Contacts had to be established with those that used the product, the people on the line, but slowly – the buyer was a conservative type and didn't take kindly to people going behind his back. Then came a piece of luck for the supplier – the line was stopped for half a day due to shortages of the right materials. People were suddenly looking for suggestions and the gates began to open. Six months of patient meetings finally paid off and supply from all four units began on a coordinated basis.

Moral of the story?

It was all down to a lucky break? Not at all. The beauty of KAM is that it helps suppliers to make their own luck. This supplier was well prepared for the lucky break, and pounced. They were ready because of a long-term effort, a significant investment from the KA manager in the can business, from senior management, and in time, from the other three businesses.

Slowly but surely the company's resources were realigned to meet an opportunity. Once the objective of company-wide KAM was accepted, it was only a matter of time before the successes began to roll.

APPLICATION EXERCISE

Consider the recent history of your own company's interactions with its key accounts:

- What are your own examples of good outcomes?
  - What can be learned from these examples, and replicated in the future?
- What are your own examples of bad, sad, or ugly outcomes?
  - What can be learned from these examples, and avoided in future?

Part IV

Achieving key supplier status

11

The purchasing revolution

In Part I of this book, we described a journey as seen from the perspective of the supplier, and yet we have continually referred to KAM as an activity requiring a certain mutuality of intent *between* supplier and customer – so what of the customer's view on all this?

Why should they let you in? Why should they allow you the access beyond the purchasing function involved in any of the 'one-on-many', 'cotton-reel' or 'diamond team' models of relationship? Why should they allow you the kind of knowledge about your true value that can only reduce their ability to use some of the 'sharper' tactics in the professional purchaser's book of tricks?

There are indeed a significant number of reasons why they might not allow any of these things:

- They might regard such relationships as a 'weapon' used by suppliers in order to secure greater power and influence in negotiations (*and they may well be right*).
- They might lose the benefits of 'dividing and ruling' a disorganized supplier (*hopefully right again*).
- They might value an individual contact (the sales rep) more than they do the company (*a situation that should rightly concern any supplier*).
- They might see you as 'muscling in' on their market (*which may be precisely your intention*).

- It might not suit the way that they buy (*and what if they do just want a straight transaction – a volume for a price?*).

And the real killer for any supplier's KAM ambitions:

- We might allow such things with a 'key supplier'… but you're not one of them.

The following chapters, making up Part IV of this book, will examine the various ways in which a supplier might hope to gain that status – key supplier (or preferred supplier, or strategic supplier) – beginning with an important observation: buyers have changed.

WHAT'S IN A NAME?

Look in the 'situations vacant' pages these days and you won't see many advertisements for 'buyers'. Companies are looking for 'procurement professionals', 'supply-side managers' and people to head up 'sourcing teams'.

Some of this may just be title snobbery, and not so very different from the 'promotion' of the sales representative to the dizzy heights of 'sales executive', 'business development manager' or even, in some sad instances where it is no more than words, 'key account manager'. But most of the time the new titles imply a new position for purchasing in the mechanics of the business.

Some comparisons between the 'buyer' of the past and the 'supply-side manager' of the present might help us to understand the changes taking place (with apologies to some buyers of the past, those who were ahead of their time and with whom the rest of the world is only now catching up).

Involvement: past and present

A number of studies in the late 1990s (a very typical one was carried out by ICI) discovered that when a business was engaged in new product development (NPD), as much as 80 per cent of the spend with suppliers was committed *before* anyone from purchasing became involved. Buyers, it seemed, were often called in with the specifications already set and the suppliers agreed, their task being to draw up the formal contracts, and perhaps secure an extra 5 per cent discount if they were wily enough!

It was supposed that a buyer would not be able to contribute any more than that in the complex world of NPD. It was quite likely that the 'buying office' was situated in a building set apart from the other commercial functions, quite possibly in a Portakabin, and equipped with furniture no longer required by sales and marketing.

Modern supply-side managers will be expected to be involved from the outset of any significant new product development and their office is more likely to be within the heart of the business (increasingly they occupy the space most adjacent to the board), though one head of purchasing did confess to me that even now the department still don't get the best furniture, but that was deliberate tactic to convey an air of poverty with which they can taunt their rich suppliers.

Strategy or tactics: past and present

I remember being sent, many years ago, on a negotiation skills training workshop that promised to teach me the 'wicked ways' and 'sneaky tactics' of professional buyers. I learned about the 'nibble' and about 'unbundling', and all great fun it was too, but if you are thinking of a training event for your team on the ways of the modern buyer, make sure it's about purchasing strategy not the tactics.

The modern buyer has much the same task of 'managing the future' (see Figure 4.1, Chapter 4) as the modern seller. They must aim to marshal the right resources against the right business opportunities, and all in pursuit of the business objectives. They might consider their resources as their suppliers, and their task one of matching those resources to the right opportunities within their business. They might call this 'supply base optimization' (see Chapter 14).

Performance measures: past and present

Old-fashioned buyers were typically measured on their ability to win discounts and their efficiency in handling transactions. The lower the prices they paid and the more transactions they handled, the greater their abilities. Having lots of suppliers was a good way to be regarded as important. Moreover, buyers were not expected to know what happened to the items they bought, beyond their arrival in the company's warehouse. Truly was it said of many such buyers that they were people who 'knew the price of everything and the value of nothing'.

Supply-side managers are more likely to be judged on their selection of suppliers, in particular their ability to reduce the number of those suppliers, and so reduce the number of the resultant transactions. Cost reduction through supply chain management (SCM) and the concept of *total costs in use* (see Chapter 12) may be seen as of much greater value to the business than the lowest prices. 'Value received' is of paramount importance, and that entails a responsibility for the items purchased well down their chain of use, often right to the end customer.

Knowledge: past and present

People still speak of those legendary buyers who were the world's leading authorities on such things as corrugated card, surfactants, cocoa beans or xanthum gum. Very often they knew more about these items than the companies that supplied them, and some spent more time speaking at international conferences than in their own buying office.

There is no criticism implied in that last observation, yet in other areas they were seriously ill informed. Many could not say, with any precision, what they actually spent by category of product or service, or at least, not until the supplier brought in their sales statistics. While this was most often due to poor systems for monitoring and reporting, it also resulted from the fact that plenty of other people in the business made purchases without the buyer's knowledge (such people were of course the natural 'prey' of the hunter-killer salesperson), and in many cases it happened simply because buyers didn't feel they needed to know.

To visit a modern purchasing function is to visit one of the most IT-intensive parts of the business. Systems exist to report expenditure by product, by category, by supplier, by site, by region, by business, by manufacturing process and so on, and the information is used to manage both the suppliers (through 'spend maps' and 'positioning matrices' – see Chapter 14) and the business.

Supply-side managers talk of 'governance': their desire to control all purchases, whether of products or services – something of a shock in recent times to suppliers of things such as IT or business consultancy – and woe betide any salesperson that tries to subvert the purchasing systems by going direct to an end user!

Vendor ratings: past and present

It was once one of life's games that a salesperson had to try to guess the criteria used by buyers to make their choices. Everyone knew about price of course, but after that the mists might gather. It wasn't the buyer's job to tell suppliers, unless it suited them to do so in the heat of a negotiation. It was the *seller's* job to find out, and usually through hard experience: failing to match up to an expectation would bring a rare glimpse of what was required.

Supply-side managers might take a very different approach. They might look to their better suppliers to set the standards for supply, and ask them to monitor their own performance against those standards. They might talk of 'lead suppliers', or 'category champions', or plain 'key suppliers', implying through these titles that high levels of openness and trust were to be expected.

Gatekeepers or facilitators: past and present

It was easy for old-fashioned buyers to be regarded as gatekeepers by suppliers and as petty bureaucrats by their own R&D or marketing people; from both perspectives they always seemed ready with a reason to slow down the process. No wonder they were brought in only at the last moment!

The problem was that poor suppliers (that is, those with products that were cheap but didn't add any further value to the business) would often stay on the list because the buyer 'liked them' and never cared if, for instance, that their products were the bane of the production people's lives. Meanwhile good suppliers (that is, ones that did add value, such as speeding the production process, or reducing wastage on the line) might never get a look in because the production people didn't know of their existence.

Supply-side managers, in contrast, have a duty to be involved in the whole business chain, involving the right suppliers with the right people in their organization. Their role is to *'add value through the supplier interface'*, a quote I saw posted behind a supply-side manager's desk, and while the language may be grating, the sentiments are spot on.

Qualifications and calibre: past and present

There was a time when the purchasing department was where you put the old horses out to grass. It was certainly not the place where new graduates fresh out of college would be actively seeking their first placements.

All that has changed. Purchasing is regarded as a place where value can be created, and where people who understand value, and can be creative, are in demand. To look at this from another point of view (and one long recognized by sales professionals), it is commonly recognized at senior management levels that more damage can be caused to a business through a poor purchasing decision than by a poor selling decision. No wonder then that the calibre of people coming into the profession has been rising in recent years.

REASONS FOR THE 'PURCHASING REVOLUTION'

All of the changes noted above are part of what can rightly be called a purchasing revolution, and a revolution that has often seen professional purchasers change and improve more significantly and faster than the sales professionals on the other side of the table.

A very dangerous situation...

There are many reasons for this, some born of bad times and a need to improve efficiency and effectiveness in a function that often lagged behind the 'sexier' functions in the business (sales and marketing or R&D were the more likely homes for 'bright young things'), others the result of new and ambitious objectives:

- In a mature business, improved purchasing can often provide the most significant opportunity for enhanced profit – greater than chasing new customers or launching new products.
- In a high-growth, high-tech business, improved purchasing practice can provide a vital key to faster new product development.
- New information technology allows more sophisticated measurement of suppliers' performance, and the arrival of 'electronic commerce' allows for a wider variety of choice in managing those suppliers.

The shifting balance of power

It has also been about power. For many years there was an equality of power between suppliers and customers, often the result of an equal ignorance of the other's true situation. The purchasing revolution has shifted that balance of power significantly in the favour of the customer, through the medium of the modern buyer and fuelled by their hugely enhanced knowledge of their suppliers.

Demands for cost breakdowns used to go unheeded (what could they do if you didn't tell them?), whereas now a demand for open book trading is harder and harder to resist. You might say that this is the result of new competitors eager to enter the market and prepared to offer things the incumbents found distasteful, and while there is some truth in that the key reason is to be found in the modern buyer's greater power through the new mechanisms of knowledge and control.

For many suppliers, the practice of KAM has been seen as a means of redressing this new imbalance, as shown in Figure 11.1.

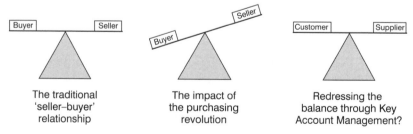

| The traditional 'seller–buyer' relationship | The impact of the purchasing revolution | Redressing the balance through Key Account Management? |

Figure 11.1 *KAM and the shifting balance of power*

Is the 'revolution' good for me, or bad for me?

On balance, the broader view taken by the modern supply-side manager, the focus on value rather than price, and the desire to involve suppliers in their processes – all of this should come as good news to 'good' suppliers and bad news to 'bad'. Moreover, the new approach will often make the task of the key account manager easier; the modern supply-side manager is far more likely than an old-fashioned buyer to take on the role of 'key supplier manager' so important to the full and proper working of a diamond team relationship (see Figure 7.9, Chapter 7).

All of that may be true, provided (and here's the rub) that the supplier understands the 'new rules' and their implications, and provided that they are considered a key supplier. If you are still dangled on the end of a piece of string by a tactical buyer using all the old tricks, only enhanced by their access to modern technology, then ask yourself whether one of the following may be true:

- Perhaps you are dealing with an old-fashioned buyer (they're still about).
- Perhaps your customer has not taken on the elements of the purchasing revolution.
- Perhaps they have, but since you are not playing to the new rules of the game, they are sticking with the old ones to keep you company.
- Perhaps you are not a key supplier.

The last point can be a killer to everything we have discussed. Not everyone deserves the treatment and the attention suggested by some aspects of the purchasing revolution – some suppliers might still be best handled by buyers who regard themselves as champions of the last surviving, and still legal, blood sport.

Knowing the new rules

The next three chapters aim to clarify the new rules, and assist your prospects of being considered a key supplier, by looking in more detail at three important aspects of the purchasing revolution:

- Supply chain management – *seeking value*.
- Purchasing organization – *centralization and rationalization*.
- Supplier positioning – *supplier management*.

APPLICATION EXERCISE

Consider the activities, behaviours and attitudes of the buyers in one of your key accounts:

- What is the nature of their involvement?
- How are they measured?
- What are their vendor ratings?
- Do they act as 'gatekeepers' or 'facilitators'?
- Would you regard them as 'traditional' or 'modern' buyers?
  - Do you identify any movement in their behaviours in either direction?
  - What are the implications of this on your own activities?
- Where is the balance of power in your relationship?
  - Why?
  - What can you do to move the balance in your favour?
- Are you considered a key supplier?
  - If yes, why?
  - If no, is such a position possible in your case, and if yes, what actions will be required to ensure that you achieve this status?

12

Supply chain management: seeking value

A product of the latter years of the last century, supply chain management (SCM, and see Figure 12.1) came to the attention of most businesses as a means of reducing costs. By removing unnecessary steps from the chain of activities, from procurement through to sales, money could be saved.

Figure 12.1 *The supply chain*

As the sophistication of SCM developed it became clear that the removal of unnecessary steps might also have the added benefit of speeding the chain, and so a second objective was added – smooth and flawless execution, with appropriate performance measures for each function along the chain, and appropriate definitions of 'operational excellence' (see Chapter 18). In more recent times a third objective has become more prominent (perhaps as the main opportunities of meeting the first and second have been exhausted over time) – that of focusing all internal activities on improving the value of the final offer to the customer or consumer.

So much for the theory, now to an observation. For most of its history, SCM has been of more interest to buyers than it has been to sellers. Indeed, mentioning SCM to sellers can be rather like raising the European Common Agricultural Policy in conversation at a dinner party.

Feeling left out?

The reasons are fairly clear if we consider the position along the chain of the two professions. The sellers are at the end of the chain and will usually think that they can contribute little to what happens before them. Worse, they might also feel that they have been handicapped by the removal of 'so-called' unnecessary steps in the chain before them – steps that they may feel added value to their own role.

Don't!

I have to say that their thoughts and feelings in this regard are often at fault. In the first place, the provision of accurate and timely forecasts can have a dramatic impact on the efficiency and effectiveness of the functions that precede them, but such things are often 'difficult' for sellers, and not only that, they can become commitments... small wonder then that they are avoided. In the second place, if the value to the customer has been impaired by the removal of anything in the chain, then the seller has done a poor job representing the interests of those customers, usually because sellers take so little interest in the chain in the first place – it is something of a circular issue.

As for the buyers, sitting at the other end, they have an obvious interest: it is their job to get the best prices and terms from suppliers, and so set the whole chain off to the best possible start. Such at least was the view of what we might call the 'old-fashioned' (or pre-revolution) buyer. This interest is shown in Figure 12.2.

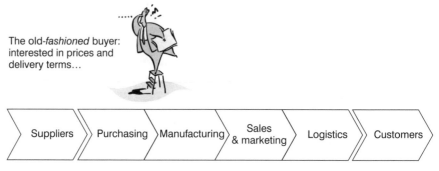

The old-*fashioned* buyer: interested in prices and delivery terms...

Suppliers — Purchasing — Manufacturing — Sales & marketing — Logistics — Customers

Figure 12.2 *The 'old-fashioned' buyer's interest...*

Compared with the seller, buyers are better placed to measure the impact of their actions on that chain, bringing another reason for their greater enthusiasm. Added to this, the ideas inherent within the purchasing revolution have served to increase their interest yet further, through the realization of the positive impact their role can have at stages all along the chain. By engaging suppliers in the important processes of their business companies can speed new product development, reduce manufacturing costs, improve product quality, raise selling prices, or improve customer satisfaction, and more. This new interest is shown in Figure 12.3.

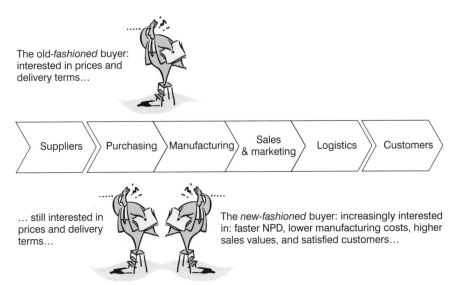

The old-*fashioned* buyer: interested in prices and delivery terms…

Suppliers ⟩ Purchasing ⟩ Manufacturing ⟩ Sales & marketing ⟩ Logistics ⟩ Customers

… still interested in prices and delivery terms…

The *new-fashioned* buyer: increasingly interested in: faster NPD, lower manufacturing costs, higher sales values, and satisfied customers…

Figure 12.3 *The 'new-fashioned' buyer's interest…*

At this point it should be clear why the supplier must become a good deal more interested in SCM. Rather than seeing it as one of the buyer's 'sticks' with which they can beat us, we should in fact be seeing in SCM the answer to many a sales professional's prayers. That is, if they are 'good' suppliers, ones that do indeed bring value to the chain beyond the buyer, recognize that value, and can articulate it in front of the right people. If they do, and can, then the prospect of key supplier status comes that much closer to reality. If they do not, and cannot find ways to do so, they may have to recognize the truth of their status as ordinary suppliers, and be content with the management style of an unapologetically 'old-fashioned' buyer.

ESCAPING PRICE… EMBRACING VALUE

There is much more to be said on this subject in Chapters 22 and 23, but for now we should consider one of the significant benefits to the 'good' supplier of the SCM-minded buyer.

Buyers negotiate on price because it is simple, because they have the advantage of knowing the range of offers from all competitors (while the individual supplier may only know their own), and because plenty of suppliers, it would seem, are all too ready to offer discounts rather than work harder to discover their true value.

One such case of needing to 'work harder' is with the principle of 'cost in use'. This is where the price is regarded as only one element of the costs to the customer; there are also the costs of storage, of physically using the product, of servicing or replacement, and a number of other elements to consider. It is quite common for the supplier with the lowest selling price to cause the customer the highest costs in those other areas, and a calculation of the total 'cost in use' might show them up as not quite the bargain they seemed.

But for the premium priced supplier to gain any advantage from this kind of analysis, they have to be able to discover and communicate their own lower cost-in-use calculation – and that is where the extra work comes in.

Consider the following scenario. You sell heavy-duty electric pumps, used by a variety of manufacturing companies in a variety of plants. Your price is €40,000 and has been for some time. One of your customers, your most important key account as it happens, has just informed you that there is a new kid on the block with a similar pump, selling at €36,000. So what do you do?

First you might ask some questions:

- Is it the same specification as yours?
  More or less it seems.
- Is the new supplier reputable?
  Very.
- Do they have similar terms and conditions?
  Almost exactly.
- Does their pump use the same amount of electricity?
  I'm afraid it does – so no 'cost-in-use' advantage there.

So do you give up at this point and reduce your price to match? Not if you are able to do a little more homework, using your contacts within the customer's supply chain. Maybe you discover the data shown in Table 12.1, relating to your own product.

The most significant item by far is the energy consumption – as much as 65 per cent of the total costs over a five-year period. But didn't we discover that the competitor's product had the same energy consumption? We did, but that is to limit yourself to the realm of a salesperson. What if this is a key account, and you are the KA manager?

Wouldn't it be worth investing time with your own R&D and manufacturing people to see whether it might be possible to develop a new pump with, let's say, a 10 per cent advantage in energy consumption over the old? They tell you that it is possible, but at a cost. You do some sums. It will cost us more, but if I can sell it for €44,000 then that will see a positive return on the investment in just over two years.

Table 12.1   *Costs in use: the pump*

Cost item	Total cost over 5 years
Purchase price:	N40,000
Spares:	N5,000
Installation costs:	N40,000
Energy consumption:	N230,000
Maintenance:	N35,000
Disposal:	N4,000
Total costs in use	**N354,000**

But wasn't the competitor down at €36,000 – how on earth can you justify raising your price to €44,000? Because a saving of 10 per cent on energy consumption is of far greater value to the customer than the saving of €4,000 (or even €8,000) per pump. That's 'cost in use' talking.

Sure there are a dozen things that could wreck such a strategy, here are just a few of them:

You have no authority to have this kind of conversation with your own people:
You're still a sales professional in that case, not a KA manager.
Your boss demands a return on customer investments within a year:
Your company isn't practising KAM yet.
The buyer only buys pumps, not the energy – so why should they care?
If they're an SCM-minded buyer they will, or should...
But if they don't, find the people who do buy energy.

ESCAPING THE LIMITATIONS OF THE 'SNAIL'

Through their interest in SCM, the buyers are taking themselves further back into the decision-making process we described in Chapter 6 as the 'snail' (see Figure 6.1), and taking their valued suppliers with them.

It is in this way that we see SCM working to the benefit of the supplier wishing for a deeper and broader relationship within a KAM approach. At the same time as gaining this advantage, the supplier takes on new responsibilities – making contacts is one thing, coming up with some substantive value is quite another.

There will be some basic tests of any supplier so involved in the customer's supply chain, one of the most basic, yet most important, being: are they easy to do business with? Fail that one and the supplier should not expect their 'penetration' to be long lasting.

Sourcing teams

As the buyer becomes more involved and moves towards the centre of the decision-making process so we might see the development of a 'sourcing team' approach, where a cross-functional team of interested parties works together on the search for appropriate suppliers, the briefing and the negotiation, their selection and their management. Such teams have been shown to bring substantial benefits – greater speed through the removal of bottlenecks, greater precision of specification, better sharing of information, greater creativity in the relationship, and better outcomes 'after the sale'.

As before, such a development should be seen as a positive benefit to the 'good' supplier, while for the supplier that wishes to hide from such complexity and win the deal on price alone, all of this can only appear as a threat.

Partnering for 'lean supply'

SCM-orientated buyers may speak of 'lean supply', the removal of non-value-added activities from the chain. The supplier that is able and willing to work with the buyer in a collaborative partnership in such a pursuit is the supplier moving themselves closer to key supplier status.

They may find that the best way for the customer to remove a non-value-added activity is to outsource it to a supplier. The supplier can see this in one of two ways: as an additional burden, or as an opportunity to bind themselves more closely to the customer. If they take the latter view (which, if the customer is a true key account, surely they must) then they will be building barriers to entry for their competitors, working on the principle of 'lock-in' as discussed in Chapter 21. Moreover, this 'lock-in' is customer inspired, not supplier inspired, and so does not come with the attendant 'threats' that an aggressive 'lock-in' approach can sometimes bring.

The customer may ask the supplier to share in the costs of improving the efficiency of their supply chain. An example of this might be a joint investment in an EDI (electronic data interface) capability in order to allow efficient electronic purchasing. Again we see the potential for 'lock-in'.

Perhaps the greatest significance for the supplier from such partnerships will be the sharing of information. The famous 'beer game' is a much-used training simulation that replicates the flow of information along a 'manufacturer to distributor to retailer to consumer' supply chain. It demonstrates admirably how something as simple as the sharing of forecasts up and down the chain, rather than simply placing orders on the next in line, can lead to significant improvements in supply, and dramatic reductions in costs such as working capital.

It can be demonstrated again and again that where information is shared, and that information leads to cost reductions through greater efficiencies in the chain, then the pressure on the supplier's price is reduced. Not removed – to hope for that would be foolishly idealistic – but reduced; and in an era of ever greater price competition from new entrants, that is surely a benefit to be cherished.

But only with key suppliers?

I mentioned being 'foolishly idealistic', and if some of what we have been discussing sounds that way to you then I can only suppose that you work in an environment where genuine collaborative partnerships between supplier and customer are rare, or perhaps nonexistent. Such environments certainly exist, and for some, what we have been discussing here may not bear such tasty fruit. But that is not a reason to ignore it altogether, but rather simply to lower your horizons on how much time and effort you will invest in such collaborations, on the basis of a lowered horizon on the potential returns.

In the 'real' world it's still about power

Much the same consideration will be going on in the customer's mind. They will not expect to be collaborating with every supplier, only those that they consider worth the effort, perhaps the ones they call their key suppliers.

For buyers, information is power, and power in the negotiation. This has always been so, hence their reluctance to share that information. That they might be prepared to be more open with some, is only for three reasons:

- It's only where they see something in it for them.
- It's only with *some*…
- With the others, the old rules still apply.

I once heard a director of purchasing criticize his team for 'leaking like a sieve'. He was telling them that they should be very aware that all this new information gained as a result of the purchasing revolution was to be used to manage their suppliers better, and not simply to give those suppliers a stronger arm at the negotiation table. This was the real world speaking. And what did he mean by managing suppliers 'better'? Well, it rather depended on the type of supplier; to some you would tell nothing, yet with others you might happily be an open book; and for more on that we should turn to Chapter 14.

APPLICATION EXERCISE

Consider the activities, behaviours, and attitudes of the buyers in one of your key accounts:

- Where in the supply chain are they most interested to make a positive impact?
  - What effect does this have on their purchasing strategy?
  - What impact does this have on your role as a supplier?
- What activities should you focus on to attain and maintain a *key supplier status*?

13

Purchasing organization: rationalization and centralization

There are fewer buyers than there used to be. This isn't a clever point about their change of role or title; it's just that there are fewer people involved in the task of buying, procurement, sourcing or whatever else you might like to call it.

The reason is simple: 'rationalization and centralization'. In the past every site had its own purchasing team, each often working quite independently of other sites. That was hard work for the seller, but also an opportunity. Today the norm is for the job to be done at one location, perhaps even globally. So why the change?

- As we have said, you need fewer buyers, so there is a cost saving.
- More importantly (perhaps), as businesses seek uniformity over their product offer so they must seek uniformity over their purchasing activity.
- The search for uniformity will almost certainly result in a reduction in supplier numbers (buyers talk of 'supplier rationalization'), and so a reduction in the transactional costs of working with suppliers – another cost saving.
- Those fewer suppliers will be asked to take on additional responsibilities – another cost saving, this time in the supply chain (see Chapter 12).

- More importantly still (probably), a central purchase means a bigger purchase, and that means better prices and bigger discounts.

Taken as a whole this is a very compelling set of reasons to centralize the purchasing function, and there are very few that have missed the chance to benefit.

SUPPLIER RATIONALIZATION

The motorcar industry started the charge towards supplier rationalization, with high-profile strategies to reduce their supply base to single figure percentages of the original number of suppliers. The knife was applied ruthlessly and implemented alongside a centralization strategy; the companies saved huge amounts of money in lower transactional costs, and secured massive discounts from their substantially fewer, but equally substantially larger, suppliers.

One purchasing director, asked how many people there were in the purchasing department, answered: 'I have over 150, but only 30 of them are on my books.' The rest came from the suppliers, many of whom had office space on the customer's premises. Not only does using the supplier's staff to do the work you used to give to your own folk save money, but since they are integrated more closely into the business operations, such objectives as 'just-in-time delivery' or 'vendor-managed inventory' become so much easier to meet.

Of course, such rationalization programmes can be carried out badly, creating havoc for all involved, whether 'winners' or 'losers'. The process can be rushed, it can be done without warning, without consultation with the suppliers or the internal customers, or without defining the rules. Trust and confidence can be blown away, and performance can suffer; a nervous or suspicious supplier is rarely the best supplier.

There is an analogy with 'personnel downsizing' where staff levels are radically reduced, particularly at middle-management levels. Horror stories abound of cases where key people are removed, essential expertise is lost and basics like customer service begin to crumble. There are also cases where such downsizing can transform a business from near death to prosperity. The difference usually lies in how the exercise is carried out.

Getting involved

Where supplier rationalization has been done well, it is usually because a period of consultation has been worked through, internally and externally, and the 'rules' drawn up to mutual agreement.

That being so, there are four things *not* to do:

- Don't be afraid to ask questions about the customer's intentions.
- Don't be afraid to give them your best advice (but be positive).
- Don't fight it.
- Don't curl up into a ball hoping it will go away.

Don't fight it...

And three things that it is essential to do:

- Be very clear about the value you bring to the customer, and how that distinguishes you from other suppliers (see Part V, and Chapters 22 and 23).
- Make sure that this value is clearly communicated to those in the decision-making process (see Chapters 7 and 8).
- Raise your status in the buyer's eyes (see Chapter 14).

You need to know

Here are some questions to ask the customer:

...aim to understand it

- Why are you rationalizing? Is it about improving supplier performance, reducing transaction costs, seeking discounts for volume, forging true alliances or something else?
- What are your targets? Final numbers, specific performance measures, supplier standards, the timetable and so on.
- What are the 'givens' and what are the 'differentiators'? What must any supplier do to stay on the list? What might make a supplier stand out from the crowd?
- Will you be 'selecting out', or 'selecting in'? Are you removing the chaff, or picking the winners?
- How do we stand right now?
- What must we do to meet your standards?
- What can we expect in return for meeting those standards?
- How do you wish us to handle 'local inconsistencies'?

Don't limit yourself to the buyer with these questions. Use your diamond team and seek out the widest possible contacts. With skill and subtlety, you might even be able to influence the targets and the standards, to suit, of course, your own performance advantages.

You might like to discuss

There are some additional questions that you might like to discuss with the customer, in order to help them avoid some of the common sins of rationalization, but take care not to sound like an opponent or a prophet of doom:

- Is this a short-term tactic that you may reverse in a few years' time, or is it for good?
- Where will all the 'rationalized out' suppliers go – to your competition?
- What if you kill a supplier?
- What if, as times change, you need them back?
- Are you increasing your risk exposure?
- With e-commerce reducing transactional cost, do you need to rationalize? (Some businesses have begun to increase their supply base, after a lengthy period of rationalization, precisely for this reason.)
- Will the remaining suppliers have sufficient capacity, and will they be as capable as they claim?

CENTRALIZATION OF THE PURCHASING ORGANIZATION

Hand in hand with supplier rationalization we usually see some form of centralization of the purchasing function. Figure 13.1 illustrates three of the more popular approaches, as well as the 'single site' approach that they might be replacing.

The lead buyer

This is where one site, business or territory takes on the main responsibility for purchasing for a wider group. The chosen lead may be selected for a number of reasons: specific expertise, largest share of purchase value, particular supplier relationship and so on. The other sites, businesses or territories will be expected to fall into line with the lead.

Corporate purchasing

This is where a new unit is established – perhaps at head office, perhaps taking some of the staff from the local purchasing teams – charged with making the decisions, managing the relationships and handling the transactions for the whole business.

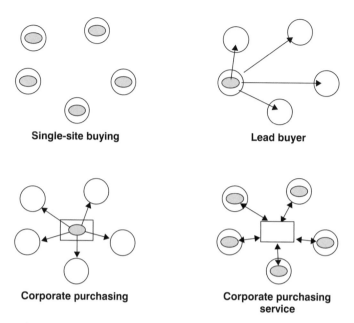

Figure 13.1 *Centralization of the purchasing organization*

Corporate purchasing service

The difference in this set up compared to the corporate purchasing model is that this new unit does not take the decisions. Individual sites and business determine their own requirements and feed them to the 'service' unit to handle the transactions.

Other options

There are of course other options and variations on the theme, but these three (or something looking very like them) do represent the majority of instances. One other that does perhaps deserve a brief mention is the 'outsourced' purchasing organization. This is where an external body is asked to perform the purchasing role, perhaps in order to gain some particular expertise. A typical example in many larger companies is the purchase of travel services through 'in-house' agencies like AMEX or Hogg Robinson, specialists in business travel.

Supplier implications

The implications for the supplier are huge. Completely different sales, service and contact strategies might be required depending on the customer's choice of organization. One organization might offer an opportunity while another might be seen as a threat, but whichever it is, an appropriate response is required.

The particular 'combinations' of their organization and your opportunity are complex enough to make any standard responses dangerous, and so the following comments and cases are intended as thought provokers only; you will of course need to find your own particular responses to suit your own particular circumstances.

Avoiding the 'unearned discount' trap

Discounts for volume... who says?

Don't be pressured into giving discounts that are not warranted. Suppose for example that a customer used to order from you through five different sites, 50 tons going to one site, 30 to another, and 20 tons to each of the remaining three. They switch to a 'lead buyer' and place one order for 140 tons, demanding a substantial discount for this higher volume. They want the 140-ton price, which must be substantially better, they say, than the 50-ton price, and certainly if compared with the 20-ton price.

Should you give them a discount? They are not ordering anything more, simply putting it through one order. Yes, there are some savings for you in that – just the one order to process and just the one invoice to raise – but is that enough to justify the kind of discount that the customer will be demanding?

If they asked you to make just the one delivery, to a central location, instead of the five separate deliveries of the previous arrangement, then there is a bigger saving for you there and some justification for a discount, but let's suppose for this example that they don't, they want it delivered as before – 50 tons, 30 tons, and three lots of 20 tons.

Sadly, history shows that most suppliers have given substantial discounts in such circumstances, with no gain to themselves. Why so stupid?

Perhaps they had five different salespeople calling on the customer, at the five different sites. The sale professional calling on the site chosen as the lead buyer is presented with a wonderful opportunity, an increase from 50 to 140 tons, and doesn't hesitate to turn to an entirely new pricing sheet. The lucky winner forgets that each of their four colleagues has seen their order go down to zero – but such is life...

Perhaps the customer's other suppliers, eager to steal your business, are prepared to offer big discounts? In such a scenario you are going to be hard pressed to resist, but at least aim to gain something in return that is better than the mere continuation of your existing business. Are there new parts of the customer's business that could be opened up to you, or new product opportunities? Can you agree on some form of 'first access' to new projects?

Think hard when presented with these 'opportunities', and do your sums properly. Most importantly, view the customer as a whole; this shouldn't be a matter of one territory's gain and another's loss, it is what happens to the total customer P&L (profit and loss account) that matters. In the case described, the difference is 'very little' and that might be the best advice on any discount proposal.

Shock, denial and then what?

You have sales to a customer in five locations: the UK, France, Germany, Spain and Italy. Each one has operated independently but they announce an intention to set up a corporate purchasing function, in pursuit of uniformity of supply.

Be prepared…

You look at your current business. In the UK you are a key supplier and life is great. In France they appear to like you and you get regular business. In Germany things are not so rosy, but the occasional order comes in. In Spain they haven't worked with you for a year, but you don't know why. In Italy they hate you – no ifs and buts, they hate you.

You know what's going to happen of course; they announce that the new unit will be based in Italy, staffed predominantly by the people from the Italian unit. What will be your response?

The first is very likely to be one of shock, but then sense prevails and you go to see your UK contact who comforts you with the following: 'Don't worry, it's some crazy idea they've had at head office. Italy! I ask you, they don't even speak English. It's never going to work. You just stay close to me and all will be OK.'

Heaving a sigh of relief and wiping the sweat from your brow you leave their office, an order for the next three months in your hand.

Six months go by, and at last the new unit is up and running in Italy. One of their first acts is to sort out a discrepancy in the UK – an unauthorized supplier (guess who), working through a local buyer who is about to be made redundant. By now, it's all too late.

There was only one proper response to be made – find out why they hate you in Italy, and do something about it. The most likely reason they hate you is you have been ignoring them, or sending a UK-based sales professional to see them once a quarter to shout, slowly…

Get yourself an Italian key account manager. (For more on this kind of scenario, see Chapter 34.)

Helping them get it right

On hearing that a customer is centralizing their purchasing function, a supplier's first reaction is often to remove their own sales professionals and other contacts. 'Our margin is about to be hit, let's at least reduce our costs,' goes the thinking. Maybe, but a little patience may be wise, to see just how the centralization goes.

Don't fight it…

If the customer opts for the 'corporate purchasing service' model (see Figure 13.1) then you would be wise to retain your contacts, as the important points of influence will remain at the individual locations. Even if they opt for one of the 'lead buyer' or straight 'corporate purchasing' approaches, you may find that your local contacts, and the local knowledge they bring, will stand you in good stead for quite some time to come. It is precisely that knowledge that may protect you from some of the overhasty and poorly considered centralization that often comes at the outset of such projects. Even more importantly, you can use that knowledge to help the customer achieve their ambitions.

Help them get it right...

You can tip them off to those parts of their own business that might have problems, or might even be about to resist their centralizing ambitions. Perhaps you might feel uneasy about being the customer's police force, 'sneaking' on those who were only recently your friends and allies. This may certainly be true for some members of your team, perhaps a salesperson that has been nurturing a local relationship for years only to see it wrenched from them by an e-mail from the customer's head office.

So what do you advise? Asking for the customer's advice might be a good first step, asking that question on our list of things we need to know (see above): 'How do you wish us to handle "local inconsistencies"?'

These are difficult issues, and will call for one of the most important capabilities in any key account manager: what we might call that of being a 'political entrepreneur'. Chapter 28 will return to a discussion of this capability, but for now, a simple explanation. The 'entrepreneur' part of the capability is about having a business sense – an eye for an opportunity, and the wherewithal to chase and capture it. The 'political' part is about the ability to handle the complexities of organizations, people and motivations. It is fair to say that most salespeople have the entrepreneurial spark, but few have the political sensitivity; the hunter-killer sales professional can often behave rather like a bull in a china shop.

There will be people issues to resolve, and there will be product and service issues to resolve. The following case study illustrates how the supplier's local knowledge can help the corporate purchasing function to do a better job.

Don't get held over a barrel...

A manufacturing company with factories at seven different locations had just set up a corporate purchasing group as its head office, a location that was remote from any of the manufacturing sites. One of its first targets was the purchase of 205-litre metal drums, an item that they used in large quantities and that would provide an excellent opportunity to flex the functions negotiating arm.

They decided to source from just one supplier (each site had usually dealt with at least two and sometimes three), and the size of the resultant order did in fact bring a handsome discount – a sound purchasing decision, or so it seemed.

Unfortunately, the buyer located at head office was not aware that each site had designed its loading bays and warehouse space to hold precise numbers of these 205-litre drums, depending on the height of the drum used. The buyer was also unaware that the drums came in different sizes (height and width) and that the untidiness of history had meant that each site had designed their spaces on the basis of different drum sizes.

When the centrally placed order was made, the chosen drum just happened to be the tallest of all the options – two centimetres taller. Not a lot, but stacked four or more high, as was the requirement, all of a sudden six of the manufacturing sites had problems.

Nobody made any comment – it was not for them to argue with head office – but a year after the decision was made it became clear that things were going wrong, and a quick study found that the extra costs incurred by the sites in handling the issue came to more than the savings from the discount for that central purchase. So, perhaps not such a smart decision after all.

Should we blame the buyer? Rather we should blame the supplier for not seizing the opportunity. Once they knew what was afoot, surely they should have moved to help the buyer make the right choice. There were options – source different sized barrels by location, get the locations to alter their loading bays, source a shorter barrel – and each of them would involve some kind of service, or provision of information, by the supplier. Might such a service be of value, and might it be used to reduce the level of discount for volume expected by the customer?

The key supplier is the one that knows the customer's objectives and, using contacts, knowledge, expertise and creativity, helps the customer to achieve those objectives.

So don't abandon your local contacts, but you may need to change their nature. Sending in salespeople might be a poor use of that resource; perhaps there are other people in your team, properly briefed, that could provide the same 'eyes and ears'? 'Properly briefed' is the key of course, and I ask you to cast your mind back to two tools introduced in Chapter 8 – the contact matrix and the GROW – the use of which will be essential in handling the kind of situation we have been discussing.

Don't abandon your local contacts

RATIONALIZATION AND CENTRALIZATION: IS IT GOOD FOR US?

In the last chapter it was argued that the move towards SCM (supply chain management) could be seen as a 'good thing' for the 'good' supplier. But what about rationalization and centralization: do we like this part of the purchasing revolution as much?

If we are honest, the answer is probably no. The old method might have allowed suppliers to divide and rule, or to be 'in' with the parts of a customer they liked, and to keep well 'out' of the others, or to have different sets of prices and terms with the same customer. It also allowed them to sleep easier at night – the risk of being thrown out of a customer, in all locations or for all products, was relatively low. The new method raises the stakes and threatens to reduce the margins.

The optimist might argue that centralization opens the door to bigger opportunities, and with a smaller selling resource. The pessimist may argue back that it does just the same for the competition and puts at risk a number of 'nice little earners'.

Whether you are an optimist or pessimist, it is not a matter of whether you like it or not; it is a question of whether your customer is doing it. If they are, then you only have one choice: support them, and with enthusiasm. If you do so then your assistance will be welcomed, and that surely can only be good for you? To resist, or even to be neutral about their ambitions, will earn you a bad reputation – after all, there will be quite enough hurdles for the buyer to jump within their own organization without their suppliers getting in the way.

Seeing the bigger picture

A supplier of a raw material to the paint industry receives an interesting call from a buyer at one of their customer's 'parents', a large chemical manufacturer based in Holland. The parent company buys this same raw material for a number of its other businesses, and is offering the supplier a chance to pitch for that business, to become involved with a number of additional industries and markets, should they be able to provide the appropriate price.

The supplier has a choice: stick with what they have, and maintain their price and margin, or go for the new and bigger opportunity, but at a lower price and margin. Some argue for the former – 'and in any case', they say, 'what do we know about these other industries?' – but wiser heads realize that much the same suggestion will be being made to the customer's other suppliers of the same materials: do they want to get into the paint industry?

Still wiser heads realize that the customer wishes to rationalize and centralize. What will be their own long-term future if they try to stand aside from that ambition?

And the wisest heads of all realize that the corporate buyer may have no experience of the paint industry (they guess correctly), and so they choose to seize the opportunity, bringing to the corporate buyer all their expertise in the paint industry, and receiving in return all the corporate buyer's expertise in the industries that are new to them.

Good KAM, good political entrepreneurship.

APPLICATION EXERCISE

Consider the activities, behaviours and attitudes of the buyers in one of your key accounts:

- What (if any) are their motivations in centralizing their purchasing operations?
    - What effect does this have on their purchasing strategy?
    - What impact does this have on your role as a supplier?
- What (if any) are their motivations in rationalizing their supply base?
    - What effect does this have on their purchasing strategy?
    - What impact does this have on your role as a supplier?
- What activities should you focus on to attain a key supplier status?

14

Supplier positioning: managing suppliers

The lives of sellers and buyers have a good deal more in common than their traditional adversarial stances might suggest.

In a pre-KAM environment, the salesperson might have worked a 'milk round' (see Chapter 7) that viewed all customers as equal, so justifying the same amount of time and attention for each customer.

In what we might call a pre-KSM (pre-key supplier management) environment, the buying office would be inundated by a constant stream of representatives, each needing attention, and an equally constant stream of orders and invoices, each needing processing, such that the time spent on the really important suppliers was often little more than the time spent on the rather more ordinary. In effect, as far as time allocation went, all suppliers were equal.

Buyers began to wake up to the problems with this situation at much the same time as suppliers were waking up to the problems of their milk rounds. What buyers have done about it however has often been more radical than the actions taken on the sales side of the table.

MAKING TIME TO MANAGE SUPPLIERS

Consider the implications for the buyer of some of the new ways of thinking we have been discussing (Chapters 11 through 13). If some suppliers are to be more formally engaged in the business supply chain, if there are to be fewer of them (supplier rationalization), and if some of them are to be granted more access and more information, then the chosen few are going to have to live up to some tough standards. It is almost inevitable that not all will meet the grade, and so buyers must now engage in 'supplier improvement' programmes, as well as all their other tasks.

From where is all the extra time required for such a task to come? And what of all those other suppliers, the more ordinary ones, still clamouring for the buyer's time?

These are of course the very same questions facing the supplier with their desire to allocate their resources more effectively to the most attractive opportunities (see Figure 4.1). From the supplier's perspective the answer has been some form of KAM. In Chapters 24 and 25 we will examine a methodology for identifying and selecting the key accounts, and for resolving the crucial question: how do we manage those customers not considered to be 'key'?

Two sides of the same coin

Buyers have gone through a very similar process of analysis in pursuit of their 'key suppliers', and in order to resolve their own mirror-image question: how do we manage those suppliers not considered to be 'key'? They will talk about 'supply-base optimization' programmes, and the identification of 'supplier types' through the use of 'supplier positioning' models.

Mirror images again of the suppliers' own thoughts, but perhaps it becomes clear at this point why the buyer's responses to much the same issues have been so much more radical than their sales counterparts: sellers may like to think that they choose their customers, but buyers really do choose their suppliers.

SUPPLIER POSITIONING MODELS

There are a variety of such models, mostly based on a four-box matrix, each using different words, or adding to the confusion by labelling the sides of the matrix in diametrically opposite ways to their fellows, but they mostly come from the same 'parent' – the Kraljic matrix. The example we will consider, shown in Figure 14.1, is itself a variant of that matrix, being one that I have encountered more often 'in practice' than the 'parent', and having the benefit of using a language more resonant to suppliers.

Your own customers might use this variant, or another, or the original Kraljic. They might use the model formally, perhaps even sharing the analysis with their suppliers, or it might be something that is considered only inside the buyer's own head. Of course, they might never have heard of

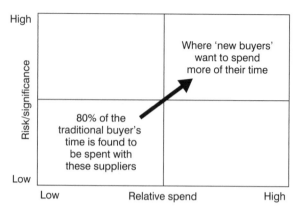

Figure 14.1 *The supplier positioning matrix*
developed from the Kraljic Matrix

the model or its variants, and yet I would be surprised if they were not acting (albeit subconsciously and imprecisely) on some of its conclusions.

It is of course the task of the KA team to discover to what extent such models are used, and how their use might impact on their own company's status as a supplier. If you find that your customer uses a different language, then from this point onwards aim to use their words, not mine.

The 80/20 rule: just as much an issue for buyers as it is for sellers

Figure 14.1 illustrates the traditional buyer's dilemma, spending the majority of their time with suppliers who are of relatively low significance and with whom their 'purchasing spend' is low – the 80/20 rule applies just as much to purchasing as it does to selling. They would much rather be spending their time with those suppliers who are of greater significance, and represent a much larger proportion of their budget.

Defining the axes

- *Relative spend* – ranks suppliers on the basis of the level of expenditure.
- *Risk/significance* – ranks suppliers on the basis of their relative importance to the customer.

The balance of power

The matrix can be seen as a study of the balance of power between supplier and customer. 'Risk/significance' reflects supplier power (the greater the significance of a supplier, the greater their power, hence the use of the word 'risk'), while 'spend' might indicate potential buyer power (the bigger the order, the bigger the hold over that supplier, although some would argue that the bigger the order the greater the dependence of that customer on the supplier, which increases supplier power). Some versions of the model will use the labels 'supplier power' (vertical) and 'buyer power' (horizontal), perhaps reflecting a hard-nosed, even combative approach to supplier relationships.

The use of the word 'risk' in the vertical axis is of great importance as it illustrates a potential misunderstanding between suppliers and customers. Suppliers will like to think that they are significant in the customer's eyes, and the more significant they are, the better their position and the better the subsequent relationship. Seen from the buyer's perspective, significance is risk – 'What if you let me down, what if you go out of business, where does that leave me?' Buyers might therefore have an aversion to too many truly significant suppliers, perhaps seeking to reduce their risk by introducing alternatives, or finding ways to commoditize the offer.

USING THE ANALYSIS

The buyer might aim to use the supplier positioning analysis for any or all of the following:

- to decide where to spend their time;
- to decide the nature of the relationship with different 'supplier types' (each box in the matrix contains a different 'supplier type');
- to determine their expectations from each different 'supplier type';
- to identify the type of activities to be engaged in with different 'supplier types';
- to identify where it is necessary to 'develop supplier capabilities';
- to consider options such as 'open-book trading';
- to manage risk;
- to determine the right sort of contract;
- to identify their 'key suppliers'.

Buyers are seeking to manage suppliers just as much as sellers want to manage customers – though they do have an advantage – they're the customer!

Any KA manager wishing to build the relationship, grow the existing business, or find new opportunities, will have to know their positioning, and how the customer intends to use that positioning. It is not an exact science of course; the risk/significance assessment in particular is likely to be rather subjective, and even the spend data can be open to interpretation, and the conclusions from the analysis are unlikely to be as clean-cut as business books and consultants might suggest, but that only argues more for the need to understand the subtleties of your customer's thinking in this regard.

Later in this chapter we will look at what buyers might expect from each supplier type, and how they might aim to work with and manage each type. This will guide us on how we might need to respond, but for the moment we need to understand a little more about the nature of the supplier positioning analysis.

WHY MEASURE SPEND?

A flippant answer may be to say that it's for much the same reason that people are said to climb mountains – because it's there. Flippant, but often true, and a demonstration of the same kind of 'sizeism' that can afflict the seller (see Chapter 3). There are better reasons, those listed below being among the most common:

- To indicate where time spent on price negotiation may pay dividends, and what the nature and outcome of that negotiation should involve. Getting a 1 per cent discount from a huge supplier will almost certainly be time better spent than securing a 20 per cent discount from a tiny one.
- To help with supplier rationalization programmes. What is the impact of concentrating more spend on fewer suppliers?
- A measure of the impact of suppliers on the customer's own financial performance – cash flow, profitability and the like.

Who is doing the measuring?

An important question to ask here is, who is doing the ranking? For example, suppose you sell latex gloves to the NHS. In the eyes of the purchasing director of one of the 'purchasing hubs' tasked with buying anything and everything for a number of hospital trusts, you might be quite small, to be found on the left-hand side of the matrix. But if the buyer of latex gloves is assessing you, and you are their largest supplier, then you will of course be positioned on the right-hand side of the matrix.

Spend mapping

Buyers might use 'spend maps' to prepare the horizontal axis of the supplier positioning matrix. The most common form is a simple ranking of suppliers, for any given product or category of products, displayed as a bar chart, as shown in Figure 14.2.

Armed with the information shown in Figure 14.2, what would you do if you were the buyer? Assuming that there are no great differences between the suppliers other than their size, then a supplier rationalization programme

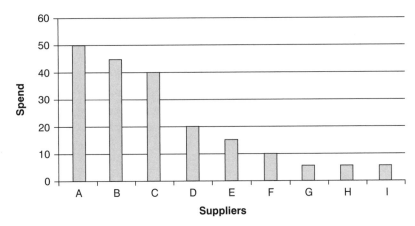

Figure 14.2 *The spend map*

looks on the cards. We might have a three-year plan (and yes, buyers do think that far ahead).

Year one – remove the five smallest suppliers (E to I) and give their business to the remaining four (A to D). We remove the smallest for several reasons:

Who needs nine suppliers?

- The relative transactional costs of working with small suppliers can be very high.
- Small suppliers can be very time consuming.
- If we remove the big suppliers we might find ourselves deluged with complaints from our own internal customers: 'Why can't I get product B any more?', and the like.

Give the business to the four remaining we said, but how much to which ones? Our aim is to get the biggest discounts possible, and so we might lean towards C and D, the increase to their business being more significant than if we gave it to A or B. What we are saying is that C and D will be hungrier, and so more forthcoming.

There is a second reason for giving it to C and D: we want to even up our supply base in preparation for the 'year two' strategy – we want four equal suppliers.

Year two is the year of the open tender, asking four equal players to fight it out among themselves, with one loser. Such fights are always keener between equals than if one party feels too small to bother or another is too big to take the contest seriously. Buyers will prepare their suppliers for the battle by a process they call 'supplier conditioning' – repeatedly telling them: 'You do realize that you are one of four equals, you do realize that you

Keep them on their toes...

are one of four equals, you do realize...'. The loser's business is divided up equally, again for a substantial discount.

In year three we might decide to reintroduce one of the smaller suppliers rationalized out in the first year of our three-year campaign. We bring back supplier G as a warning to A, B and C: don't get fat and lazy. Of course, supplier G will be eager to return and will almost certainly give us their best prices, best terms, best services – hopefully sufficiently generous to put the three larger players to shame – and so we turn back to them for similar improvements.

And so the 'game' goes on, a game with only one winner, the buyer.

Handling the game?

How do we avoid such ruthless treatment? Well, if we have no competitive advantage, if we are insignificant in the buyer's eyes, or if there is no difficulty in them swapping us with another, then we probably won't. In other words, the secret lies in the vertical axis of the 'supplier positioning' matrix.

WHY MEASURE RISK/SIGNIFICANCE?

Buyers need to know how dependent they are on their suppliers, and so know how they need to treat them – roughly (common enough), or with kid-gloves (rarely!) – or more importantly, how they must manage them, or potentially even change them.

Why your 'significance' might just make them nervous

Suppose there is only one supplier for a particular product, a monopoly holder; the significance of that supplier is clearly enormous, so too the level of risk for the buyer. Life without that supplier would be inconceivable. Where there are many alternative suppliers, the risk involved in any one of them letting the buyer down is lower, and so the significance of any individual supplier is lower.

This is of course a rather simplistic scenario. In most cases, ranking the suppliers will involve a number of considerations or factors – this is a more complex axis than that of 'relative spend'. Learning the factors used by your own customer will be of huge value to you as not only will you be able to judge your own status, you will also be better placed to predict your customer's concerns, and so their behaviour. Indeed, a fairly good way of learning about their choice of factors is to look out for what seems to bother them most.

The following is a general list of the sort of factors (and by no means exhaustive) that might be used:

● The number of suppliers.
● Geographic location – distant suppliers might imply greater risk.

- Dependence on a particular technology or type of solution – are there alternatives?
- The criticality of their product to our own product/process.
- Supplier brand names or trade marks used by the customer – Intel has a great significance to many a PC manufacturer.
- Patents, copyrights.
- Are the suppliers also competitors?
- Do the suppliers work with our competitors?
- The amount of time required to switch suppliers: if it takes a day, they're not that significant; if it takes a year, then they have a significant hold over us.
- The supplier's financial stability.
- Politics – are they the MD's favourite…?
- The existence of contracts.

MANAGING SUPPLIERS

Figure 14.3 shows the kind of labels that might be applied to the four 'supplier types' in the supplier positioning matrix.

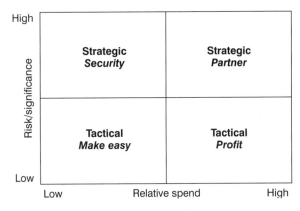

Figure 14.3 *Supplier types*

Explaining the labels

- **Tactical *Make easy*:** such suppliers don't deserve much time or attention, and ideally will be largely self-managing (any supplier that proves difficult to work with is a dead supplier).
- **Tactical *Profit*:** getting the best financial deal is the top (perhaps only) priority with such suppliers (look out for some fairly robust management styles!).

- **Strategic *Security*:** ensuring security and consistency of supply is crucial (price may be of low importance if a supplier can be 100 per cent reliable, or perhaps they supply a critical ingredient, perhaps a 'brand within a brand': Lycra® to a clothing manufacturer, Intel® to a PC manufacturer).
- **Strategic *Partner*:** the ones to spend the time with, working on future-orientated projects (the most likely place to find key suppliers and diamond team relationships).

Determining the approach

For each supplier type the buyer will have a different answer to the following questions (we have encountered this list before of course):

- How much time should I spend with them?
- What type of relationship do I require?
- How might I use 'e-commerce' technology?
- How will I behave?
- What are my expectations?
- Must I actively manage them to improve?
- Should I insist on 'open-book' trading?
- Must I reduce my risk?
- What sort of contract?
- Are they key suppliers?

Table 14.1 suggests some 'typical' answers and outcomes, though these are of course dependent on specific circumstances.

A good way to understand the dynamics of this matrix is to consider your own position as a buyer. Try to place different items that you spend money on throughout the year in the most appropriate box and then think about how you approach those purchases. Where do you position the house, shoes, petrol, the annual holiday, baked beans, the TV licence, medicine, beer, the car, your family, life insurance, books, milk, newspapers, wine, soap, and so on.

How do you go about those expenditures? For myself, I spend a good deal more time (and money!) on books than I do on baked beans, and expect a good deal more in return, from them, and from the bookshop. Running out of soap would be a bad thing, and I'm partial to some particular smells, so there's always plenty of that about the place, and I don't even know the price. There's no point stockpiling petrol, and in any case I buy whichever brand is cheapest at the time because they are all the same.

Professional buyers go about this analysis with a little more precision than the average consumer, but never forget that they are human too, and the vertical positioning in particular is often subject to personal likes and dislikes.

Table 14.1 *Possible answers and outcomes*

	Tactical **Make easy**	*Tactical* **Profit**	*Strategic* **Security**	*Strategic* **Partner**
Time	Minimum	Enough to secure the best financial deal	Enough to ensure security of supply	Maximum
Relationship	None – keep remote	Limit to 'bow-tie' Tough negotiations	Depending on need Possible 'diamond'?	'Diamond' most likely
E-commerce	Reducing supplier 'noise'	Doing deals with a broadening supplier base	Sharing information Telemetry	Collaborative partnering
Behaviour	Expect independent self-management	Competitive – rotate suppliers?	Collaborative – support suppliers	Collaborative – partner with suppliers
Expectations	Make it easy	Best financial deal	100% security Consignment stock?	Partnership for future gain
Managed improvement	'Shape up or ship out…'	'Shape up or ship out…'	Joint improvement projects	Joint investment
Open-book trading	Important if considering a sole supplier arrangement	A tactic to reduce supplier margins	Not a top priority, unless the supplier has problems	A genuine intention to improve supplier efficiency
Risk	Allow sole supplier	Maintain rivals	Seek or maintain alternatives	Seek or maintain alternatives
Contract	Possibly long-term but with tough penalty clauses	Short-term	Long-term, with clear clauses on handling problems	Long-term, with a focus on shared responsibilities
Key supplier status	Unlikely	If long-term lowest price…?	Possibly, if no alternatives	Probably, but not for all

Time and effort

Buyers have aimed to escape the 80/20 rule by forcing the bottom-left quadrant suppliers through easy-to-purchase channels – the use of electronic commerce, or the provision of purchase cards to staff being examples – perhaps even outsourcing the purchasing task to a third party.

The freed-up time is given to those suppliers that really matter: predominantly the top-right suppliers, but also to those in the bottom-right if there is a worthwhile price negotiation to be had. Alternatively, the buyer may focus on those in the top left if it's important to get control over what the buyer might refer to as 'bottleneck' items – such as products that can bring the plant to a grinding halt if they're not immediately accessible.

Relationships

If you are positioned top-right then our discussions regarding diamond team relationships (Chapter 7) are probably already familiar to you – the customer may well have been drawing you into a more complex relationship to suit the nature of their expectations. It is quite likely that a 'key supplier manager' will exist (an issue that we discussed in Chapter 7, observing that without one, building diamond teams is so much harder).

Don't expect anything more than a bow-tie in bottom-right; this is how buyers aim to win the arm-wrestling contest over price and volume.

Suppliers in the top two boxes can expect greater access to senior management, and will probably be treated with more respect (though don't bank on a personalized parking space and paid lunch on *every* visit).

Using e-commerce

Figure 14.4 shows the different nature and intent of e-commerce, depending on the supplier's position. The earliest use of e-commerce was to reduce supplier noise (bottom-left), followed by its use in price and terms negotiation (bottom-right) where it earned itself something of a bad name due to some inappropriate usage by inexperienced buyers (and sellers). An important aspect of its use in 'doing deals' is the way that it has expanded the supplier base after a period of rationalization – the high transactional costs that led to that rationalization are not apparent when using internet tendering and the like.

More recently we see more ambitious use of the technology, for sharing information, for improving forecasting and ordering (telemetry – remote ordering systems such as the use of bar-codes in retailers, or capacity sensors in bulk silos) and for building collaborative relationships (top-left and top-right).

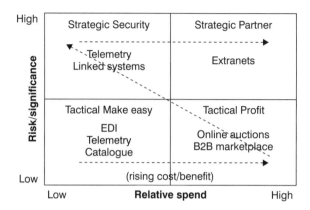

Figure 14.4 *Supplier positioning and e-commerce*

Managed improvement: developing suppliers' capabilities

Buyers have always demanded improvements, but in the past their job may have been merely to demand. Today, many buyers have taken on the responsibility of actively managing supplier performance improvements.

This is particularly common in the retail industry, where major retailers effectively manage some of their own label suppliers: the customer sets the standards and the specification; they manage the forecasts and so the production schedules; they initiate new product developments; and, perhaps of greatest significance, they manage the suppliers' margins.

In the bottom-left quadrant it may be that in pursuit of greater 'ease' the buyer wishes to develop a capable sole supplier. The supplier may need to expand their product range to allow the customer to rationalize their supply base. They may need to help that supplier to integrate their processes, through the development of IT capabilities, perhaps installing an electronic data interchange (EDI) system that allows the supplier direct access to the customer.

Security of supply is the name of the game in the top-left quadrant, and this is not easily found with some suppliers in the food industry. In the early days of organic food production the supermarkets often found that their potential suppliers did not have the commercial set-up to cope with their demands. Sainsbury's in particular were very active in improving such suppliers' capabilities, particularly their business processes, offering training and investment through organic supplier 'clubs'.

In the top-right quadrant, joint investment in development projects is a common activity. Buyers eager to see a faster flow of new products might help suppliers with the financial investment by providing people, giving guarantees of business, or offering themselves for pilot trials. In return, they will expect some form of special arrangement, perhaps exclusivity.

This gets to the very nub of relationships in this box: the supplier has undoubted privileges, but they come with attendant responsibilities. The customer may let you get very close to them, only provided you agree not to supply their competitors. Anyone who works closely with companies such as Coca-Cola or Procter & Gamble will recognize that theme.

Through the 1980s and 1990s, Marks & Spencer led the way in the retail trade, managing some of their strategic partners to the point that those suppliers thought, talked and acted like Marks & Spencer – true synergy. Some suppliers became very reliant on Marks & Spencer, put their trust in the customer's judgement, and allowed the customer to determine their ranges, quality standards, service levels, even their margins.

Was this good for suppliers? Many benefited enormously, as in the case study below. Others found themselves severely burnt when Marks & Spencer's fortunes were reversed in 1999. The decision to look to cheaper more varied and more creative suppliers in their clothing lines hit some of their incumbent 'partners' very hard.

Improving the supplier, instead of punishing them

When Marks & Spencer introduced a new kitchen product, only to find that the supplier had miscalculated their costs and were making a loss on supplying something that was now a great success and with a price fixed in their catalogue, many a retailer would have called that 'an education' for the supplier. But M&S went about helping their supplier to re-engineer the product to lower costs, while they themselves reduced their margin. The result? A long-term relationship with long-term profitability on both sides.

Close management of suppliers, in the way practised by M&S, can gain much in the way of control and efficiency, but it also implies a risk: in this case the risk of losing an 'independent' supplier's flair and innovation. Much of the retailer's woes in those years can be put down to a kind of cloning that went on between customer and supplier. When a customer takes on all the responsibility for things such as their supplier's product development, then they just have to get it right because there isn't anyone else to come up with the ideas. A successful relationship in this box must recognize the potential perils as well as the benefits of such closeness; only then can it guard against them.

The bottom-right quadrant may not seem the most fertile ground for trying to develop suppliers' capabilities – strong-arm tactics being the more likely course of action you might think – but even here buyers can be positive in their assistance. Helping a supplier to build greater scale, and so improve efficiency and reduce prices, is an obvious win–win. The buyer might offer a longer-term contract than would normally be expected, with carefully managed increases in volume in return for steadily decreasing prices.

Open-book trading

Buyers have always tried to get cost breakdowns from suppliers. This is a very old-fashioned but highly effective way of getting price reductions. The 'trick' was to get the supplier, often through an indiscretion, to disclose the costs of various parts of their package – perhaps the delivery costs, the packaging costs, or even the costs of the salespeople. Then, choose part of the product or service that you can do without and demand a discount for this new 'stripped down' package.

Once, this was a buyer's 'trick', now it is increasingly a formal requirement, called 'open-book trading', a sometimes abused, and often misunderstood process of managed supplier improvement.

Are they out to get you, or out to help you? Are their enquiries a genuine desire to help you improve your own efficiency and so reduce your own costs, or do they want to reduce your margin? We are clearly in the world of 'it depends', and this scenario calls for every ounce of the KA team's knowledge and sensitivity.

Do you refuse to play? What if your competitors are only too happy to oblige? Do you agree, but try to confuse the customer with complex data? This is no more than a stalling tactic, and a none-too-popular one at that. So do you agree to give the breakdowns? Consider the pressure exerted over a merchandising team in the case study below.

A supplier of a big brand name consumer product found their back against the wall with their largest customer, a national retailer. The salesperson was being told that they 'never did anything' to help their customer and it was about time things changed. Being in a corner, the salesperson 'broke', protesting: 'But that's not true; just our merchandising team alone costs us over £200,000 a year.' This was correct. Indeed, the merchandising sales team was of high value to the customer – they took orders, stocked shelves, built displays and handled complaints. But that was not the point and, a few weeks later, the salesperson was summoned to a meeting with the buying directors. 'We have been considering your services to us,' they began, 'and we have decided that we no longer require your sales team to take orders in our stores. We will do it ourselves, starting next month, and we would like you to compensate us for our extra work, from the £200,000 that we will be saving you.' This was not strictly true as the sales force covered other customers as well and the supplier would see no such savings, but that was not the point. The sales force was removed and a substantial payment made to the retailer. The story gets worse. After a few months, it was clear to the supplier that sales were declining. The retailer was not as diligent in their duties as the supplier's sales team and the salesperson was forced to go back to the directors. 'Can we put our sales team back in?' was the plea. 'Of course! Start tomorrow,' came the answer, 'but don't expect your money back...'

The price of innocence...

This was trickery – the customer valued the merchandising team almost as much as the supplier did, but were prepared to live without it for a while if they could gain such levels of 'compensation'.

The suppliers with the most to fear from open-book trading are those that have high-cost activities that do not give value to the customer. If we were feeling harsh, we might say it was their own fault if they got caught out – and buyers often do feel harsh.

If you are an efficient supplier, what do you have to hide? Indeed (as the buyer would argue), you can only shine if you are compared to your competitors. It is rather like the arguments in favour of individuals carrying identity cards; the only people with anything to fear are those who wish to conceal their identity for some 'dissident' purpose. But it is also the case that 'honest' people might object to the notion through feelings of independence, pride or 'honour'. Fine sentiments for independent citizens, but no way to run a KAM relationship.

Perhaps a bigger worry is that such 'open books' allow the customer to calculate your margins, and from there on in it can be a downward spiral. Often the best 'defence' to such strategies is to focus on the customer's costs, and to reduce them to such an extent that the buyer sees no point in enquiring into yours. We are back to the 'cost-in-use' arguments introduced in Chapter 12.

Managing risk

The management of risk is an increasingly important expectation on modern buyers, and they will make full use of the supplier positioning matrix in determining their best course of action in each supply circumstance.

Very significant... Consider a supplier of a critical ingredient to a big-brand consumer food product. It's a flavour that gives the unique taste so strongly identified with that brand, and it also happens to account for less than half a per cent of total expenditure on the materials for the final product.

This is of course a top-left supplier with a vengeance. Margins are good (no buyer is going to risk supply of such a product by switching to another supplier for the sake of a 5 per cent discount), and they have a long-term contract as a sole supplier. In return they give exclusivity, and 100 per cent reliability and consistency are assured.

> Such a situation existed for many years with a particular supplier/customer. From the buyer's perspective this was of course pure risk, to be so dependent in such a critical area (a 'bottleneck' item), but they were stuck with an arrangement that had been established by their R&D colleagues more years ago than anyone could remember.
> One day, the supplier had problems with their own supply base and failed to deliver. Everyone blamed the buyer for the fact that the production line was

halted, and then worse, the next batch, made in a hurry, was out of spec and an emergency product recall was instituted.

The supplier made much of the fact that this was the first such instance in over eight years, but the anxious buyer considered once was enough and seized control. There were to be no more sole supplier arrangements, indeed no supplier was to have more than 50 per cent of the business, and the incumbent supplier would have to give their recipe to the new competitors.

...but far too risky

Another way of reducing risk in the top-left quadrant has been noted in the section above on using e-commerce. Telemetry (remote and automated re-ordering) can help to smooth the supply of 'bottleneck' items, but here we see the sometimes two-edged sword of such activities; buyers aim to reduce their risk, while suppliers succeed in 'locking-in' the customer through such an automated process, so increasing the 'risk' to the buyers.

In a bottom-left 'tactical make easy' situation there may be plenty of fish in the sea – let's say we are looking at stationery suppliers – and the total spend is relatively small. The buyer may grant sole supplier status in such a case, and manage the risk through a contract with tough performance standards and a speedy exit clause if the supplier lets them down.

Top-right suppliers present the highest level of risk, and as such the buyer will assess them against a range of performance standards, and as we saw in the previous section may step in to actively manage supplier improvement programmes if anything falls below par. Suppliers in this box are often surprised to hear buyers asking them how they train their staff, or what health and safety measures they have in place. If they knew more about their positioning then they wouldn't be so surprised...

Bottom-right suppliers present the least risk and so provide fertile ground for the most 'robust' of tactics (suppliers might use the word 'brutal'). If a supplier lets you down, you fire them. If you feel exposed by having your business with too few suppliers you simply share it out to more – and you don't expect any price increases from the first lot.

Removing risk?

A number of high-profile cases in recent years have made clear the buyer's role in removing risk from certain situations. It has become increasingly common for companies to take positions on the 'bigger issues' such as health, the environment, fair trade, and social conditions for workers and suppliers around the globe, all of which bring a new responsibility to the buyer's desk. If it is claimed that all suppliers are vetted to ensure good employment practices, then this must be managed with great care – the alternative is an embarrassing headline in the newspapers. If it is discovered that toys made in China contain high levels of lead in their paint, then it is the buyer who will suffer the wrath of the board (and pretty much everyone else's, including the customers).

For the buyer, some issues are no longer to be left open to chance, or the hope that suppliers won't let them down. Suppliers must adhere to increasingly stringent guidelines, and those that appear to resent their imposition will find themselves dropped. But here we are often in areas that cannot be managed entirely by buyers' edicts. Suppliers that can demonstrate their ability to self-monitor and manage to high standards, and to remove risk on behalf of the buyer, will be much smiled upon.

Key suppliers: being appropriate

Being 'key' is first and foremost about being appropriate

The majority of key suppliers (and they will be few in numbers – less than 5 per cent of the total supplier base, and commonly less than 2 per cent) will be found in the top-right quadrant, but not exclusively so. The secret to attaining this status if you are positioned elsewhere is to be entirely appropriate to your positioning.

If you have the lowest price, and can guarantee the same for the next five years, then you might expect to be well courted despite being a bottom-right supplier. To be the sharpest on the block you probably need to have the lowest costs of supply in the business and you will be expected to pass on your efficiencies to the customer.

If you can take on the task of ensuring supply across a full category of products, self-managed and dependably, then if those products are bottom-left (office stationery is a typical example) you may well find yourself in a sole supplier situation. Be supremely easy to do business with; install remote ordering systems, communicate through e-mail, don't overburden customers with your presence. Be there when required and keep out of the way when not. Don't try to force complex relationships on the customer, unless they lead to easier transactions. Show willingness to take on those administrative tasks that perhaps traditionally have been the buyer's – think about offering to set, and police, your own standards (but don't be too pushy!).

Be 100 per cent reliable in an area where the customer has reason to be nervous (top-left) and although you may be a relatively small supplier you might find yourself very well rewarded. But be warned, *100 per cent* reliability is the name of the game in this quadrant – nothing less than perfection will be acceptable (as we saw in the case of the flavour supplier discussed earlier). You might expect to be asked for some form of consignment stock or 'vendor-managed inventory', which can be expensive but can also help to tie you in to the customer.

And what is 'appropriate' as a top-right supplier? Let's start with some negatives: never assume your indispensability, don't be arrogant and don't become complacent. All three are common sins, and the longer the relationship continues the more easily are the sins committed. After that, the list of positive requirements may be very long – these relationships require significant investments of time and effort from both parties. Aim to establish contacts at the most senior level, and try to focus on the long term. Bring the customer your new ideas, first. Above all, get the relationship right. A 'tactical make easy' supplier that gets it wrong will be a nuisance, but a 'strategic partner' that gets it wrong will be a disaster.

If we consider the nature of the top-right relationship in one particular industry, that of key suppliers to major grocery retailers, we will see the practice of what is called 'category management', where both supplier and retailer join in focusing time and energies on identifying and meeting consumer needs from the broadest standpoint (the whole product category, not just the particular supplier's brand).

One of the most highly publicized examples of such a partnership is that between Proctor & Gamble as supplier and Wal-Mart as customer in the United States. Both had reputations as fairly 'confrontational' negotiators, based on the strength of their positions, but in the late 1980s they decided to work things a new way. Wal-Mart began to provide P&G with information on the sales of P&G products, detailed stuff – volumes, returns, profit, regional variations – all of huge value to the supplier. Wal-Mart then allowed P&G to take responsibility for managing their stock, placing orders, determining levels, even allocating space in store. The benefits were huge. For Wal-Mart, the new arrangement removed 'stock-outs', reduced transaction costs and passed such savings on to customers through an 'everyday low price' policy agreed with P&G. For P&G, they got very close to a customer that represented a significant chunk of their total revenue. Hugely improved forecasts allowed them to make significant enhancements to their supply chain, and perhaps of greatest importance, they received a first class education in the challenges and dynamics of the retail industry.	**Getting it right**

POSITIONING IS ONE THING – BUT LIFE GOES ON

Suppliers are sometimes surprised when, after being assured that they are a key supplier, and after being shown their top scores against the buyer's vendor ratings, the decision goes against them. This is not necessarily about the buyer breaking their word, which is sometimes mumbled by the exiting supplier; rather it might suggest a certain innocence on the supplier's part.

Hewlett Packard is an example of a company that is very open in discussing its vendor ratings with its more significant suppliers: specific and tangible standards are set, regular reviews are held, suppliers are expected to manage their own performance improvement, and everyone knows where they stand. But this is not to say that the top-ranking suppliers are guaranteed the order.

Buyers use such rankings as a guide to their management of suppliers, not as a means of making their decisions. To win the business a top-right positioning and a high ranking against the vendor ratings will help, but suppliers should never forget the importance of each individual sale – sometimes buyers get an offer they just cannot refuse.

And sometimes the world just changes. A buyer that has treated you as a partner for months or even years appears to turn against you, demanding savage price cuts and radical improvements in services. A betrayal? More likely it is due to a period of poor trading conditions for the customer, or perhaps they have just lost a major deal, or they might have cash-flow problems resulting from an expensive acquisition or investment. Of course, these are the kind of things that any alert KA manager should be fully aware of, and well before the buyer's demands arise, allowing them to consider appropriate palliative actions designed to avert the crisis. Just as for a stand-up-comedian, good timing can be the mark of genius in a KA manager.

So long as we sell to human beings there will be irrational and emotional decisions, and cries of 'not fair'. We might better regard such things as the impact of the less tangible factors, and sometimes the intangible can make a good deal of sense. A buyer that makes a choice based on like or dislike of a seller might also be making another judgement: 'I need to work with these people over the long term, in a close and collaborative relationship, and I don't see this one lasting the pace...'

Is trust the basis of an irrational or emotional decision? A lack of trust is certainly a sound reason to say no. Maintaining trust is the result of continual vigilance, of attention to the small things, of keeping promises big and small. Trust can be destroyed by laziness, by complacency and by inattention. Trust in business is not unlike trust in life: you may win the affections of another through a steady flow of chocolates and flowers, but what impression do you give when after 20 years of inattention you turn up at home one day with a bunch of flowers in your hand?

BEHAVE APPROPRIATELY, BUT PLAN YOUR ESCAPE

The advice earlier in this chapter was to behave appropriately to your positioning if you were aiming to be thought a key supplier, but perhaps the actions required are not attractive to you, or perhaps your business strategy points in other directions. In such a case you may wish to shift your positioning, to escape the buyer's 'pigeonholing' of your capabilities. This is of course possible, by increasing your significance and so 'moving north' in the matrix, but it will almost certainly be something of a long haul.

One of business life's 'truths' should always be remembered: the customer's *perception* of your position is more important than the fact. Where they see you is where you are. Perhaps they place you in the bottom-left quadrant, whereas you know that your unique technology actually places you top-left. Don't expect to be able to just tell them. Take every opportunity, and every potential contact, to slowly drip feed the information required for them to change their view. Wait patiently for the opportunity to demonstrate your incomparability, but then be ready to pounce.

A second truth has already been referred to: don't expect the buyer to take delight in your increasing significance. Figure 14.5 shows the differing intentions of sellers (wishing to argue their uniqueness) and buyers (wishing to argue your proximity to a commodity). Buyers will not want too many suppliers in those upper two boxes, so demonstrations of your importance to them will need to be handled with care if you are not to make them nervous. Gaining the support of those in the customer that see your true value, arming them with the necessary information, and asking them to brief the buyer, may be a better strategy than telling the buyers yourself.

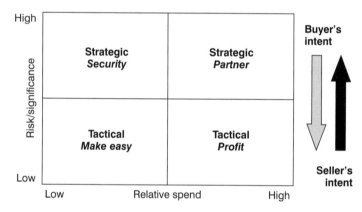

Figure 14.5 *The differing intentions of sellers and buyers*

Moving north

Much of the rest of this book is devoted to advice on how to raise your significance. The chapters in Part V, 'Achieving strategic supplier status', look at doing this from the perspective of the whole company and not just in the buyer's eyes. The chapters in Part VI, 'The value proposition', suggest ways of building your proposition to express greater value, and so raise your tangible significance to the customer.

APPLICATION EXERCISE

Consider the activities, behaviours, and attitudes of the buyers in one of your key accounts:

- How do they position you?
  - What effect does this have on their purchasing strategy?
  - What impact does this have on your role as a supplier?
- What activities should you focus on to attain a *key supplier status*?
- How can you increase your significance to the buyer, without raising their fears?

Part V

Achieving strategic supplier status

15

Being of strategic value

Throughout Chapters 11 to 14 we have been concerned with making a positive impact on the customer's purchasing strategy. Our aim to achieve 'key supplier status' has been as judged by the customer's purchasing professionals. In these next chapters it is time to move up a level, to consider our impact on the customer's *business strategy*, in pursuit of what we might call 'strategic supplier status'. We must consider how we are judged by the customer as a whole, across all functions, and in particular at the most senior level.

We will need to consider a whole new set of performance criteria, summarized in what we will call the 'diagnostic toolkit' (as discussed later) – a series of analytical tools that will enable us to judge our impact on the customer's business strategy.

TIMES CHANGE

But first, why the need for this higher status: isn't it enough to be top of the buyer's league table? The truth is that we need something more secure. Buyers can be fickle. Buyers can be changed. Buyers are not always in charge (despite what they may tell us to the contrary), and their purchasing criteria can be changed for them by some very short-term forces – a few bad months of trading, shifts in supply and demand, the arrival of a new supplier…

Competitive advantage can be short lived. It hardly seems credible that OTIF (those four little letters that have focused so many suppliers' minds – 'on time in full') should once have been a source of competitive advantage. Today it is so much the standard requirement from ever-vigilant customers that we easily forget how some suppliers were once able to use it as a means of ousting less efficient competition. Indeed, in many markets it was the supplier and not the customer who introduced the measure, as evidence of their competitive superiority.

Times change. Laws that once favoured you turn against you; competitors in decline find new leases of life, superior products become ordinary, the buyer who loved you leaves you. This is particularly true where a supplier has become 'lazy', perhaps having enjoyed for too long a position of power and security. Customer dissatisfaction, pent up over a period of time, can suddenly blow its lid. (Much the same can happen to governments at general election time.)

Who needs to listen to customers, if you're the best?

There was once a hugely successful company making slide rules (for those of you too young to remember, slide rules were calculating 'machines' using logarithmic scales and highly engineered sliding parts, before the days of electronic calculators), and as there were not too many alternative tools for calculation (logarithmic tables and the abacus being about it), they effectively held their customers to ransom.

Retailers were obliged to stock this leading brand and schools were obliged to buy them for their pupils, who were put through the agonies of learning how to use them despite the fact that they, like everybody, hankered for something better, something easier to use.

Some customers said as much to the slide rule manufacturer, but the letters and the phone calls never made it down to the R&D department. There, they spent their time working on making even better slide rules, with 'slidier' slidy bits, clearer printing, a smarter case – and steadfastly refused to listen. Who needed to listen to customers when you made the best slide rules in the world?

Change came in the guise of the electronic pocket calculator and customers were only too happy to jump ship – they 'snapped'. I was one of the throngs of schoolchildren eager to break my slide rule into pieces! Seen any slide rules lately?

WHEN CUSTOMERS 'SNAP'

When there is very little competition, and customers have few options for changing their suppliers, dissatisfaction has to be quite high before customers put in the effort of finding an alternative. There is inertia in the market, as shown by the low competition curve in Figure 15.1.

Add competition – new suppliers eager to win new customers – and the picture changes. Now, small lapses in a supplier's performance can result in

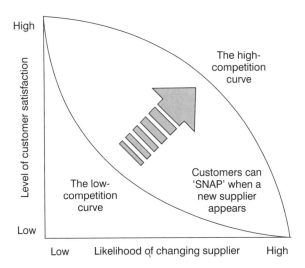

Figure 15.1 *When customers 'snap'*

the loss of the business. Relatively small increases in customers' dissatis-faction can cause them to 'snap'. The market has become fluid.

If there has been a long period of low competition among suppliers, perhaps even a monopoly, and worse, an arrogant incumbent supplier, then you might expect to find customers at their most twitchy, and most ready to 'snap'.

> Before the deregulation of the energy supply industry in the UK, British Gas had a virtual monopoly of industrial customers. Within months of deregulation industrial customers were starting to leave, but there were few plans in place to keep them from departing, and still fewer for winning them back. The notion of customers 'snapping' was just too foreign to a supplier that had enjoyed such forced 'loyalty' for so long.
>
> More recently, with the consumer market up for grabs, we can see the gas suppliers behaving a lot more aggressively to retain customers, and win new ones, and well beyond the bounds of the gas industry.

One leak British Gas found hard to fix

Such things can happen to 'key suppliers', if the appellation 'key' is simply the result of there being no alternatives. It should never happen to a 'strategic supplier', not if the appellation 'strategic' is the result of the supplier having a deep-seated and positive impact on the customer's business strategy.

How this can be assessed and achieved is the subject of this and the following chapters in Part V.

WHEN CUSTOMERS MERGE

One of the toughest challenges for suppliers in recent times has been to deal with the fallout when two quite separate customers merge (make one of the two a key customer of the competition and the challenge is yet greater). Such things can find a poorly prepared supplier caught like a deer in the headlights.

Who will be 'in' and who will be 'out' in this new world? Who should we back – our old friends, or our 'new' friends? Will they simply demand bigger discounts? Will they rationalize their sites, their products, their buyers, their suppliers?

Any supplier that has relied on a sales-driven 'bow-tie' relationship (as described in Chapter 7) may find these kind of questions rather daunting, or worse, make poorly informed guesses based on the views of their current contacts. Suppliers that have taken care to build a depth and a breadth of relationship, particularly at a senior level, will find themselves so much better placed when the world changes. They might even find that they are called in for early-day briefings on which way the winds are blowing.

In some markets, where mergers and takeovers have become almost the norm, this alone may be a justification for a diamond team approach (see Chapter 7), and yet even having such relationships in place may still not be enough to ensure your position. Nothing can guarantee security of tenure at such times, but the odds will be heavily in favour of those suppliers that can demonstrate their strategic value to the new entity. Note: you must demonstrate your strategic value to the *new* entity. It will not be enough to claim that you *were* a strategic supplier to one or to the other – that is all history now.

The ability to make a rapid assessment of the new and emerging business strategy, and to align your proposition to ensure a positive impact, will be of significant importance. It is the purpose of this and the following chapters of Part V to help you with that assessment and alignment.

BEING OF STRATEGIC VALUE

The tale of two hospitals ...

Two competitors are each trying to sell an x-ray machine to a private hospital. One costs £400,000, the other £550,000, and they apparently do much the same job.

The buyer, an old-fashioned type with no time for supplier positioning models, calls it a 'no brainer' and goes for the cheaper machine, feeling happy with a good day's work that saved the hospital £150,000.

Over the next two years the x-ray machine is serviced eight times, each time at a cost of £10,000, and required a major overhaul costing £20,000. Oddly enough, the buyer doesn't care; servicing costs come out of the radiology department's budget and are not the buying department's responsibility.

> The machine has broken down on two occasions, resulting in major patient logjams, a lot of ill will towards the hospital and one very expensive court case for negligence. Oddly enough, the buyer doesn't care; again the department is not responsible for patient-processing targets and its staff rarely go to court or read the newspapers.
>
> A competing hospital in the next town bought the more expensive x-ray machine. The service contract requires only two services a year, each at £5,000, and the machine has never broken down. The hospital has no patient logjams, and no bad press.
>
> They are doing well, and stealing customers from the hospital with the cheaper machine and the PR problems. Not surprisingly, people want to go to the hospital that isn't in the newspapers.

This tale of two hospitals is all about value, but there are two rather different types. The first is the type of value that saved money – the lower servicing costs, which over time will make the more expensive machine the better buy.

The second is perhaps the more important type of value, the defence of the hospital's reputation. I once heard a hospital manager say: 'If the customers feel they can trust us then they don't begrudge having more expensive coffee in the waiting room. They don't even mind if they have to pay for things that other hospitals do for free – but do badly.'

The supplier that helps build trust with the hospital's public will have every chance of being regarded as a strategic supplier. Imagine the position of a supplier that provided the means of removing MRSA from hospitals!

The task of any key account team is to identify what would be considered as strategic value by their own customer. Each customer's view will be unique, resulting from the uniqueness of their *competitive position* and of their *business strategy*.

The customer's competitive position

What are they up against? Michael Porter has provided us with a robust model for assessing the nature of the competitive challenges faced by a business. His famous 'five forces' are shown in Figure 15.2.

Porter argues that a business operates within the ferment and flux of five different forces that combine to determine profitability. The KA team must understand how each impacts their customer, and how they might be able to help the customer build protective barriers against these forces:

- How might they give competitive advantage against the existing players?
- How might they help prevent new entrants?

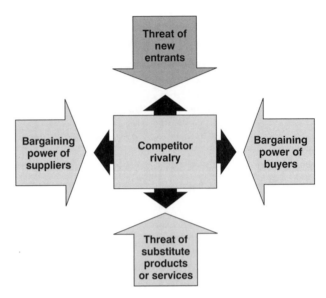

Figure 15.2 *Michael Porter's 'five forces'*

- How might they help prevent substitute products?
- How might they help reduce the power of buyers?
- How might they help reduce the power of suppliers?

The last may seem a peculiar goal, but it is of course one fully in the hands of the supplier!

These are the big picture questions to be understood, on behalf of the customer. Which of these forces keeps the customer awake at nights? The ability of a supplier to promise a good night's sleep can be of great significance in the pursuit of a strategic supplier status.

How could you help?

As an exercise, consider the forces impacting on a UK grocery retail chain, and ask what impact a typical supplier might be able to have on reducing those forces:

Current competitors
Nowhere is there a more heated 'battle of the giants' than between the big players in this market. The fallout manifests itself in price wars, ever more generous loyalty cards and a race to launch new products and services, all of which can take a heavy toll on margins.

The threat of new entrants
New forces are continually hovering, spotting gaps in the market left by the ever-repositioning major players. We have seen Aldi and Netto promising cut-price shopping, and Wal-Mart threatening to bring its 'category busting' tactics to the

UK through its acquisition of Asda. Not all of these new entrants are as successful as their aggressive launch plans promise, but their very presence reshapes the competitive dynamics of the market.

The threat of substitute products or services
Will it or won't it – will the internet and home shopping replace the supermarket as we know it?

The bargaining power of customers
Consumer pressure grows daily, fanned by the media, demanding more ecologically sound products, no GM ingredients, fairer trade with Third World suppliers, healthier food, better-labelled products, tastier food and cheaper food.

The bargaining power of suppliers
At the other end of the supply chain, major suppliers can wield enormous power, whether through brand names (who could envisage a major supermarket without Coca-Cola or Cadbury's?) or simply through the scale of their operations.
  So, how could you help, and come to be considered a strategic supplier?

The customer's business strategy

How often have you complained of not knowing your own company's strategy? Then why should your customer's staff be any better informed? Maybe they're not, and to rely on the views and comments of any one individual (particularly the buyer!) would be taking a big risk. Nor is it about reading the chairman's statement in the company report.

A true understanding of any company's business strategy will only come from conversations with a breadth of contacts across a range of functions, and particularly at a senior level. Even then we must recognize that there can be internal disputes that will colour the tangible outcomes, and sometimes significant time lags between the stated ambitions of the board and the practical actions of those charged with implementation.

THE DIAGNOSTIC TOOLKIT

On top of all that, business strategy is no small study. The key account team is in need of a quick means of assessing and acting, which brings us to the 'diagnostic toolkit' shown in Figure 15.3.

Business strategy, at the level we wish to understand it, might be said to be the outcome of three questions, each with its own issues and each with its own analytical 'models' to aid our understanding.

Strategy	Question	Analysis
Markets & products	How are they growing?	Ansoff matrix Product life cycle
Competitive advantage	How do they aim to win?	Michael Porter Money-making-logic
Value drivers	What drives them?	Wiersema Culture

Figure 15.3 *The customer's business strategy: a 'diagnostic toolkit'*

The following chapters will address each of these three questions in turn:

- How are they growing?
- How do they aim to win?
- What drives them?

In each case the aim is to understand how a supplier can build a more significant and 'strategic' position through the pursuit of a positive impact.

Following on from that analysis, we will conclude Part V with a consideration of how likely it is that we will have a strong 'shared future' with the customer, as a result of our ability, or not, to make a relevant and positive impact on their wider business ambitions and concerns.

APPLICATION EXERCISE

Conduct Porter's analysis for one of your own key accounts, seeking to identify the key issues that impact on their competitive position:

- The current competitors:
  - the threat of new entrants;
  - the threat of substitutes;
  - the bargaining power of customers;
  - the bargaining power of suppliers.
- Where can you best help them to combat those forces?
  - What value do you bring to their business by doing so?
  - Can you use this value to move your status towards that of a strategic supplier?
- What reward do you expect for your efforts?

16

How are they growing?

GROWTH AND RISK

For any business wishing to grow there are four choices with regard to what it has to sell and where it chooses to sell it, expressed by the four boxes in the Ansoff matrix shown in Figure 16.1, and named after its developer, Igor Ansoff. The options are:

- *Market penetration*: sell more of existing products into existing markets.
- *Market extension*: sell existing products into new markets.
- *New product development (NPD)*: sell new products into existing markets.
- *Diversification*: sell new products into new markets.

The purpose of the matrix is to help us recognize the different levels of risk involved in each growth strategy; the percentage figures in each box indicate the likely level of success of the strategy. In other words, risk increases as we move around the matrix.

Provided that there is more business to be had in your existing market (you do not already 'own' 100 per cent) then a 'penetration' strategy is usually the safest option: you already have a presence, you know the requirements, and you can plan your activities with the confidence of experience.

As your chosen growth strategy moves around the matrix, from penetration to 'market extension', to new product development (NPD) and finally to 'diversification', the chances of success go down (or the risk of

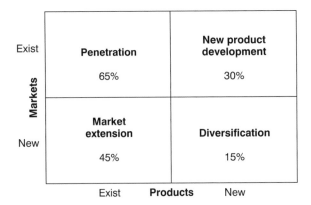

Figure 16.1 *The Ansoff matrix*

failure increases, whichever way you prefer to regard it). The reasons for this are many, but in essence it is as simple as this: the top-left box is 'home' (your existing market and your existing products), and with each step away from home (into new markets, and then new products, and then both new products and new markets) you are moving further into the unknown.

For the supplier in pursuit of strategic supplier status the use of this analysis is twofold. First, to identify the nature of the customer's growth strategy, and so understand the nature and extent of the risks they are taking. Such an understanding will tell us a lot about their likely needs, their priorities, and their probable attitudes and behaviours with regard to suppliers. Second, and even more importantly, it will help us to assess our own potential for making a positive contribution to that growth strategy, and in particular the extent to which we can help the customer reduce their risk and so improve their chances of success.

Reducing the customer's risk

What kind of customer do you prefer? The sort who grows through penetration and so is most likely to succeed, or the sort who might be taking more ambitious steps in the area of market extension, NPD, or diversification, and who might very well fail in their attempt? The latter could of course take you with them in their failure, wasting your time and your resources, so do we choose for the safer bet of the penetrators? The problem with those in the top-left box is that their demands on suppliers might be rather limited: lower prices, lower prices and lower prices... Those being more ambitious might look for more, in their efforts to manage and reduce their risk, and that may open the door to a genuine 'value sell'.

It's the classic trade-off, low risk and low reward, or higher risk and higher reward. Perhaps the best answer to 'who you prefer' is to aim for a

Risk is good, if you can help reduce it for your customer!

balanced portfolio, some promising certainty, with others suggesting a more challenging investment. But who might be most likely to regard us as a strategic supplier: the safe bet, or the risk taker?

Consider the customer's perspective. Some form of risk is necessary if they wish to grow, but any sensible business will always seek to manage or contain that risk. There are many things that can be done to manage risk:

- market research;
- market testing;
- joint ventures with experienced partners;
- taking on experienced staff, or training;
- seeking help from the suppliers.

This last point gives us our clue of course; perhaps it is with those customers taking risk that we have the most opportunity to 'shine' as a strategic supplier. What that involves will of course differ depending on their method of growth. The customer looking at new markets for their existing products (market extension) will be seeking suppliers that have knowledge and experience in those places – 'guides and consultants' as well as suppliers.

The customer looking towards NPD will want suppliers that can be trusted with confidential information, that offer relevant innovation, perhaps financial support, but most importantly of all, suppliers that will be fast. The secret of NPD is speed to market and any supplier that slows them down will be frowned upon. Imagine a customer dealing with a supplier through a bow-tie relation (see Chapter 7); how do they view their supplier in terms of their speed? Figure 16.2 suggests the answer.

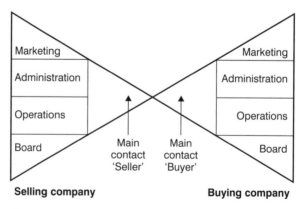

Figure 16.2 *The 'sand-timer' or 'logjam' relationship*

The bow-tie can look to them like a sand-timer or logjam, a holder-up or a slower-down of progress. The diamond relationship (see Chapter 7) is far more likely to assure them that they have access to the people that can make things happen for them.

Those looking at diversification will want the most of all, and might prove to be the most valuable of your customers if you can help them. The importance of matching the customer's aspirations is paramount in this scenario. If you bore them with your ability to deliver three times a week, and offer them extended credit provided they don't ask for any short-notice services, then you should not be surprised to be shown the door.

Of course, all these scenarios will involve the supplier in a level of risk, and perhaps investment long before the merest sniff of a sale. You will be asked to commit time, energy and perhaps even money to a venture that could fail. Only you can judge the situation, which suggests another skill required by the KA team – that of risk analysis and assessment.

> Consider a supplier of complex molecular raw materials to the pharmaceutical industry. One of their greatest challenges is knowing how much effort to put into a piece of work for a customer setting out on a new drug development. Will the customer's drug succeed? There are mountains of tests, regulatory approvals and efficacy trials to get through. It could be years before any appreciable volume of business is established. 'Jam tomorrow' is a common hope. Much of the success of such a supplier will be based on their ability to make complex assessments, assessments that will require the supplier to know their customer as well as the customer knows themselves. The questions that need answering are hardly the sort that can be discussed by a seller and buyer across a negotiating table. The supplier will almost certainly need to have a thorough and deep diamond relationship, which itself will only be granted as a result of achieving some kind of key or strategic supplier status. We are of course in the realm of the chicken and the egg…

Reducing your own risk depends on your ability to assess the customer's level of risk

What the customer advises

Sir Richard Branson give some very clear advice to the company pursuing the diversification course, and he should know, having taken Virgin through more diversifications than most (record label to airline to cola manufacturer to personal equity plan seller to mobile phones… and so on), and with significantly more success than Ansoff's analysis would suggest. The secret?

- Do more market research than anyone thinks is necessary.
- Have a brand that acts as a 'halo' around each new activity.
- Seek help from expert suppliers.

Partnerships are key to Virgin. Virgin brings the brand name; the supplier brings the market expertise. The supplier is expected to take on a good deal of the risk (in some cases, the majority) and should they fail in any way then Virgin retains the right to step in.

GROWTH AND THE PRODUCT LIFE CYCLE (PLC)

Looking for the clues...

Once the supplier has understood the nature of the customer's risk, their next step, in pursuit of strategic supplier status, is to understand the specific requirements arising as the customer's product or service moves through its life cycle. Figure 16.3 shows a standard PLC, with the introduction followed by growth, moving into maturity and then into saturation and decline.

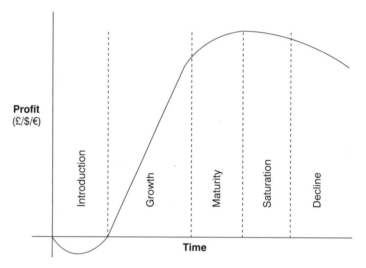

Figure 16.3   *The product life cycle*

Each stage calls for specific management tasks (usually the responsibility of the marketing department), and perhaps for some specific requirements of their suppliers. Figure 16.4 suggests some typical examples of such requirements.

Introduction

As we noted when discussing the NPD box of the Ansoff matrix, innovation is important in the process of development, and speed is vital. At introduction itself the customer must depend on suppliers to keep their promises – any failure can be very expensive indeed.

Consider a food manufacturer launching a new product. Their retail customers may only give them two weeks in which to prove themselves.

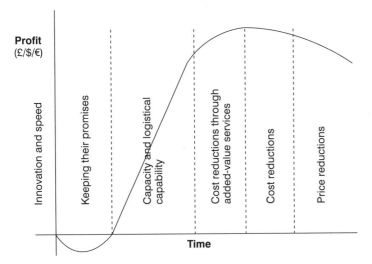

Figure 16.4 *The customer's requirements through the PLC*

Imagine the catastrophe of one of the manufacturer's suppliers holding their launch up by just two days... 'What's two days?' asks the supplier – possibly the difference between success and failure. At no other stage is 'on time in full' so important.

Growth

As the customer's product moves into the growth phase, the biggest problem can sometimes be dealing with unexpected success. Forecasting is one thing, but nobody wants to hold back a runaway success just because the forecast was for less. Suppliers are chosen on the basis of their ability to keep pace with growth and those that frown and complain when forecasts are exceeded will not be doing themselves any favours in the strategic supplier stakes.

Maturity

Maturity often sees the professional buyer enter the scene in earnest. The customer is in search of increased efficiency and cost control. Supply chain management (see Chapter 12) will be much in evidence. The buyer may just ask for price reductions, and the unthinking supplier may just oblige. The more aware supplier will realize that at this point in the customer's PLC, cost reductions can be of greater value than price reduction. The difference? Perhaps the supplier can provide a service, or a quality of product, that reduces the customer's costs, a product enhancement that reduces customer down time in their production, or reduces wastage, or speeds the process in some other way. The supplier should perhaps even be able to sell such a 'solution' at a premium.

Avoiding maturity

Of course, products don't have to mature, they can be rejuvenated, relaunched, repackaged, enhanced, even replaced. This raises three important issues for the supplier:

1. Should they be pressing the customer into these actions?
2. If so, who should they be pressing?
3. When is the right time?

The answers will, of course, depend on a host of factors, but more often than not they will be: 1) yes; 2) marketing; and 3) as early as possible. A true strategic supplier will not wait for their customer's product to reach maturity before suggesting the means to give it a new lease of life. Strategic suppliers should always be looking ahead, should always be stretching the boundaries, and should have the realism to recognize that things take time to happen.

Saturation and decline

When the writing is on the wall for a product the buyer will be looking to reduce costs by the most straightforward of means – price. The future value in the product is not sufficient to justify more complex solutions that might involve new investment. The supplier that can guarantee price cuts projected into the future will be given a lot of airtime.

As decline truly sets in and volumes start to reduce, some suppliers may be of a mind to raise prices. They may succeed, and may gain some short-term reward, but it is unlikely that they will be considered in any way as strategic suppliers.

Why should you care, if the customer's product is on the way out? Well, perhaps the customer has other products at earlier stages of their PLCs, and the supplier would hope to be rewarded for their loyalty and assistance by a generous share of those more interesting projects. It all depends on the relationship.

Avoiding the lowest common denominator

There is a particular challenge for a supplier that does business with a customer that has different products at all stages of the PLC. It is very easy to lose focus on the different circumstances and needs, and to then succumb to the lowest common denominator – price pressure.

If a buyer wins a price concession from you on a product at saturation or decline, then why shouldn't they chance their arm at one for a product in the growth stage? Your being a strategic supplier doesn't mean they won't try such a tactic, but it is to be hoped that being a strategic supplier will mean that both you and the customer are properly aware of the true value of your contributions, at each separate stage of the PLC.

Matching the proposition

The skilled observer of the customer's PLC will begin to match their whole value proposition to customers at the different stages.

For customers at the introduction and growth stage, the supplier might offer truly tailored and innovative solutions, being prepared to invest in anticipation of a long-term return.

For customers moving towards maturity, if it is not possible to help them escape maturity (see above), more cost-effective solutions may be required. Perhaps the supplier will aim to offer already proven solutions, so reducing their own investment and costs, perhaps sharing those reductions with the customer through lower prices. Perhaps they can offer additional services that reduce the customer's costs.

For customers fully into maturity and heading for saturation and decline the options may be more limited. The offer of value solutions may not be attractive to the customer, and the supplier will be keen to restrict their investment at this late stage. A possible option is to offer the customer an alternative lower-priced range, perhaps a 'fighting brand', with limited or no services. The key to success for the supplier using such a fighting brand is to keep very tight discipline on what is offered. Stripped down must mean stripped down, all additional services must be paid for, and the pursuit of ever lower costs through scale and operational excellence will be key targets.

Observation and identification in the real world

Drawing out the curve of a PLC after the event, once the product is dead and gone, is easy; but how about knowing where it is while it is still active? What tells you that it has moved from introduction to growth, or that it is approaching maturity? It is a jigsaw of clues that the KA team must put together:

- What do the sales statistics tell you?
- What do the customer's demands tell you?
- What do your other contacts tell you?

Before introduction your main contacts may be with marketing or R&D. As the growth stage is entered you might find yourself more in contact with the customer's operations departments – production and distribution. As maturity closes in, expect more contact with the buyer.

APPLICATION EXERCISE

Using the Ansoff matrix, consider the growth strategy of one of your key accounts:

- What is the nature of that growth strategy, and what level of risk does it imply?
- How can you act to reduce or mitigate that risk, and so move towards strategic supplier status?
- Who from your team needs to be involved with whom from their team in order to make this positive impact?
- What reward do you expect for your efforts?

Where is your customer's business/product in the PLC?

- What needs from suppliers does that position imply?
- What actions should you focus on to move towards strategic supplier status?
- Who from your team needs to be involved with whom from their team in order to make this positive impact?
- What reward do you expect for your efforts?

17

How do they aim to win?

PORTER AND COMPETITIVE ADVANTAGE

In Chapter 15 we looked at Michael Porter's model (see Figure 15.2) for assessing the external forces that can impact on a business, so affecting its competitive position and its profitability. Here we will consider the responses that Porter suggests can be made to those forces, and consider how a supplier can assist their customer with those responses, in pursuit of strategic supplier status.

There are two principle strategies, both described as a potential source of competitive advantage:

- being the lowest-cost supplier;
- being a differentiated supplier.

Success is not necessarily the result of the choice itself – either strategy can work in a variety of circumstances – rather it is the result of the ability to focus the whole business on whichever route is chosen. Failure usually comes when a business vacillates between the two, becoming an 'in-betweeny', often the result of functions or departments working in opposition to each other.

The implications for the budding strategic supplier and their activities are clear: aim to support the chosen strategy, and in particular avoid becoming entrapped in any internal disputes over direction or priorities.

Being the lowest-cost supplier

Don't confuse this with being the lowest priced. An expert practitioner of this strategy once said to me: 'The trick is to be the lowest-cost supplier, but not to let the customer know!' Getting the operational costs down, from procurement through manufacture and on to selling and distribution improves margins when times are good, protects margins when times are bad, and allows the use of the low-price weapon when times call for competitive aggression.

There are many courses of action. Wal-Mart developed IT systems that allowed them to eliminate significant costs from procurement – fully automating the process from the point at which the customer's purchase is swiped through the checkout's bar-code scanner. Dell Computers have taken huge costs out of the supply of computer hardware as a result of their significant use of the internet as a sales medium. EasyJet and Ryanair have done the same in the airline industry.

In each case the requirement on their suppliers (at least, those suppliers relevant to these issues) was not necessarily to reduce prices, but to help them with their investment in the necessary capabilities. This is vital to remember: a customer pursuing a lowest-cost supplier strategy is looking first and foremost for suppliers that will help them achieve that goal. If the supplier has nothing to offer other than low prices then so be it, but a truly strategic supplier will be able, and expected, to offer more.

A 'lowest-cost' strategy may not always be looking for the 'lowest price' supplier...

There are plenty of myths about why Chinese manufacturing is so low cost, mostly to do with wage levels. While this is true in many industries it is far from the principle reason in the textile industry – one of the lowest cost of them all. Tour a modern Chinese textiles factory and the first surprise is how few staff there are in the first place. These are highly automated concerns, using mechanization on the largest scale, and the latest technology throughout. Compare this to the often shabby state of a 'Western' textiles factory (such as still survive) and you have the answer.

Lowest cost is more often achieved through investment than disinvestment, and even more so if it is to be sustainable lowest cost. Any fool can fire the sales force to save costs – and many do.

Suppliers that can help with such investments, or that can reduce their customer's costs through the provision of products and services with superior performance, will almost certainly stand more chance of being regarded as strategic than those who simply offer low prices.

I once sold to a buyer who called their suppliers the 'soft underbelly' of the market: the place you could always poke with a sharp stick when times were tough and cost reduction the target. Poor suppliers will succumb to such pressure; they have little alternative. A strategic supplier will seek to reduce their customers' costs by more creative means.

Lowest costs can also come from economies of scale, perhaps driven by low prices, and if this is the customer's route to success then they will need suppliers that can cope with the increasing volumes required. The supplier that can best keep pace will stand the best chance of being considered strategic.

Being a differentiated supplier

There are three very important letters in the words 'lowest-cost supplier' – 'est'. It is not enough to be a low-cost supplier to win with this strategy; you have to be the lowest. There can only be one victor in the battle. The ambition to be a differentiated supplier provides much greater scope and choice, and with it much greater variety of supplier response.

The customer may choose to differentiate itself through the quality of its product, the breadth of its offer, the expertise of its staff, the sophistication of its technology, the strength of its brand, the range of its distribution, the frequency of its new product development, and so the list goes on. The supplier must choose carefully the nature of its value proposition if it is to make the right kind of impact to warrant the status of a strategic supplier.

Consider a company that wishes to develop Key Account Management as a key ingredient in its differentiation strategy, seeking to build diamond relationships that will bring knowledge, security and competitive advantage. The company is seeking help from a training provider. Will it choose a provider that suggests the use of an off-the-shelf and online training package because it will cut the costs of travel associated with sales training, or will it choose a provider that will work closely with it to tailor the training to the specific needs? My own company knows the answer to that one, and in cases where the customer has the wrong answer we can be certain that they will be no key account of ours.

Consider the aspirations of a large printing company. The printers want to offer an exciting, innovative range of unique 'finishes', achieved through the type of paper used. They don't expect huge volumes from this venture, but they do see the benefits of what they call the 'halo' effect, as customers' perceptions of their standard services are enhanced as a result of these 'new technologies'. They have dozens of paper suppliers, but the right one for this job will be hard to find. It must be a supplier with an ability to develop new products. It must be prepared to offer them exclusively. The volumes for these new finishes may be small. But the supplier that will do all this will be held in great esteem and might very well expect to see some rewards through other parts of their business with the printer.

THE CUSTOMER'S MONEY-MAKING LOGIC

It may sound obvious, but knowing how the customer aims to make their money is vital. What may seem less obvious is how often suppliers fail to grasp the essence of the customer's 'money-making logic'. It is almost as Alvin Toffler once said: 'profits, like sausages, are esteemed most by those who know least about what goes into them.'

The reason for this surprising lack of understanding will often lie at the door of the buyer, who may be inclined to suggest various different money-making logics if doing so will gain them some advantage over the seller. That such subterfuge does not ultimately help the customer is something that has frustrated sales professionals for as long as there have been sales professionals, but such is life when the customer is in pursuit of a short-term gain.

Getting under the real skin of such matters will involve, as so often said already, a broad range of contacts, a thorough understanding of the customer's market, their business operations, and their decision-making processes.

There are so many choices (Figure 17.1 suggests just some of them for a business aiming to improve profitability, and those only as they result from two broad options among many) that I will limit my comments to a short cautionary tale, and a lesson from my own sales experience.

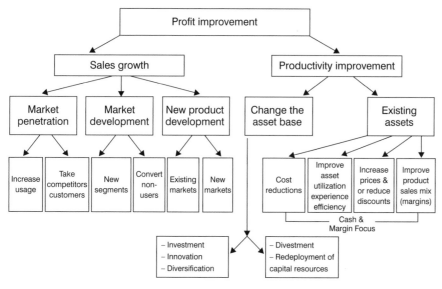

Figure 17.1 *Choices for improving profitability*

The tale of the zero margins

The peril of assumptions

My first sales job was selling decorative paint to retailers in the UK. For the most part identifying their money-making logic was easy; there were those who aimed to pile it high and sell it cheap, and those who aimed for higher margins by offering range and service, with a range of subtle distinctions in between. I had one customer however, a cash-and-carry, that seemed to use neither of these standard approaches.

On inspecting their selling prices I was horrified to find that they were selling at zero margins, which meant that, considering their costs of handling, they were losing money on every sale. I was convinced there must be some mistake, but didn't want to cause a potential crisis by raising the point, so made subtle enquiries. The result: there was no mistake – the prices were as they intended. And so I saw the disaster looming; before long they would discover their losses and drop my products like hot bricks.

I resolved to do something about it by persuading them to alter their range. At the present time they stocked almost exclusively white paint, the highest volume seller but also the part of the range permitting the lowest margins due to fierce competition. If I could get them to take on a range of colours, surely they would start to make real profits?

For six months I persuaded, cajoled, badgered, nagged and bullied, all to no avail. I even suggested a trial of colours on sale-or-return and was astonished by their rejection of my generosity (I had made the offer without asking my boss, who I was sure would have banned my suggestion). Indeed, I sensed more than resistance, there was definite resentment at my suggestions.

Finally they took me aside and gave me a little education. I was reminded that they had negotiated particularly long payment terms – 90 days instead of the normal 30 – and that as a cash-and-carry they offered no form of credit. White paint turned over fast, and faster than the invoice arrived, meaning that my product gave them a very nice cash generator. If I cared to look at their other ranges, they said, continuing my education, I would note that they did much the same on all lines. Their money-making logic was the generation of cash that they put to other, more remunerative uses, in other parts of their business empire.

My efforts to get them to stock slow-moving colours were entirely counter to that logic – so no surprise at their resentment and frustration.

Once I knew the truth of the matter we proceeded from strength to strength. So why had they not told me in the first place? Well, I hadn't asked, happy with my assumptions, and they were happy to see me struggle because who knew what I might have offered in an attempt to improve their position.

Nothing like this would happen in your business of course.

APPLICATION EXERCISE

Using Porter's analysis, consider the nature of the competitive advantage sought by one of your key accounts:

- How do they aim to win:
    - lowest-cost supplier;
    - differentiated supplier?
- How can you best contribute towards their ambitions, and so move towards strategic supplier status?
- Who from your team needs to be involved with whom from their team in order to make this positive impact?
- What reward do you expect for your efforts?

Consider the nature of the profitability of one of your key accounts:

- What is the basis of their money-making logic?
- How can you best contribute towards their ambitions, and so move towards strategic supplier status?
- Who from your team needs to be involved with whom from their team in order to make this positive impact?
- What reward do you expect for your efforts?

18

What drives them?

In the last three chapters we have stressed that the route towards strategic supplier status involves finding a close and burning relevance to the customer's sense of value, to their ambitions for growth, and to their means of competitive advantage. Never was this idea of matching and contributing more important than in the matter of this chapter: what drives them.

VALUE DRIVERS

Here we will get to grips with their essential business values and culture, and it is when walking in this neck of the woods that we must do our utmost to make sure we come down on the right side of relevant or irrelevant, or put another way, partner or alien.

So, what makes their business hum? What values distinguish it and drive it, and how do those values help their staff to decide what to do each day?

Treacy and Weirsema, in their book *The Discipline of Market Leaders*, identify three key business or 'value drivers'. All may be present in any successful business, but in really successful businesses, one or other of these drivers tends to stand out, distinguishing the business for their staff, their investors and their customers:

- operational excellence;
- product leadership;

● customer intimacy.

Operational excellence

Operational excellence is about doing what you do, well. It is about effective processes, smooth mechanics and the efficiency with which products or services are brought to market. Efficiencies of production, economies of scale, uniformity and conformance, accurate forecasting, slick distribution, fast response – these are the sort of things that might be important to a business that is seeking operational excellence. Such 'excellence' can bring significant competitive advantage in a market where reliability is important or price is competitive. In the main, businesses in the mass market – the no-frills, low-hassle, low-price arena – will be driven by this value.

> IKEA achieves huge efficiencies through their logistics chain, from manufacture to store. Adding to this, in store, the self-selection, self-collection formula completes the operational excellence of the supply chain, reflected in excellent value for customers. International uniformity (Swedish product names like Gutvik and Sprallig make it all the way to Australia), modular ranges and a carefully honed (limited, but it doesn't seem so) offer are some of the watchwords.

One size fits all...

Product leadership

Product leadership is about producing the best, leading-edge or market-dominant products. Businesses with high rates of innovation and patent application often have this value at their heart. It is hard to imagine a successful pharmaceuticals company that is not driven by this value. Investment in successful NPD is the key to success; the market for 'nearly there' or 'almost as good as the best one' drugs is rarely good.

One of the biggest threats for a business driven by this value is that of falling behind; it is necessary to continually push the boundaries of performance – and be seen to be doing so.

> 3M have long been famous for their policy of allowing employees significant periods of 'free time', and access to significant resources, in pursuit of new ideas and new products. NPD is their lifeblood, and indeed they claim that the lion's share of their profits in only five years time will come from products only in development (or not even yet imagined) today.

Pushing the boundaries...

Customer intimacy

Customer intimacy is the ability to identify with specific customer needs and match products and services accordingly. What distinguishes the customer-intimate business is their stated determination to develop close customer relationships and to act on the resultant knowledge at all levels of their operation. They will probably have a wide menu of products and services and the ability to mix and match these to suit individual customer requirements – or perhaps they will go further than this and offer a totally bespoke service.

There is a limit to how many customers this can be done for and a customer-intimate business will think carefully about segmentation and key account identification. Something else that often distinguishes a business driven by customer intimacy is their willingness to share risks with their customers and to expect a concomitant share of the rewards.

Truly tailor-made...

A supplier of fragrances to the perfume industry will deal with some very demanding and very particular customers. Each of the customer's products is unique, and the fragrance within is equally unique – there are very few, if any, off-the-shelf solutions. The perfumer's art is as much one of black magic as chemistry and the supplier must be able to identify with this. Customer intimacy is essential for success; absolute identification with the customer's needs and the ability to focus the whole organization on meeting them.

Many of the customers will themselves be driven by product leadership – branding is all – and suppliers have to demonstrate an intimacy with the demands created by that situation. Truly customer-intimate suppliers must be able to identify with value drivers in their customers that may be quite different from their own.

Choosing the leader

The theory goes that any business may be driven by any mix of these drivers, but that in most cases a choice must be made as to which is the 'lead' driver. There is no right answer in the choice, but there is a right way to go about the activities resulting from the choice – consistently across the whole business.

IMPLICATIONS FOR THE WOULD-BE STRATEGIC SUPPLIER

The supplier with an ability to make a positive contribution will be highly valued, provided their contribution is relevant and appropriately targeted.

Businesses driven by operational excellence will be looking for ideas that impact positively on their own supply chain. You might expect an emphasis on systems, logistics, inventory management and e-commerce.

Those driven by product leadership will be focused more on ideas that make a positive impact on their own products. Look for their interest in joint NPD through supplier partnerships, and a focus on lead times. Expect them to ask about your innovation capability, and to want to spend time with your own R&D people.

Finally, you might expect a business driven by customer intimacy to be interested in ideas that have an impact on their customers, or improve their own ability to have a positive impact on their customers. They may be looking for responsive and flexible suppliers that can demonstrate their expertise in particular markets, through to the end users.

These are of course generalizations, but here is an unfailing rule: 'good ideas' from suppliers that ignore the customer's drivers are in fact 'bad ideas'.

A friend of mine once worked behind the counter at McDonald's, perhaps the supreme example of a company driven by operational excellence. Their ability to replicate the product unfailingly, on every continent of the world, is a remarkable achievement. My friend was young and keen to make a good impression so, one morning, as a sign of his initiative, he took a bottle of his mother's best home-made pickle in and placed it on the counter. Customers were offered a free scoop from the jar to add to their burgers.

The tale of the burger...

My friend did not last long with McDonald's. This was the wrong kind of initiative. Now, if he had found a way to improve the uniformity of the buns, or reduce the cooking time of the fries by 5 per cent, and followed that up with such genius once a week, then perhaps he would now be on their board.

Selling to McDonald's, driven by operational excellence, is a different experience from selling to Subway or to Pret a Manger, who are both driven by customer intimacy. The 'good ideas' will be different, the value hotspots will be different, and the resultant value propositions should be different.

IDENTIFYING THE DRIVERS

It's easy to be relevant, once you know what to match up to, but sometimes the clues are not all that clear. You want to know what drives them, so you ask the buyers. Do they know? Do they tell you the whole truth and nothing but the truth? So you ask the production people, and they tell you it's operational excellence. You ask the R&D people, and they tell you it's product leadership. You ask the salespeople, and they tell you it's customer intimacy (and it's not so different in your own company I'm guessing!).

The point is that each function has its own mix of drivers, and if we deal with only one function we might rest easy with that thought, but if our proposition has impacts across a number of functions (and for true strategic suppliers this is very likely to be the case), then the task of identification gets harder.

In the end, it's a jigsaw puzzle, and the more points of contact you have, the more senior contacts you get in their management hierarchy, and the more you discuss these issues within your own KA team, the more chance you have of completing the puzzle.

Handling the clashes

As a supplier gets closer to the heart of their customer so they find themselves drawn into internal debates, arguments and cross-functional clashes. We discussed the problem when speaking of penetrating the customer's decision-making process (Chapter 6), and talked of the need for a 'political' sensitivity in the KA team. The same applies here.

Working with a customer that has a clear business strategy, and one that is translated into these drivers, is always so much easier. Those businesses that are less able to define where they are headed, and how they will get there, will probably also exhibit a vague mixture of these values, often to their own cost. Suppliers are often able to see the resultant clashes more readily than the customer. They can see that the customer-intimate sales force is promising product and service variations that are in open conflict with the folk in production and distribution, driven by operational excellence.

An understanding of these drivers may enable you, as the supplier, to help. You know that the fault does not lie in the people concerned, but in the different values, and how those translate into performance targets. If the business truly wishes to be customer intimate, then the measures used to assess the contribution of the production folk will have to change, perhaps focusing on their flexibility rather than their occupacity (the measure of how near the plant is to full capacity). Equally, if they wish to be operational excellent, then perhaps it is the sales team chasing the wrong orders, which is probably down to how they are targeted and rewarded.

Making the choice does not mean that you throw the other values out of the window, but rather that you aim to make them more appropriate to the main driver. Basketball teams talk of measuring 'the assists', meaning taking account of who contributed to getting the ball through the hoop, not just the scorer. The same approach might work well in handling the clashes between drivers within a business team.

The toughest task is dealing with the internal compromises; compromises that you know will lead to a suboptimal outcome. Patience will be a virtue, and help in finding the opportunity to discuss these compromises at a senior level, with ideas as to how they could be averted, perhaps through changes to performance measures as discussed.

This is not to say that it is impossible to achieve top performance against more than one driver. The theory of 'mass customization' would be argued in defence of this aim.

A manufacturer of bathroom sealants knows that the customer wants a broad range of colours, but many of those colours will only ever be sold in small quantities, and each additional colour required has a significant negative impact on the plant's operational excellence. A combination of the purchasing, marketing and production teams comes up with a solution whereby almost the whole manufacturing process focuses on the production of just one colour, with the addition of the different pigments actioned right at the end of the process to achieve the required colour range. And what did this have to do with the purchasing team? The solution came from a supplier of pigments that was aware of the issue, understood the drivers, and developed an appropriate technology: achieving a strategic supplier status.

Mass customization

Does it matter what *you* are?

Might your own driver clash with the customer's? Only if you are unaware of the possibility. Successful supplier–customer relationships can be formed by any mixture of drivers, provided the focus in the relationship remains on the customers. The danger is for those suppliers who become too obsessed with their own drivers.

GE has for some time now been positioning itself as a corporate leader in addressing climate change. Their chairman, Jeffrey Immelt, has had cause of late to reflect on their ambitions with regard to how they have positioned themselves with customers. Some of those customers have been making it plain that they are growing tired of GE's 'lectures'. 'Can't you just shut up and sell us stuff?' they have said to Mr Immelt, and he goes on: 'That would be a paraphrase, maybe with a few blanks in between.'

Getting carried away...

Or how about your own performance of KAM; might your choice of driver impact on that? It might seem that the principles and disciplines of KAM tend towards a customer-intimate driver, and while that would certainly add force to the KAM ambitions, it is entirely possible for KAM to exist and thrive in a business driven by operational excellence or product leadership.

A supplier driven by operational excellence will seek activities that both meet customer needs and suit their own strengths and abilities – matching market opportunity with business resources. The same can be said of the business driven by product leadership. Nobody would argue that a business with a brilliant list of product innovations could survive without nurturing their customer relationships (at least not for long – see Chapter 10, 'The bad story').

THE CULTURAL MATCH

To be regarded as strategic supplier, must the supplier be in the same 'mould' as the customer; must they be alike on a cultural level? To quote the song, 'It ain't necessarily so', and plenty of successful relationships exist between absolute opposites; and yet it is fair to say that such relationships can sometimes have their moments of doubt, when both sides might wish for something more than that tangible demonstration of business value; when the customer wants to feel they are working with 'like souls'. A preference to work with suppliers from the customer's home country rather than from abroad is in this sense often more than a simple matter of the efficiencies of geographic proximity.

To be viewed as a truly strategic supplier it may be necessary to practise some level of 'cultural mirroring'. If this is not possible or desirable on the supplier's part then it may be necessary to review how far this particular relationship can develop.

By understanding the customer's business strategy and acting to make a positive impact on it, the supplier will in some way already have developed a closer 'cultural match'. But culture goes beyond business strategy, being sometimes substantial and deep-seated as in the case of organizational or national culture, sometimes a matter of surface details such as dress codes.

Some factors are clearly going to be easier to match than others, and some are more deserving of the attempt than others. Remembering to dress up or down when visiting the customer is simple enough (and the way to avoid much discomfort), while changing your organization's structure to mirror the customer's is a much bigger throw (and may not even be necessary).

The following list suggests the kind of areas that you might need to examine (with some inevitably vague definitions against a notional spectrum in each case), first to understand the customer's culture, and then to assess the likelihood or desirability of a match. How far you go will be entirely down to your own circumstances, capabilities and ambitions. There is no golden rule, other than to observe and understand – once that is done, the necessary actions become much clearer:

- Dress code: informal – formal – uniform.
- Entertainment: none – internal only – supplier provided.
- Meeting venues: the customer's – neutral – the supplier's.
- Meeting style: 1:1 – ad hoc – teams.
- Organizational structure: Hierarchies – teams – flat.
- Management control: open – federal – centralized.
- Management style: empowered – process led – individualistic.
- Internal communications: informal – ad hoc – formal.
- Career development: ad hoc – fluid – structured.
- Time horizons: short – medium – long.
- Attitude to risk: averse – shared with suppliers – entrepreneurial.
- Growth aspirations: low – medium – high.
- Growth methodology: organic – mixed – acquisition.
- Ethics: weak – pragmatic – strong.

APPLICATION EXERCISE

Using Wiersema's model, consider the nature of the value drivers of one of your key accounts:

- What is their lead value driver?
- How can you ensure that your own value proposition enhances that driver, and so move towards strategic supplier status?
- Who from your team needs to be involved with whom from their team in order to make this positive impact?
- What reward do you expect for your efforts?

Consider the nature of your customer's business culture, and how it compares to your own:

- What (if any) are the mismatches between their's and yours?
  - Does this matter?
  - If so, what actions must you take to build a closer match?

19

A shared future?

Customers have plenty of suppliers to choose from; only the best will be recognized as strategic suppliers, and only the very best will be regarded that way over a long period of time. Such a position may sound great, but don't imagine it doesn't come at a cost. The cost can be in time, energy, investment in continual improvement and renewal, and of course, just plain money. It will be for you to decide whether the rewards are justification enough. I did hear one KA manager say to their customer, on being appointed as the customer's number one supplier: 'Well, that's very good to hear, but I guess that this is where it starts to get expensive...'

If you feel that you will be unable to make the kind of impact we have been discussing, or that the cost of doing so will be too high, then you might just decide to stay as an ordinary supplier; there's no sin in that, and a good living can be made. The only sin is in failing to achieve what you are able to achieve.

The purpose of this chapter is help you in your assessment of what is possible, and how much you may need to change to achieve what we will call a 'shared future' with the customer.

THE SHARED-FUTURE ANALYSIS

The analysis is completed using the form shown in Figure 19.1. This is a kind of a SWOT analysis, but one demanding a good deal more analytical rigour than the usual SWOT (which too often tends towards wishful thinking and an internal focus), forcing us to make the link between the customer's oppor-tunities and threats (the external focus) and our own strengths and weak-nesses as they are perceived by the customer (the true reality).

		The customer's opportunities and ambitions				The customer's threats and concerns			
+ sign(s) *We make a positive impact on their ambitions or reduce their concerns*	**– sign(s)** *We detract from their ambitions, or compound their concerns*	1.	2.	3.	4.	1.	2.	3.	4.
Our strengths, as perceived by the customer	1.		+++		+			+++	
	2.								
	3.	+++			++				
	4.						++		+
Our weaknesses, as perceived by the customer	1.					– – –		– –	
	2.								
	3.	– – –			– – –				
	4.						–		

Figure 19.1 *The shared-future analysis*

Their opportunities and threats

Start by putting your own business out of your mind and putting yourself entirely in the customer's shoes. This is vital. Now try to identify the things that excite the customer about their future, their opportunities, their ambi-tions, their hopes. Remember, keep your own business out of your thoughts; these are the customer's own ambitions, not yours, and nor are they the ambitions you would like them to have because they suit your own!

Next step; what are the things that concern them about their future, the threats to their business, the things that they worry about, that they might be losing sleep over?

It is quite possible that you will not know the answers to these questions, and if that is so your next course of action is very clear: find out. Ask the customer, and have all the members of the KA team do the same. Read the customer's annual report and their in-house newspapers; these can be gold mines for learning about their current ambitions and fixations.

To some degree this analysis summarizes many of the questions we have been asking throughout the last few chapters; what forces are impacting on their competitive position, how do they aim to respond, how do they aim to grow, how mature is their product offer, how do they wish to drive their business? As such, the tool is an excellent one to consolidate a good deal of complex analysis already undertaken.

Your strengths and weaknesses – in their eyes

Now turn to your own company, but keep yourself in the customer's shoes. What do they like about you? What are your strengths? Equally, what do they not like about you? What are your weaknesses?

Again, there is no substitute for talking with the customer, but this takes some subtlety. The aim is not to get them focused on a long list of complaints and insecurities!

Before moving to the next step, stop for a bout of honest reflection. Are these really their perceptions of you? What would they say when you were out of the room? We are about to use this analysis to determine our direction for the foreseeable future – it will be as well to have it right.

A shared future?

Now consider each vertical column (their opportunities, their threats) in turn, working down through your own capabilities (strengths and weaknesses). At each junction indicate with a plus sign where your strength makes a positive contribution to their opportunity or ambition, or where your strength helps to reduce a threat or relieve them of a worry (use a scale of one to three plus signs to represent the size of the contribution). Do the same with minus signs where your weakness either detracts from an ambition or makes worse something that worries the customer already.

So, to the all-important question: do you help or hinder their progress? Do you reduce or exacerbate their concerns?

Where you show minuses, you must ask whether these can be resolved, and at what cost. It is one of the facts of life in business that no amount of plusses will work in your favour so long as there is one significant minus blotting your copybook. The actions required will involve correcting the weakness, but just as importantly you must give time to letting the customer know the weakness has been corrected. This is an area where perceptions can be more important than fact, and memories of bad performance are long.

Where you show plusses, aim to talk these up. Plusses where you help them with their ambitions are obviously good news, plusses where you relieve them of worries can be even better news; it is much the same principle as regards blots on copybooks.

In the final analysis, does the balance of plusses and minuses argue for a shared future based on mutual respect and partnership, or does it suggest a long battle over shortcomings? We have been thinking of KAM as an investment, and this analysis will help make plain the size and nature of the investment required. You will wish to invest in customers where there is a good potential future, but you may also need to invest in the rectification of weaknesses. There are no easy choices here, but the analysis will help you to identify them, and to establish some priorities for action.

Finding the right proposition

A French-based food manufacturer was looking to expand their operation into the UK. This was a very clear and publicly stated ambition, but they also had a major concern, and one that they didn't shout from the rooftops. They were worried by what they saw as a continual series of food scares in the UK market, and worried that becoming involved in any such scares might have a negative impact on their reputation at home.

They were looking for a UK supplier of some vital materials and services, and arranged a number of supplier presentations. One of these potential suppliers also had some business with the customer in France, and so was able to learn something of the customer's concerns from their French colleagues.

The UK supplier assessed their strengths and weaknesses, as they would be seen through the customer's eyes. High on the debit side was their price; they had a reputation for being most expensive in the market. High on the credit side was their own track record on health and safety; they were spotless. Their analysis of the correlations between their own various strengths and weaknesses and the customer's ambitions and worries encouraged them to major in their presentation on their health and safety record as being the most relevant to the customer's biggest concern. Needless to say, they won the contract.

Do we enhance the customer's competitive position, and should we?

In assessing our contribution to their ambitions, a common question arises: is it the purpose of KAM to help certain customers to prevail over others? Consider the implications of saying yes – you actively intend to make some of your other customers (actual or potential) less competitive. If you are very confident in the identification of your key accounts, perhaps based on the criterion 'who will be the winners in this market?' then maybe the answer is yes. But take care: how many 'winners' can there be? Must we be fair to all, or are some customers more equal than others?

In some industries this is an area where large customers, those with dominant market positions, will try to influence their suppliers to help them, to their competitors' loss, through persuasion and pressure. Suppliers to the likes of Coca-Cola, Procter and Gamble, Kellogg's or Hewlett Packard will know how difficult it is to be a strategic supplier while also actively chasing the customers' competitors.

Managing business review sessions

The shared-future analysis presents an excellent summary of the relative positions between supplier and customer, and as such can be used very effectively to prepare for those difficult customer sessions – the business reviews. Indeed, if you were a true strategic supplier, then such an analysis would be an open discussion between both parties. To go further, any supplier that feels the need to hide such analysis from the customer's eyes is probably heading for a fall.

Don't keep it to yourself

THE COMPETITION

One of my all time favourite comedy shows is that eternal classic, *Dad's Army*. I am reminded of a scene from one of the earliest episodes where Captain Mainwaring is lecturing his platoon on how to deal with an enemy tank, using the slim resources they have to hand. He briefs them on how they can decoy the tank, how they can obscure its view with a burning blanket, how they can use a crowbar to prise off the turret, and how they can deliver a deadly Molotov cocktail through the opening. It is the reaction of Private Walker that brings it to mind: 'While we're doing all that, what will the tank be doing?'

While you are doing all your analysis, and making all those positive impacts, what will the competition be doing? Probably much the same, and perhaps better, which can of course negate all of your good (and expensive) efforts at a stroke.

As well as completing the shared-future analysis for your own position you should aim to complete it for the competition, using the same customer opportunities and threats of course, but now assessing the competition's strengths and weaknesses.

Figure 19.2 shows an expanded version of the shared-future analysis, incorporating the competitor's position.

Now answer three key questions:

- How do you compare?
- What can you do about it?
- Will it be worth the effort?

+ **sign(s)** *We/they make a positive impact on their ambitions or reduce their concerns*	– **sign(s)** *We/they detract from their ambitions, or compound their concerns*	The customer's opportunities and ambitions				The customer's threats and concerns			
		1.	2.	3.	4.	1.	2.	3.	4.
Our strengths, as perceived by the customer	1.								
	2.								
	3.								
	4.								
Our weaknesses, as perceived by the customer	1.								
	2.								
	3.								
	4.								
The competitor's strengths, as perceived by the customer	1.								
	2.								
	3.								
	4.								
The competitor's weaknesses, as perceived by the customer	1.								
	2.								
	3.								
	4.								

Figure 19.2 *The competitive view*

APPLICATION EXERCISE

Consider the overall business strategy of one of your key accounts:

- Do we know what excites them about their future – their ambitions?
- Do we know what worries them about their future – their fears?
- Do we know how they regard us – good and poor?
- Do we understand how we contribute (or not) to their ambitions?
- Do we understand how we help to mitigate (or not) their fears?
- Complete the shared-future matrix:
  - What does it indicate should be your priority activities?
  - How can you use this analysis to develop your value proposition?

Part VI

The value proposition

20

The customer's total business experience

The chapters in Part VI of this book deal with what is, or should be, the culmination of all the efforts of KAM described so far: the value proposition. All the efforts taken to build a deep and broad relationship, to understand the customer's market and business, to identify and match their values and their drivers, all of this is to help us develop a better, a more appropriate, and a more rewarding value proposition.

Figure 20.1 recalls the KAM model introduced at the close of Chapter 4, reminding us that the task of developing the value proposition is to do with the return on our KAM investment.

Being in front of the right people will avail us little if we are not saying the right things. Having made the investment in time and effort to make contact with those that we believe will be most important to our future, wouldn't it be tragic if we were just to trot out the same proposition that we had rehearsed back in the days of a bow-tie relationship and the limited knowledge and understanding that went with it?

Value propositions will be seen to improve over time, provided they are permitted the vital ingredient – customer involvement. At their outset, perhaps as they leave the offices of our own R&D department, they tend to be heavy with 'features', those 'facts' about the product beloved of the technical folk and the specification sheet (I realize that I am once more in the world of the stereotype, so feel free to soften the edges of my description if

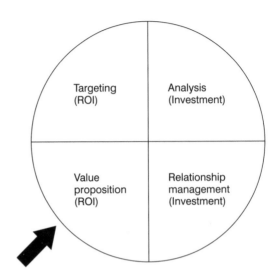

Figure 20.1 *The KAM model: the value proposition*

your own circumstances are better than this). Features are unbending, but perhaps this was of no concern to the technical people as they make up a proposition intended to meet the needs of all customers. We might call this the 'take it or leave it' proposition.

One of the key purposes of the KAM journey is to help us refine that proposition. Let's consider an example. The 'take it or leave it' proposition is for a bag of fertilizer sold to commercial farmers, the leading 'feature' of this product being the magic ingredient 'Oomph'.

The product is handed to the marketing team, and they start to do what they have to do if this product is ever going to be a success, determine what it actually does for the customer – the product's 'benefits'. The benefits might of course differ dependent on the farmer in mind, and so we have the basis (albeit the very early stages) of a market segmentation strategy. Perhaps after a little more work courtesy of the technical team we find that 'Oomph' has moved on a stage, reformulated to be of particular benefit to wheat farmers. Perhaps it is now called 'Oomph plus'.

As the sales team becomes more involved, knowledge of the customer's circumstances develops further. The more enquiring of the sales professionals might uncover deeper and more specific needs among the variety of wheat farmers. Some farmers wish to reduce their use of fertilizers and would smile on a low-application formulation of 'Oomph plus'. The sales team talks to their marketing technical colleagues, urging the development of a 'tailored solution' for this particular group of customers.

Throughout this process the value proposition is developing, from a simple 'feature' through to a specific 'benefit', and on to a 'tailored solution', but what is not clear is whether the subsequent rewards are worth the extra effort. Such developments are not uncommon, with increasing complexity and costs, and a fairly haphazard approach to the opportunities. It might work, or it might just cost you time and money.

IDENTIFYING THE CUSTOMER'S TBE (TOTAL BUSINESS EXPERIENCE)

There is a stage to which we might take the value proposition that is beyond any of these, a stage more impactful and rewarding than features, benefits or tailored solutions. We will call this the stage the customer's 'total business experience' (TBE).

To get here will almost certainly require the kind of KAM processes described so far. We must start with an understanding of the customer's problems that goes beyond the customer's own understanding. Next, the development of the solutions to those problems will almost certainly require a team effort well beyond the realm of the sales force. And beyond that comes the implementation and the reward for our investment.

Returning to our fertilizer example; your work with a small number of key accounts helps you to understand their true attitudes, and needs. Fertilizer, it seems, is boring, and no amount of 'Oomph' will ever make it anything else. Furthermore, the task of applying the fertilizer is even duller, hugely time consuming, and a very low-grade task in the great scheme of things. Little wonder that fertilizer suppliers have never been regarded as people of any great significance. In fact, your efforts with 'Oomph plus' have made things worse as these more 'sophisticated' products can make it harder for the farmer to pass the application task on to a jobbing contractor.

In short, the customer's 'total business experience' is not a good one, but it is about to be made a good deal better now that the supplier understands the full picture. There is no more talk about 'Oomph' or 'Oomph Plus'; indeed, you rarely mention the product at all, for now your business is in providing an outsourced fertilizer application service for your key accounts. You charge by measured results and not by the volume of material. Indeed, your joint aspiration to use less fertilizer and improve performance leads to the continual development of better formulations, and formulations that can be of benefit to all customers. Not only do we see that less truly is more, but we see the practice of KAM reach its ultimate goal.

Building your significance

So, how does this TBE approach differ from a plain 'solution'? The divide between a feature and a benefit is bridged once the customer's interests come into the picture; we talk less about products and more about positive effects. Similarly, the divide between a benefit and a solution is bridged when we start to consider the customer's problems; we talk less about general effects (however positive they might be) and focus on a specific requirement.

So far the conversations will have been about known issues and known needs. By looking into the customer's TBE we can take the conversation to a new level, discussing needs that may not yet have been identified or antici-pated, and onto issues that might remain unarticulated but are nonetheless of greater significance than the kind of problems flushed out by a bow-tie seller/buyer conversation. We talk less about solving problems and more about improving the business.

The offers are still solutions, but of a kind that will have the customer looking at their provider in a new light. The supplier will have enhanced their significance, which takes us back to an ambition noted in Chapter 14 where we considered the way in which the professional purchaser positions their suppliers. It will be worth a quick recap.

Figure 20.2 shows the purchaser's 'positioning matrix', and we are reminded of the supplier's ambition to raise their significance (to move north) in order to attain a more strategic position.

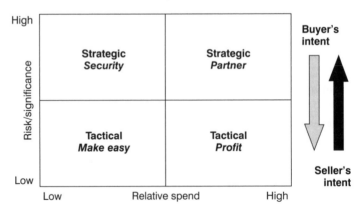

Figure 20.2 *Supplier positioning: the differing intentions of sellers and buyers*

Let us suppose that you are positioned in the bottom-right but aspire to be in the top-right. I am your customer and you are selling me petrol for my car. I spend a lot on petrol (hence placing it to the right) but have no belief that any one brand of petrol is better than any other – they are all of equal insignifi-cance as far as I can judge (hence placing it to the bottom).

You try to increase your significance to me by several means, and histori-
cally we can see what these have been – a man in white overalls on the pump
and Green Shield stamps (for those who go back that far), free glasses (an
icon of the 1970s), additives and product performance claims (mostly
ignored, except by a very few 'techno-cognoscenti'), an on-site shop (newspapers and cigarettes), loyalty cards, an on-site convenience store, a coffee
shop, an on-site Tesco or Marks & Spencer, a cash dispensing machine, clean
toilets, and so it goes on.

Beyond petrol...

Some of those grab me, some of them don't. I never have gone for loyalty
cards but the cash machine works for me, as does the Marks & Spencer – I
buy my petrol where I can get my money more conveniently, and where I
can spend it as quickly!

The ones that work (for me) are the ones that have a positive impact on
my total business experience of the petrol station – influencing the reason I
stopped there in the first place, and offering me a reason for lingering there.
The supplier with the right package (and solutions of this nature tend to be
packages rather than individual benefit/solutions) now find themselves
placed top-right in my supplier positioning matrix.

Figure 20.3 expresses this developing value proposition as a series of
concentric rings.

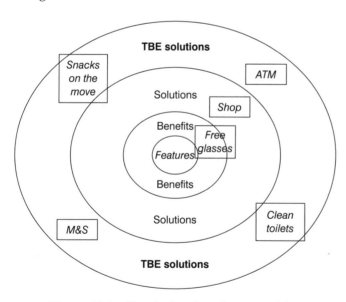

Figure 20.3 _Developing the value proposition_

Of course, market circumstances and events can influence my view. When
a recent scare over contaminants in petrol hit the petrol stations attached
to a particular supermarket chain, I, like many others, suddenly raised the

significance of those suppliers offering premium brands distinguished by their product formulations – though the shift was relatively short lived for most.

The key question is: what do those things on the outer edge of Figure 20.3 have to do with petrol? The answer is: nothing. What they have everything to do with is the nature of the customer's experience while selecting, purchasing and using that petrol – the TBE.

The idea that a supplier can identify the right package for the customer without some form of KAM is a difficult one; it is the intimate knowledge of the customer's market and business developed through a KA diamond team approach that provides the basis for a TBE solution, and it is the intimate knowledge of their values and drivers that ensures the appropriateness of that solution. One of my customers talks of their ambition to 'resonate' with the customer, and I cannot think of a better way to achieve such harmony.

Developing a broader capability

The pursuit of a positive impact on the customer's TBE often tends towards the development of packages and skills that enhance the supplier's overall capability. There are two very obvious benefits of this:

- the option to offer this enhanced capability to others;
- the creation of a competitive advantage based on the team, not the product.

Beyond oil...

Once upon a time oil companies just supplied oil, but as their processes became more sophisticated, and as their involvement on the customer's site deepened, so some of them found that they had developed a new and broader expertise: managing fluid supplies on a customer's site. For their key accounts, BP will offer to manage the customer's total 'fluid requirements'. This will almost certainly involve taking responsibility for the supply of products outside their own portfolio, perhaps in some cases even working with a competitor's products. The focus moves to reducing the volumes of product required and improving efficiencies of use; to providing value rather than lowest prices. Indeed, the price of the product itself becomes of less and less relevance as the broader services are charged for in more creative, more holistic ways.

Failing to see the wood for the trees

Suppliers that focus on their own products and benefits can find themselves staring at lots of trees while failing to see the 'wood' of the customer's broader needs. Market research is meant to bring a clarity of view, but so often it can be guilty of just staring at trees.

Suppose you were in the car business and were thinking of launching an 'off-road' vehicle. You commission an agency to find out how many people need to drive 'off road' and how often. The answers come back – almost none, and hardly at all (which happens to be the truth of the matter). So you abandon your idea and miss one of the biggest growth sectors of the car market in recent years.

In the early years of the 20th century, Benz conducted one of the first market research studies into the potential car market in the UK. They concluded that total sales of all cars would never exceed 1,000. The reason? A shortage of chauffeurs.

The questions are too precise, the scope too limited, and all because of the wrong focus. A few years back many suppliers of fresh produce to multiple supermarkets were guilty of such lack of scope, as the case study below indicates.

Retailers would often complain about the receipt of damaged goods, a particular problem with soft fruit, while the suppliers would argue that the customers' demands for ready-to-eat freshness almost mandated a certain amount of damage. The suppliers concentrated on the freshness issue, and the complaints went on.

Beyond the supplier...

No surprise that the retailers took the problem into their own hands, going above the heads of their suppliers, and approaching a supplier of plastic crates. They insisted that their fresh produce suppliers should purchase and use these crates in the delivery of their products, reducing damage dramatically, and also ensuring a uniform method of supply at their backdoors. The solution was imposed by a customer frustrated by their suppliers' inability to understand their TBE. No surprise either that the solution was entirely a cost to the suppliers with no prospect of being rewarded for their newly enhanced performance.

Knowing the customer's problem better than they know it themselves

This is something of a Holy Grail of KAM, and cannot be achieved simply by asking the customer what they want. Customers don't always know what they want, or what might be possible, and even if they do they might not articulate their real problems – it might make them look awkward, or shallow. Knowing the customer's problem better than they know it themselves comes from a proper investigation of the customer's total business experience.

My own company once commissioned a piece of research to see why training managers chose particular training suppliers. The answers seemed very worthy – value for money, value for time, leading edge and all the rest, only we knew that wasn't the truth, at least not the truth that went to the root of their desired experience. The truth of the matter was that many training managers chose the supplier least likely to make them look foolish. See it from their standpoint: they arrange an event, they commit people's time – it is their reputation that is on the line if the trainer turns out to be an embarrassment.

How did we know that? Because we focused on what the training manager wanted from the total experience of doing business with us – their TBE.

APPLICATION EXERCISE

- Identify the *total business experience* desired by one of your key accounts
- How close is your current value proposition to matching their requirement?
  - What problems do you resolve for them?
  - What value does that deliver?
  - What reward do you receive?
  - Is that reward equitable?
- What capabilities might you need to develop in order to ensure a closer match?
  - How can you build your positive significance to the customer?

21

The customer's activity cycle

There are some important questions to ask if we want to properly understand the customer's TBE (as introduced in Chapter 20):

- Do they have problems with the way they buy from us?
- Do they have problems with the way they receive and use our products?
- Do they have problems when selling their own products in their own markets?

The emphasis here is clearly on identifying their problems. There is no solution without a problem – something known by every sales professional who has ever had to sell their company's latest 'cure for a disease the customer doesn't even know they have'.

Figure 21.1 illustrates the tool that we will use to answer these three questions, identify the problems, and so focus our minds on solutions that are wholly relevant – the 'customer's activity cycle'.

The small crosses around the circle (or repeating cycle) represent the activities of the customer in doing business with their supplier. Every step must be noted, in as much detail as possible, as it is often among the minutia of business transactions that the gold dust of added-value solutions is to be found.

The cycle is divided into three sections: 'before', 'during' and 'after'. The precise dividing points are fluid, and for you to decide with your own customer in mind, but in general they might represent:

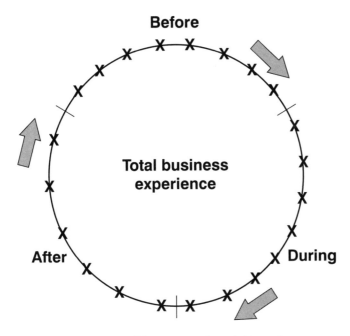

Figure 21.1   *The customer's activity cycle*

- *Before*: all the steps and activities taken by the customer with regard to their supplier's products and services, up to the placing of an order on the supplier. These include, for example, their generation of ideas, identification of needs, supplier selection process, setting of vendor ratings, trials and supplier negotiations.
- *During*: all the subsequent steps and activities taken by the customer with regard to their supplier's products and services, up to the completion of their own product. These include, for example, the receipt of goods, quality control checks, storage and manufacturing.
- *After*: all the steps and activities taken by the customer with regard to their supplier's products and services, in selling their own product in their own market.

Note, these are the customer's activities, not your own. This is a tool for helping us to understand the customer's TBE *first*, and then our potential for making a positive impact, not the other way around.

Many people will say that they have no interaction with the customer in the 'after' portion of this cycle. Think more broadly: if you have supplied a raw material, then you are intimately involved in the customer's 'after' – your product is inside their product, and is either contributing to that product's success, or is instrumental in its failure.

When sitting down to complete this exercise, as you must, it soon becomes clear how well you understand the customer's TBE, or how poorly. It is quite common for the steps at the 'late before' and 'early during' to be very apparent – this is the stuff of your daily transactions – but for the picture to become less clear as we move either backwards or forwards around the activity cycle. This limited knowledge is illustrated in Figure 21.2.

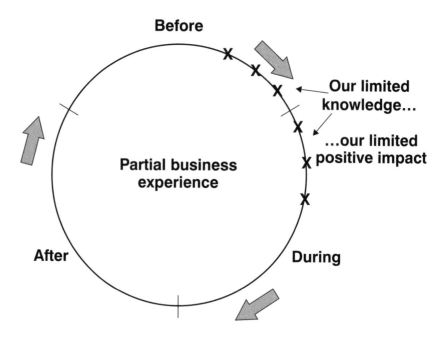

Figure 21.2 *Limited knowledge: limited positive impact*

This is a problem, and for several reasons. This is the part of the customer's activity cycle where everybody tends to focus, you and your competitors, so finding competitive advantage is increasingly difficult. It is where you very likely have already done what there is to do to solve problems and smooth the path between supplier and customer; not too many more bright ideas remain to be found. It is also where the 'familiarity' of these activities can lead the customer to reduce your existing added-value contributions to a list of 'givens'; familiarity in this regard breeds, not so much contempt as commoditization.

The opportunity (doesn't every problem suggest one?) is for you to broaden your understanding, and potentially to find points of interaction where substantial new value can be delivered, and uniquely. Figure 21.3 illustrates the kind of 'cradle to grave' impact that might be an ideal outcome in some cases, but we should never confuse the number of interactions with their quality, and quality is judged in this respect by their appropriateness: do they resonate with the customer?

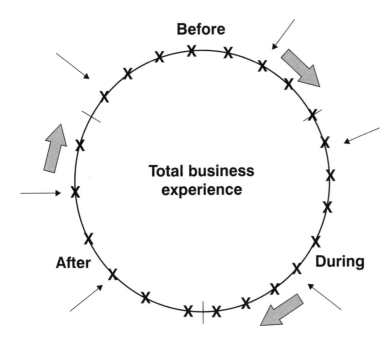

Figure 21.3 *'Cradle to grave' positive impact?*

COMPLETING THE EXERCISE

We are however getting a little ahead of ourselves. The key to making this tool work for you is to take it in stages. Resist the temptation to leap at 'bright ideas' before you have properly mapped out the full cycle, step by step, detail by detail, ploddingly and meticulously. There are in fact 10 distinct stages to this exercise:

1. Select a customer, a product and a circumstance, and then map out the customer's activities, in as much detail as possible (the focus on a specific product is important – mapping your whole relationship across a range of products could get too complicated for any meaningful results).
2. Identify the gaps in your knowledge and takes steps to fill them.
3. Identify the points in the cycle where the customer experiences problems (this is vital, see below).
4. Consider what things you already do to address these problems:
    - How successful are they?
    - What value do you add?
    - Do you get an appropriate reward?
      (Also consider your competitor's position against these problems: do they do a better or worse job than you?)

5.   Then, and only then, move on to consider the range of new actions that could be taken, to make new positive impacts on the customer's problems.

6.   Assessing and screening the ideas:
   –   The costs to you:
   –   Your capabilities and the investment required:
      –   Do you have the capability?
      –   Can it be developed?
      –   Is there a partner to work with?
      –   Might that in fact be the customer?
   –   The value given to the customer:
      –   Does it remove a problem?
      –   Does it reduce their risk?
      –   Does it extend their life cycle?
      –   Does it impact on their value drivers?
      –   Does it make a positive impact on their business strategy?
      –   Does it 'resonate' with the customer?
   –   The likely reward.
   –   The sustainability of these ideas against competitor response.
   –   The extent to which they achieve 'lock-in' (see below).
   –   Will the ideas be usable with other customers, so expanding your wider capability?

7.   Identify the actions (the package) that will represent your value proposition.

8.   Assess the nature of the impact that you will make on the customer's total business experience.

9.   Determine the reward due for all your hard work.

10   Implementation.

Problems, problems, problems...

**No problem?
No solution!**

Step three is without doubt the most critical: the identification of problems. We have spoken before about the sin of curing diseases the customer doesn't know they have, and might never have – observing the discipline of step three will help you to avoid this sin.

It is a sin particularly apparent in 'clever' companies, those with plenty of 'bright ideas'. I was on a long-haul flight recently, and was amazed by the technology of a passenger entertainment system that allowed me to watch, simultaneously, up to 20 (I think it was) movies. By simultaneously I mean, five minutes of one, freeze it, 10 minutes of another, freeze it, back to the first for another burst, open up a third, and so on. Brilliant technology, but what problem was it aiming to solve? Rather than enhancing my flight its complexity bamboozled me and simply made me feel inadequate. Perhaps it was aimed at teenagers, and if so it was no better an idea – there are not many teenagers travelling business class on long-haul flights.

Figure 21.4 illustrates an activity cycle with the problems highlighted. This is where to put your effort, curing diseases that most certainly afflict the customer.

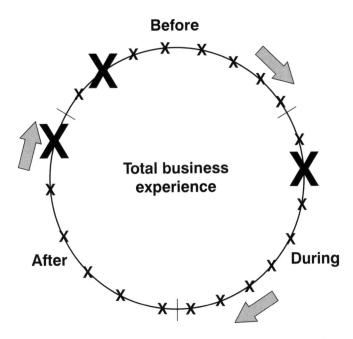

Figure 21.4 *The problems in the customer's activity circle*

Lock-in

This is a matter of huge importance. Any supplier can do things that are of value to the customer, but whether they bring sustainable competitive advantage is another matter. Extended credit is certainly of value to a customer, but it is very easy for a competitor to match or even offer more. Such added value is short-lived, the competitive advantage is not sustainable, and worst of all, it can start a process that will spiral out of control as competing suppliers vie to improve on the last offer.

Sustainable competitive advantage comes from activities that encourage loyalty and that competitors are not able to match without costly effort. *Buying* loyalty rarely works. Frequent-flyer miles are said to be about loyalty, but they are very often false loyalty; the customer goes elsewhere as soon as the scheme is stopped. Worse, everyone can do them.

The secret of 'lock-in' is to find an activity or service that customers value and would rather not perform themselves, that no competitor offers, and that doesn't involve handing the supplier too much power. It is a delicate balance; 'lock-in' implies supplier power, and suppliers should tread carefully.

One of the most famous examples of a misplaced attempt at lock-in was that of Apple. Apple had a truly splendid operating system but they wanted to hang on to it and use its strength to sell their own machines; in other words, you could only have it if you bought an Apple computer. This effectively restricted the value that consumers could receive and when Microsoft allowed MS DOS to be put on any machine you liked, they won the day.

Lock-in can be unpopular if it is used for obviously selfish ends. Much of the complaint against the development of genetically modified seeds in the early days was that they were designed to force a link to the use of the seed supplier's own pesticides and herbicides. The infamous 'terminator gene' was an extreme example, being a genetically modified seed that would prevent the crop from producing new seeds. Consider the sale of this product in the Third World and it is easy to see why that particular attempt at lock-in was withdrawn.

INVOLVING THE TEAM

The best way to approach the exercise is with a team, and of course the KA team is the ideal. Each member will have a different angle and view. You may be pleasantly surprised by the 'corporate knowledge' of the team, and what better way to pool such knowledge, and to demonstrate a common purpose? Promote debates and encourage others to go away to fill in the gaps. Go beyond the immediate 'core' team; if you don't know what happens right at the start of the cycle, the very early 'before', think about asking your own buyers – what would they be doing at such a stage of a potential purchase?

INVOLVING THE CUSTOMER

Once you have made progress as a team, by far the best way to ensure the relevance and resonance of your thinking is to involve the customer. This is something that requires careful consideration; timing is important, as is whom you involve, and most of all, the importance of managing their expectations.

First of all, the timing. Don't involve the customer before you yourself have command of both the process and the content. You can look very foolish not knowing 'what happens next' in the customer's order of events. Don't involve the customer if you have no intention of actioning any of the ideas for some time to come – that is surely the best way to disappoint them.

As for whom to involve, the ideal would be the combined diamond team. But if you manage to gather such a group, be sure not to waste their time by a pre-planned sales pitch loosely disguised as an activity cycle session! This is an opportunity, perhaps one of the best you will have, to understand each other. I have facilitated such sessions, and am no longer surprised at the frequency of the comment, voiced on both sides, 'Well, we never knew you did that…'. Think about using an external facilitator, and avoid at all costs being seen to take over the session, to manipulate the customer's thoughts or views.

A good session will come up with plenty of new ideas, and it is fairly certain that you will have no intention of pursuing them all. So manage the customer's expectations before you begin. This is an exploratory session, not a promise to action everything that is said. A good way to proceed might be to agree beforehand how you will deal with the hoped-for list of ideas. Are they just ideas? Should they be evaluated? What are the criteria for that evaluation? How will you define value received? Is the customer more interested in the 'before', the 'during' or the 'after'? Must they be possible from current capabilities, or will the supplier consider investing in new capabilities? Should there be joint development of ideas? This conversation alone will be of huge value in developing a mutual understanding.

THE ACTIVITY CYCLE IN PRACTICE

Each application of this tool will be unique, as unique as the business concerned and the problems highlighted. The purpose of the following examples is not to establish any kind of blueprint for your own exercise, but simply to illustrate the kind of things it can achieve.

Flying the Atlantic

You're travelling on business – what might be your problems? Wasting hours getting through the complexity of airport car parks and shuttle buses? Hanging around in an airport environment where it is impossible to work? Not enough space to work on the plane? A flat PC battery after only two hours on the plane? Eight hours without e-mail? Arriving too tired to do a good job?

Airlines have analysed the activity cycles of such passengers and the result has been a range of services from home pick-ups to business lounges, from on-board seating plans with workspace and hook-ups for laptops to pyjamas and eiderdowns.

But what if you are travelling on holiday; is any of that stuff of interest to you? Probably not, and the airline will conduct another activity cycle to identify the right package for such travellers. A particular favourite of mine is the facility provided by Virgin Atlantic to check in for your return flight from Orlando, Florida, *inside* the Disney Parks. The problem identified was the last day of the holiday, which was not part of the holiday at all. Now you can have another day with Mickey Mouse, an extra day's holiday, free.

And what if your real issue is that you are a diabetic, and long-haul flights are a major problem for taking your insulin? Insulin needs to be taken at particular times, often relative to when you eat, but airlines make you eat when they want you to eat. That is no problem on some airlines, those that allow you to choose the time of your meal, and so secure the loyalty of such passengers.

The moral of these particular examples is: value is in the eye of the beholder, and value propositions are customer specific.

Crossing the Irish Sea

The ferries from Eire to the UK see a lot of racehorse traffic, and in the past a lot of worried-looking stable lads. Consider their problem. They're responsible for several million pounds worth of horse and they have to leave it down in the hold while they fret upstairs, worrying about what it might be doing to itself.

The solution, identified after a careful analysis of what such travellers went through on their trips, was the provision of a video camera to put in the horsebox, linked to viewers in specially equipped lounges for the stable lads.

Learning over time

The penetration of the digital camera into our lives illustrates how a value proposition can develop over time, as the interactions with the customer's activity cycle unfold. At its first appearance the talk was about the new technology inside the camera – classic features. Before long the benefits were being promoted: smaller and lighter cameras for one, an issue at the 'before' stage of the activity cycle. Then the discussion moved on to the 'during', and the way that photographs could be instantly viewed, like an ultra-high-speed Polaroid, and without the attendant complexity. But perhaps the real secret of their success is to be found in an interaction at the 'after' stage of the activity cycle. It's not in the taking that they are found to be so much better than film cameras, it is in the ability to select which shots to keep, which to delete, and which to turn into prints, or store on PCs. The digital camera is the supreme achievement to date of a tool for 'making and keeping memories'.

Category management

Suppliers to the retail industry talk of 'category management', the idea that they should base their propositions on a combination of the retailer's and the consumer's perceptions of value received, all of which is considered against the broader canvas of the market segment, not simply the supplier's own product. A good category manager is interested in the total health of the category, not just any one product within that category. The activity cycle is a great way to understand these issues.

A food supplier like Kraft combine their knowledge of the consumer (after) with their knowledge of the retailer (before and during) to deliver a high-value proposition to both. In the United States, Kraft have segmented their consumers into six broad types based on their shopping behaviour. The company have then designed specific ranges of products to appeal to these six types in different ways. Working with the retailer, they assess what balance of these six types shop in each of the retailer's stores, and plan the store's range and layout accordingly. By looking beyond their immediate customer (the retailer), Kraft is able to add value to that customer, and to the final consumer offer.

Securing and sharing the value in the chain

Ideas in the 'after' stage of the activity cycle are ideas that may impact on the customer's customer, or even beyond. It can be hard to measure the precise impact of such ideas 'down the chain', and even harder to calculate precise values to different players, but if you wish to secure your just reward then the effort may be justified.

Companies with an excellent track record of gaining a fair share of the value put into a chain, despite their position some way from the end consumer, include DuPont, with materials such as Teflon (and before its sale, Lycra), and perhaps the most notable, Intel, with their ubiquitous 'Intel Inside' stickers.

When Toyota launched the Lexus car in the United States, they wanted dealers to offer levels of customer service that would leave competitors standing. They knew this would mean dealers having to invest in new systems, people, training and so on. Their solution was to allow dealers a substantially higher margin on selling the Lexus than was the industry norm, with the proviso that this margin went towards customer service improvements – a fair share of the value created by the whole Lexus package.

Gaining advantage or avoiding disadvantage?

So far we have discussed this exercise as a means of gaining advantage; finding things that are unique to you: what we might call the 'differentiators'.

But we should also consider its use in ensuring that we don't suffer disadvantage, by identifying those things that must be in place: what we might call the 'givens'.

Avoiding disadvantage is as important as gaining advantage, and may well involve attention to a more mundane list of activities: just the sort that might be discounted as administrative, clerical or even, if we're honest, dull. Making sure, for instance, that invoices are raised in a way that corresponds to the customer's requirements will rarely win you the account, but it may well help secure your position, and failing to do it will certainly lead to your disadvantage against those who can.

It is surprising, and worrying, just how much of the already short time available for communication between seller and buyer can be occupied by the discussion of such shortcomings. Worse than the time spent, such shortcomings can close the customer's eyes and ears to any claims on the supplier's part to be delivering added value. Who hasn't heard a customer tell them to 'Get your day-to-day act together before attempting anything clever'?

Making it easy for the customer to do business with you is a vitally important part of KAM, and the activity cycle tool can be used to identify the critical factors in that process.

APPLICATION EXERCISE

This is a significant exercise, best completed by the account team, working on a specific customer product or issue.

- Draw out the customer's activity cycle:
  - Identify the gaps in your knowledge.
  - How do you plan to fill these gaps?
- Where do they experience problems?
  - Do your existing activities impact on those problems?
  - Do your existing activities add value?
  - What reward do you get for these activities?
- What activities could add further value?
  - Try to identify at least one new activity for each stage: before/during/after.
- How will you decide which of these activities to take forward?
  - Do you have the necessary knowledge to make these happen?
  - Do you have the necessary contacts and influence to make these happen?
- What benefits would be gained by working this exercise through *with* the customer?
  - Who would you like to involve?
  - How can you make it happen?
  - How will you avoid the risk of building false expectations?

22

Measuring the value

If you are going to be as clever as the last two chapters will hopefully help you to be, then you had also better be certain to get the right reward for your brilliance. The secret to getting the right reward for a value proposition is not to be found at the negotiating table, it is to be found in knowledge. Know who receives your value. Know what they get from it. Know what they can do with it. Know what 'price' they put on it. Know how to measure it, and in their terms.

Most purchasers will concede that value received is more important than spend, so why do they persist with using spend in their analysis and arguments? 'Because they can', is a blunt but realistic answer. Can you really expect a busy buyer to measure the value received from your proposition? For many, accessing the spend data used in the Kraljic matrix style of analysis discussed in Chapter 14 is effort enough; 'value' can be seen as too complex a notion to be pinned down. They might not have the time, or the means, and some will not even have the inclination. Measuring value is something you will need to do for them.

The argument in favour of measuring value is a strong one, and it is one I learned from my mother. She gave me some sound advice when the time came to leave home: 'Always buy a good pair of shoes and a good bed; you'll spend half your life in one and half in the other.'

Well, she got the ratio wrong, but the principle was right – never skimp on the essentials; it will always catch up with you in the end. That cheap pair of shoes, the ones that split at the vital moment causing me to trip and drop the priceless vase I was carrying, would be pretty poor value, all things considered. The cheap bed that loses me sleep, gives me backache, makes me grumpy and then argumentative, and loses me my job, would be fairly disastrous value.

Yes, the argument is a strong one, and modern buyers (or supply side managers) will have it in their remit to look at the impact of their purchases on the whole supply chain, but more often than not it is still up to the supplier to provide the evidence.

USING THE RIGHT LANGUAGE

The first step towards measuring your value is to make sure that you will be doing it in the customer's terms; you must speak their language. It is not so very long ago that breweries would approach their retail customers with good news like the following:

> 'Good news, last month you purchased 5,000 more barrels of our beer than in the same month last year.'
>
> 'No we didn't,' came the reply from the customer.
>
> 'Sorry, I don't understand – here's the evidence in my sales statistics – look, 5,000 barrels more.'
>
> Once again came the same reply, 'No we didn't'.
>
> The sales person was getting restive at this point at what seemed to be a breakdown in trust, but before they could put their foot in things any further the buyer came to their rescue:
>
> 'I don't recall a single one of your barrels coming into a single one of our stores. We bought cans, and bottles and four-packs, but no barrels. That's how you brewers measure your volume, but we're in a different business.'

The sins of a brewer...

The lesson was well learned; how could you hope to measure and communicate something as subtle as value if you were not even using the same terminology?

UNDERSTANDING THE CIRCUMSTANCES

The next step is to understand the nature of the customer's circumstances. Consider the hospital that was described in the case study in Chapter 15. The buyer was responsible only for the initial cost of the x-ray machines and went for the cheaper of the two models. Its failings over the next two years cost the hospital heavily in service costs, delays, litigation and reputation, but these problems were no concern of the buyer. As perhaps you will recall, the neighbouring hospital trust took a longer view and bought a more expensive machine; it was well repaid by lower costs in use and greater reliability that helped enhance the reputation of that trust.

Hospitals increasingly have to fight for their customers, like anyone else, and what brings customers in is a feeling that they will be well cared for. Not surprisingly, people want to go to the hospital that isn't in the newspapers.

The KA team must understand the nature of its customer's circumstance before it can know what points of its proposition can be termed as 'of value'.

UNDERSTANDING THE COST IN USE

'It's not my selling price that matters; it's what this product will save you over its lifetime.' Such is the claim of every premium-priced sales professional, and if there is measurable evidence of the savings then it will be a good cost-in-use proposition.

Consider again the example we mentioned in Chapter 12, where you sell large-scale industrial pumps at €40,000 a time. Over five years each one uses the best part of €250,000 worth of electricity. Now, which would do the customer more good, giving them a 10 per cent discount off the purchase price, or investing your money in developing a pump that was 10 per cent more energy efficient?

The former saves the customer €4,000 today; the latter saves them €25,000 over the next five years. It's a good cost-in-use argument, but only some customers will value it, and that is an important point to remember: value is in the eye of the beholder. Don't expect a customer with cash flow problems to think the energy efficiency argument a good one.

Then there is the point of who in the customer cares about this. What if the buyer just buys pumps, not electricity? If it doesn't impact on their budget or their performance measures then perhaps they wouldn't care so much about you saving them €25,000?

Cost-in-use propositions need to do more than just measure the value; they must also target the right people, the people that see the benefit of the savings – and so we are back to penetrating snails (see Chapter 6).

PROVIDING THE MEASURE

Figure 22.1 shows the reason why office printer 'Model C' dominates that heavy-user market segment. It is the second most expensive to buy, but its superior efficiency in using toner makes it an excellent cost-in-use proposition, if you are a heavy user. But the real secret of its success is the way that the supplier has educated its customers to recognize that value, and to be able to compare it to all comers.

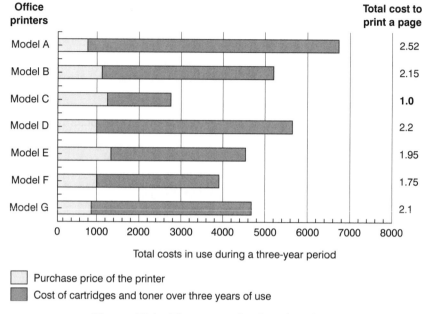

Figure 22.1 *The measured value of a printer*

Model C doesn't talk about its selling price much, nor even the reduced cost in use that results from its efficient toner use. It has a far simpler message, as demonstrated by the figure shown in the right-hand column: the cost of printing a page of paper. The supplier of Model C has done the buyer's work for them by providing an easy, evidenced and comparable measure of value.

What would be your equivalent to this: your own product or service proposition, with your customers? You should aim for something that matches up to the following criteria:

- Is it measurable and quantifiable?
- Can it be presented using their terms?
- Does it matter to the customer?
- Do you have a sustainable competitive advantage?
- Will you be able to secure an appropriate reward?

If the answers to all these questions are satisfactory, then there is just one more to ask: who from your KA team needs to be in contact with whom from the customer's team in order to identify, measure and demonstrate the value, and to secure the appropriate reward? It is very clear that value propositions and diamond teams must go hand in hand.

APPLICATION EXERCISE

Consider the nature of your value to the customer, and your ability to demonstrate and measure its impact, and so determine your proper reward:

- What 'features' of your offer can you use to demonstrate value received by the customer:
  - that are measurable and quantifiable;
  - that matter to the customer (ie, these features are genuine benefits);
  - where you have a competitive advantage;
  - where you will get an appropriate reward?
- Who from your team needs to be in contact with whom from their team, in order to demonstrate your value, and to secure the appropriate reward?

23

Making the proposal

Proposals are opportunities to show that you have listened, and under-stood. Management consultants are often criticized for simply playing back to their clients what they were told at the briefing stage. If that is all they do then the criticism is fully justified, but if this is their preliminary 'opening', before the meat of the proposition, designed to show that they have listened and understood, then the only justified criticism might be of a certain lack of skill in their ways and means, not of their intentions.

Proposals come at all stages of the relationship. At the early stages they will tend towards demonstrations of understanding and suitability. At later stages they will become more specific and detailed, but whatever the stage the temptation to allow your proposal to become a boast must be resisted. Remember: proposals are opportunities to show that you have listened, and understood.

Above all else, show that you have listened…

MANAGING CHANGE

Some sales professionals feel that in order to get the customer to change, to persuade them to switch from the competitors' product to their own, they have to boast, at least to some extent. How else can customers be made to recognize our superiority?

There is a better way. Selling is about managing change, and managing change is about converting negative thoughts to positive ones. Let's start with the negative thoughts – deep dissatisfaction with what you have at present, with what we might call the status quo. If that's where your customer is, then great: you already have the first part of the 'change equation' in place.

Figure 23.1 shows the 'change equation', a simple idea that people will change, shift from one position to another, only if a sequence of thoughts is in place. First, they must be dissatisfied with what they have already. People don't buy beds simply because they see a good price in a shop window. They buy a bed because their existing one is too small, too lumpy, too noisy – bed sales professionals talk of it as a 'distress purchase'.

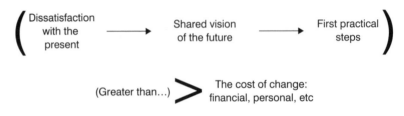

Figure 23.1 *The change equation*

The sales professional's job is to go out sowing seeds of dissatisfaction (just as professional advertisers do – making us feel too fat, too old, too tired), but if that was all they did then they would be unpopular folk indeed. They need to move on to the next part of the equation: the shared vision of the future. How could things be? Wouldn't be great if you had a bed three times the size? It might not seem attainable at this point, but no matter, this is a 'vision' of what could be.

The key word here is 'shared'. You know what you want them to want, but do they?

Getting ahead of your customer...

> When Alexander Graham Bell invented the telephone, he toured the United States showing it off to what he hoped would be interested businessmen. After one such session, he was approached by an apparent enthusiast: 'Mr Bell, I really like your new toy. It's my daughter's birthday party tomorrow and I would be very grateful if you would come along to show it.'
>
> Well, the great man was incensed: 'It is not a toy!' he exploded. 'Don't you realize that this will revolutionize communications and your business? Just think, with one of these you can talk to a customer 300 miles away.'
>
> The businessman thought for a moment and then answered: 'But, Mr Bell, I don't have any customers 300 miles away...'

Alexander Graham Bell was ahead of his customers, and this slowed him down. He needed to look at the world through their eyes, not his own, and that can be hard for an inventor or a visionary. The needs were there, deep inside, but they were what we might call latent needs. A little later in this chapter we will look how such needs can be coaxed out of the customer, through skilful questioning.

Next comes the 'first practical steps' part of the change equation. Change can be daunting, so why not make it easier for the customer by providing a lower entry point? Don't ask them to buy here and now, ask them to trial. Don't ask them to commit, ask them to read about it. Don't ask them to devote hours of their time, ask for a five-minute conversation.

All of this – the dissatisfaction, the shared vision, and the first practical steps – must add up to something greater than the cost of change. The cost might be money, or it might be ego, or a dozen other things. The mathematicians among you will have spotted that this isn't in fact an equation, but an inequality – one side has to be greater than the other for it to work – and that suggests the options open to the persuader. First, reduce the cost of change: a lower price perhaps? Or second, increase the other side of the inequality: more dissatisfaction, a more splendid vision or an easier first step…

The way to do this is through a questioning strategy, but before we look at what that involves we must conduct another piece of enquiry: how do you stack up against the competition?

THE PROPOSAL ANALYSIS

The change equation will help you assess how your proposal may be received, perhaps compared to the buyer's simplest choice – doing nothing. But what if you are up against another kind of alternative, a competitive offer?

The question to address is: do you have a competitive advantage, in the customer's eyes? The answer is to be found in a simple piece of analysis, illustrated in Figure 23.2. The proposal analysis provides a simple means of making this comparison and then judging where your relative strengths and weaknesses lie. This will be vital when you come to presenting your case or defending yourself against competitors' claims.

Let us use the example shown in Figure 23.2 that has you trying to sell a flipchart stand to a training company. The training company's staff are comparing your offer to the purchase of an overhead projector.

First, list their needs. To ensure that you consider all the customer's needs (and not just the ones that you think your proposal stacks up well against) it will be helpful to think as broadly as possible . What are their needs for performance, what are their financial needs, and of course, the needs suggested by an understanding of the 'total business experience' sought (see Chapter 20)?

The customer's needs	Your proposal	Competitor's proposal	DMU member	DMU member
	Flipchart	OHP	Trainer	Delegate
Performance:				
Clarity of presentation in a room of up to 20 people	1	1		
Usable in a variety of environments	2	1		X
Easy to prepare	0	2		
Portable	0	2		
Financial:				
Purchase price below £200	1	1	X	
Low running costs	1	2	X	
Other/TBE:				
I want to look professional	1	1	X	X
I want to be in control	2	1	XX	
Total Score:	**8**	**11**		

Figure 23.2 *The proposal analysis*

Once the needs are determined, you must score your proposal in comparison to the competitor's, with a score of 2 meaning the proposal meets the need well, a score of 1 meaning it is OK and 0 meaning it is poor or doesn't meet the need at all.

Adding up the scores you may find yourself in a losing position, but all is not lost! Next you should consider the members of the DMU (decision-making unit). Might there be differences of need or opinion? In our example, two members of the DMU are considered – the trainer who will use the equipment (and is eager to please their audience), and an imaginary delegate at a training event (who does not want to be bored rigid), who will experience the output of the tool used. Note any particular interest with an X, or XX for a very significant interest.

Let us look at what we have (Figure 23.2). So far, it isn't looking too good for the flipchart business. If the buyer were a computer, you would have lost on points. Fortunately, the buyer is human and you have some choices:

- Argue with the customer's assessment: 'But you're wrong, it's *very* easy to prepare!' Rarely a good idea.

- Downgrade the competitor's offer: 'But have you seen the price of bulbs?' An even worse idea – this just gets the customer defending the competitor.
- Raise the importance of those needs where your offer shows a clear strength. The best plan by far.

There are many ways to do this, but let's consider two:

- finding 'coalitions' of interest in the DMU;
- the 'CICS' questioning strategy.

First, the 'coalition of interests' approach. Are there any issues or needs where your offer can satisfy all, or most, of the important members of the DMU? Are there points in your offer that provide a compromise for different members of that DMU?

In our example, the issue of being able to use the presentation tool in a variety of environments might just be the answer. Delegates at an event don't want to be victims of a one-way lecture from someone armed with a folder full of slides. And what if the weather was so wonderful that they wanted to take the course outside? Your proposal would allow the trainer greater flexibility and the delegates a more enjoyable experience – grounds for a good coalition of interests.

In the next section we consider the questioning strategy approach.

THE 'CICS' QUESTIONING STRATEGY

Questioning is a skill, to be learned through practice and feedback; it is not enough simply to know the mechanical process, and the skills required can certainly not be learned from a book. With this health warning in mind, the following deals only with the mechanical process and is intended as no more than the start of a discussion to be had within the KA team.

The best proposals are never lectures. Questions lie at the heart of persuasion and are a vital part of building genuine partnerships. We might aim to prepare a questioning strategy that will help raise the importance, in the customer's view, of those needs where your proposal makes the strongest case (as learned from the proposal analysis).

This is a four-part questioning strategy (the acronym CICS refers to the four key words highlighted below):

1. Identify the customer's current **Circumstances**. (In our flipchart versus overhead projector example – in what circumstances will they be using this tool? Is it for presentation? Is it for recording of comments? Is it to stimulate and manage discussion?)

2. Uncover existing or potential **Issues** in the customer's mind. (What kind of problems do you experience when running training events? What can you do when attention is flagging? How do delegates feel about being on the receiving end of a lecture?)

3. What might be the future **Consequence** of these issues? (What are the worst outcomes of these issues? What happens to the learning experience once attention has wandered? How do you feel about 'losing control'? What do they think of you?)

4. Explore the possible **Solutions**. (Might a flipchart presentation at such a stage help you to regain attention and take control, and make you very popular into the bargain?)

This is of course a huge simplification of a questioning process that might take some time. CICS is not a slick mechanical process, but an aid to your thinking – as much a planning tool as an actual order of events. Increase the complexity of the sale, and such a questioning strategy could extend over several meetings.

Take great care not to use such a strategy as a means of 'laying traps', the 'now I've got you' school of selling. Nothing will stop the customer from answering your questions faster than making them think you are walking them out on to a branch of a tree, in preparation for sawing it off at the trunk!

It is also a strategy that must involve the whole KA team. Every customer interaction is to some extent a part of this strategy, whether identifying the circumstances, uncovering the issues, elaborating on the possible consequences or exploring the solutions.

APPLICATION EXERCISE

Consider the value proposition to one of your key accounts:

- Do you have all the elements of the change equation?
  - Which elements are missing?
  - Which elements need enhancing?
- Draw up a benefit analysis:
  - Where are your strengths?
  - Where are the competitor's strengths?
- Do you need to change your value proposition, or can you target your existing proposition more effectively?
- How can you raise the level of importance of those aspects of the customer's needs that will play to your strengths?
- Prepare an appropriate CICS sales/questioning strategy.

Part VII

Targeting: customer classification and distinction

24

Customer classification

It is surprising how many businesses set off on the KAM journey without having identified their key accounts. It is as if the task of selection is too troublesome, so they just get on with it, with everyone. The result is, of course, no Key Account Management.

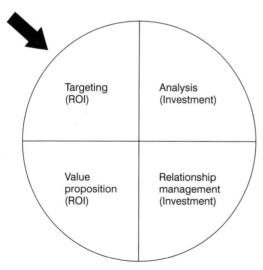

Figure 24.1   *The KAM model – targeting*

Figure 24.1 reminds us of the fourth part of the KAM model – targeting – and that it is a key factor in ensuring the proper return on our KAM investment. Done with too many, the KAM investment is diluted, and the returns negligible. Done with the wrong customers, the investment will be wasted.

This is something to get right, and perhaps that is another explanation for the reluctance of some to tackle the task: the fear of getting it wrong. It is certainly a task that will provoke internal debate and even arguments (the most common being over who *isn't* a key account rather than who *is*), but managed properly those arguments can be the precursor of something very important: alignment of all functions to an agreed list.

The six-step process

Figure 24.2 gives a six-step process to help navigate the way through the mass of questions, analysis and debate, and help avoid the inevitable traps that lie in wait, with the ultimate objective of an agreed customer classification and agreed actions against those classifications.

Step 1. Know your objectives for KAM.

Step 2. Market segmentation.

Step 3. Assemble the classification and selection team.

Step 4. The 'KAISM' – Classifying your customers:

i. Identify the *customers' attractiveness*.

ii. Assess your *relative strength*.

Step 5. Customer distinction strategies.

Step 6. Communication, alignment and implementation.

Figure 24.2 *The six-step process*

STEPS 1 AND 2: OBJECTIVES AND MARKET SEGMENTATION

These are essential preliminaries that should almost go without saying, and yet too often people leap into the choice of 'who is' and 'who isn't' without being clear on these fundamentals.

Step 1: Objectives

The objectives for KAM may be very clear to you – after all the thought you have been giving it – but are they equally clear to others in the organization? You see it as an essential process for winning new customers (let's say), someone else sees it as a means to developing better value propositions, while yet another sees it as a matter of profit enhancement. The more people you ask the more objectives you uncover (and that was only across the sales team!).

Make sure you have alignment on this fundamental point before proceeding too much further. It is of course quite possible to have multiple objectives, but be sure that they are not in conflict with each other, and avoid the situation where some people accept a list, for an easy life, but resolutely promote their own objective to the top and ignore the rest.

Step 2: Market segmentation

This comes first, before any identification of key accounts. The reason is simple: there is no such thing as a key account in a market segment that is not attractive or important to you.

There should be a clear planning hierarchy, from marketing plan to segment plans, and then to key account plans, as illustrated in Figure 24.3.

In Segment A there are two key accounts, in Segment B there are none (this is a low-priority segment) and in Segment C only one key account. The targeting process is not about neatness, or sharing things out evenly; it is about ensuring the investment is put where it will bring the best return.

Segmentation will help in the selection of key accounts for many reasons; here are just a few for starters:

- A key account is the most important customer in an attractive and important segment, not just one of the business's big customers.
- Segmentation will help us define what 'most important customer' means. Customer attractiveness can vary across segments; 'big' might be important in one segment but a problem in another.
- When comparing the virtues of different customers, segmentation helps us to compare apples to apples. The alternative is to use size as the driving factor.

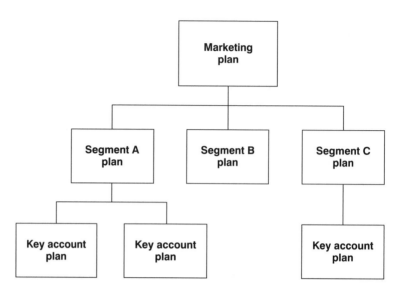

Figure 24.3 *The planning hierarchy*

Segmentation lies at the heart of all good marketing strategies. It allows the business to focus its resources efficiently and effectively, allows the development of targeted marketing mixes (the famous four p's: product, place, price and promotion), enhances your chance of securing competitive advantage, perhaps even a unique market position, and helps to foster operational excellence (perhaps also economies of scale).

Segmentation is clearly 'a good thing' and so it may be worth taking a moment to define just what is meant by a 'market segment'. A market segment is not defined by your products, nor your technologies, but by your customers. A market segment is a group of customers that shares a similar set of needs, attitudes and behaviours, and that can therefore be served by a consistent marketing mix (those four p's).

One segment, one key account?

It is at this point that a fascinating question can be asked: how many key accounts do you *need* per segment? The question was 'need', not 'should you have', and if your segmentation has been done properly, won't the answer be, 'only one'? By investing the team's time and effort into only one KA per segment, such a focus of attention will surely help you to gain a deeper and a better understanding than by focusing it on several? And as the needs, attitudes and behaviours of each customer in the segment are the same, won't it be the case that once you identify the winning value proposition for that one KA, you have identified it for all?

The logic of this theory is sound enough; the problem lies in the fact that market segmentation is rarely done that well or that precisely. If only it was!

This is of course very close to the idea of a key account as a 'lead' customer, helping you to develop solutions that can be applied to all, and whether as a result of inadequate segmentation, or the fact that some customers resolutely refuse to be pigeonholed by the marketing department, a recent trend has been to regard each key account as a segment in itself. A fully cross-functional KA team, developing tailored value propositions, makes it effectively so.

Benefits beyond the selection stage

Once customers are classified and key accounts identified, good market segmentation continues to be of assistance to the effective application of a KAM strategy. Much could be said in its favour, but I will restrict myself to two key points:

- Segmentation will permit a much clearer definition of service standards for all classifications of customers, so providing a focus for the all-important support functions.
- The development of such standards, particularly for key accounts, will help avoid the slide into the chaos of an 'anything goes' attitude.

Finally, in this short discussion of segmentation and its relationship to KAM, the development of key accounts as segments in themselves can be seen to be having some very positive effects on the wider practice of marketing in many companies.

There is a move away from the idea of marketing through a prescribed package (the marketing mix) towards marketing as relationship management, based on high levels of trust and collaboration, leading towards joint development of value propositions. Christian Gronroos, a leading writer on this new kind of 'relationship marketing', calls it 'the mutual exchange and fulfilment of promises'. Grand words, but not a bad basis for a long-term key account relationship.

STEP 3: ASSEMBLE THE CLASSIFICATION AND SELECTION TEAM

The wrong people can be asked to make the decisions. How about asking the sales team to decide?

Salespeople naturally have positions to defend, and careers to build. Everyone wants their own accounts to be seen as key; surely that way lies promotion?

267

Salespeople may have very clear ideas – it is to be hoped that they do – but what about the views of other functions, the functions that will be called on to support the KA process? Perhaps you are in sales and perhaps you already think you know your key accounts, maybe you are certain; but what if the rest of your business doesn't seem to see it your way?

Getting everyone to agree

I learned this lesson in the first few months of my selling career. I sold decorative paint to independent retailers out in rural East Anglia where I was warned there would be little I could do to rouse customers from their comfortable slumber. I determined to prove those warnings wrong by identifying those customers worthy of extra attention, my key accounts. After poring over my sales statistics and pushing pins of different colours into a map of my territory I went off to inform my local distribution depot, absolutely certain of my analysis.

For 10 minutes or so (perhaps longer – time goes quickly when you are lecturing people) I briefed them on the customers that they must now regard as more important than the rest, my key accounts, only to reel back in amazement as they contradicted my identification of almost every customer. For me, a sales rep, a key account was one where I could expect a large order as the result of my call. For my distribution colleagues this was the sin of sending eager young reps out in the first place! For them, a key account was a customer so regular and so consistent in their order pattern that they could form the backbone of their workload planning.

We agreed to differ and I went away wiser on one very important issue – it was highly unlikely that key accounts could be identified by single criterion, and certainly not from the narrow perspective of any one function. Fortunately, I was dealing with rather small independent retailers in a quiet corner of the country, not the global customers that might have determined our whole future. Even more fortunately, I learned a lesson in this quiet corner that was of enormous benefit later in my career when dealing with much larger and more significant fish. There is a time to learn from your mistakes, and a time to get it right.

The ideal team?

The ideal team is only ever ideal for the purpose for which it is formed. There is in fact a dual purpose for this team:

- To identify and select the key accounts on the basis of a combination of intimate customer knowledge and a clear vision of future strategy and goals.
- To give that selection sufficient authority for it to mean something across the business. Selection without implementation will be meaningless.

This suggests the need for a fairly senior team, and it must in fact be the responsibility of the most senior managers to see that the right decisions are made, but do you therefore ask them to make those decisions? How senior must be the classification and selection team? Consider two scenarios.

In the first, the team is a group of senior managers who approach the task very much with their eyes on the recently agreed five-year plan. 'Vision' abounds, but the sales force asks: 'What do they know about our customers?'

Senior management vision...

In the second scenario, it is a group from sales and customer service that makes up the selection team, and their efforts reflect their intimate knowledge of the customers. 'Fine', say the bosses, 'but what about tomorrow's customers? Where's the vision?'

...coal-face knowledge

The ideal team must be able to combine both vision and knowledge. One problem is that 'knowledge' will exist in a lot of places, and any attempt to gather it all together in one team would result in an unworkable monster. Perhaps the solution is a core team (no more than four or five people), probably with a bias towards 'vision', which calls on the knowledge of others as and when it is required.

A final thought – the more senior the selection team, the more likely that their conclusions will make an impact – and that is surely one of the key purposes of this whole selection activity?

STEP 4: THE 'KAISM': CLASSIFYING YOUR CUSTOMERS

(The weblink associated with this book contains a software package designed to help with the process described in this step.)

A, B, C, or perhaps Gold, Silver, Bronze: typical classifications used to indicate customer importance and priorities. Do they work? Probably not, as they fall foul of the sin of 'one-dimensionalism' (a term I have just invented, but a sin that has been long in existence). This is the sin of thinking that you select your key accounts based on criteria of how attractive they are – Gold is more attractive than Silver, and so it goes on.

The real problem is with the word 'select'. I once had a lengthy debate with a client as to whether 'select' was in fact the right word. 'You have obviously been very lucky in your sales career,' he said to me. 'I have never selected a customer in my life; they've always selected me.'

He was right of course; as we have seen in Part IV and the chapters dealing with key supplier status (Chapters 11 through 14), customers do just as much 'selecting' of us as we do of them, and which is the more important of the selections? But couldn't this kind of consideration take us into a horribly fatalistic dead-end where any customer that doesn't regard us as important can never be regarded as a key account (and that might mean all of them for some!)? That would simply be another manifestation of the sin of 'one-dimensionalism'.

The answer is to be found in the four-box matrix ('two-dimensionalism' is *not* a sin) illustrated in Figure 24.4 – the KAISM (key account identification and selection matrix) and a different word – 'classification'

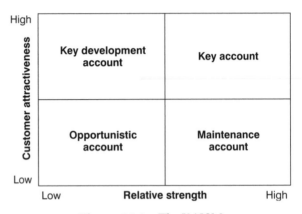

Figure 24.4   *The KAISM*

Here we take the two dimensions discussed – their attractiveness to us (the vertical axis), and our attractiveness to them, or what we will call 'relative strength' (the horizontal axis) – and combine them to give us four classifications of customer:

- *Key accounts* are those where the attraction is mutual – we like the look of them, and they rate us more strongly than they do our competitors.
- *Key development accounts* are those that we have strong ambitions for, but who currently prefer one or more of our competitors.
- *Maintenance accounts* are those that rate us highly, but that we don't view as our more attractive prospects.
- *Opportunistic accounts* are those where neither regards the other as of great attraction.

We can now see the danger of one-dimensionalism, in either direction. Most businesses will rate their customers on the vertical axis (though too many only use the criterion of size), but that does not help us distinguish clearly enough the different kinds of approach and different levels of investment required. The horizontal axis, while much harder to establish (as we will see) is of critical importance in this regard.

Before moving on to how we establish each customer's position in this matrix we should put a little more flesh on each of the four classifications, with a comment on how many customers we might like to see in each box if we were eager to have the 'ideal portfolio'.

Key accounts

This one hardly needs defining, so a warning instead: these customers are critical to your future and they deserve energetic attention from a KA team devoted to keeping on top of a situation that can easily change. Remember the cliché: 'nothing recedes like success'.

How many should there be? Getting into double figures should be a cause for concern. If your rating system (see below, the sections on 'Customer attractiveness factors' and 'Relative strength factors') puts 75 customers into this box, you need either to refine your rating system, or to do what every classification and selection team should do after completing the mathematical part of the exercise, and that is, re-engage the brain!

Key development accounts

This is where your future could lie, if only you could improve your performance in the customers' eyes. The KA team must focus on finding out what makes the customers tick, what they want, and committing the business to providing it.

Such customers could be hard work, with all the 'chicken and egg' problems imaginable, but success will be well rewarded. They almost certainly represent the biggest investment, and the longest pay-back.

How many? Wouldn't it be nice to think you had lots of future prospects? Yes, but remember that you have finite resources, so don't spread them too thinly. If you have 20 genuine development key accounts you are probably getting to the limit.

If you really do have too many candidates in this box, you might consider taking them as a group and repeating the KAISM classification exercise again, comparing apples to apples as it were.

Some businesses appoint their most junior salespeople to look after these customers, or attach them to the responsibilities of key account managers already burdened by too many top-right key accounts – a sort of moonlighting job. If this is done because the business doesn't see much real prospect of progress, then they are usually proved right – they make no progress! Again, once the mathematics has positioned the customers, re-engage the brain.

Another common approach is to make such customers the responsibility of the tele-sales team, giving them an almost impossible task, to develop relationships that will enhance the customer's view of you – by telephone.

Success with such customers will come from applied effort, not from starving the teams of resources or expertise. If there are more customers in this classification than can actually be developed into key accounts, then you have some choices: increase your resources, or 'pick them off' as specific customer opportunities arise.

Be prepared to experiment, to trial, to allocate resources as 'test cases', always aiming to learn from each experience. Be prepared to put some on hold on the famous 'back burner', and finally, know when to admit defeat. Think of it this way: Can a truly 'unconvertible' customer be honestly called 'attractive'?

Maintenance accounts

In many ways this is the hardest classification. These are good customers, perhaps they have been loyal for years. Almost certainly they are personal favourites of plenty of your team. The tough decision, but the right one, is to pull resources and energy back from such customers because they are needed elsewhere. But this does not imply that you are in any way prepared to lose the customers. The aim is expressed clearly enough in their label: 'maintenance'.

Winning time to invest in key and key development accounts

To succeed with KAM you must free time and energy from these customers (who may well represent the bulk of your portfolio) but not to the extent that you endanger their loyalty. The decisions here are among the most difficult for any supplier.

Aim to find ways of looking after these customers that won't trap you and your team into time-consuming commitments. Aim to reduce service costs and maximize sustained earnings. Making use of inside sales resources can be an important part of the solution. Make full use of all 'remote' ordering systems, whether electronic or otherwise. The customer might even prefer such arrangements, especially if they can be arranged to be more appropriate to their needs.

You might need to consider the withdrawal of some support functions, a common one being direct contact R&D resources. I know several businesses that use the label 'key' or 'key development' account to indicate that R&D resources will be allocated, but only here. Other customers (maintenance and opportunistic), will receive the benefits of the supplier's R&D resource indirectly, perhaps through products initially designed for key accounts.

It's all in how you say it

Imagine that you have just completed the KAISM analysis and find a number of customers previously considered key now sitting in the bottom-right box. You decide to take them out of your own direct supply network and pass them to local distributors. How do you handle this 'transition'? Compare two alternative approaches.

Apologies are sent to the customer, including a letter from the MD thanking them for their loyal support and hoping that it will continue, despite the need to reorganize business operations. The distributor is given the account to work with how they see fit. Once the handover is decided on, and the necessary meetings concluded, the previous sales contact has no further contact with the customer.

Or, the supplier and the distributor make a joint presentation on the advantages to the customer of moving to a local distributor, including shorter lead times, more frequent delivery, flexible terms, product variants to suit local circumstances and more personal attention. The distributor is helped to understand their new customer by the previous sales contact, who stays in touch over a managed handover period.

How many?

In a sense, the more the merrier. These customers will provide you with the profit and the cash required to invest in the key development accounts.

Opportunistic accounts

These are customers that you will service willingly as and when it suits your priorities. You should not make wild promises that you cannot keep, nor should you treat them like nuisances. Be pleased with their custom, but recognize it for what it is: income that helps you to develop your key and key development accounts.

Such customers are always useful at those moments when you receive a 'message from management' – 'It's nearing year end and we need some volume to meet budgets.' Don't rush off to your key accounts looking for orders, turn to the opportunistic accounts; here's the right place to do short-term deals for short-term gains.

Some benefits of classification

An international supplier to the oil industry once put at stake a number of their key contracts because they were over-eager to secure a large, but one-off, deal with Russia.

They had a system of customer categorization that put the Russian customer in the opportunistic box, but it was only given lip service and not all functions agreed with the definitions. The order was large and tempting and the production people put in a superhuman effort to meet the deadlines. They made it, and they felt pretty good about it, until the complaints started to flow from their real key accounts. They had all taken their eye off the ball.

Being led astray...

273

Why not just chase hot opportunities?

Classification does not imply abandonment; it implies a planned allocation of resources. For some businesses, the people resources required for KA teams would be a big call and they must identify the real candidates for such an approach with care. Other businesses might find they have the people and so perhaps many customers could enjoy the diamond team approach, but perhaps the production resources could not cope with the variety of commitments that ensued.

The classification process must be carried out with all functions in mind, indeed, with the total business objectives and value drivers in mind.

What if your key accounts are mortal enemies?

I have seen a supplier chase and win a major customer (in this case it was Coca-Cola), only to see it almost wreck their good work by then chasing that customer's competitor (in this case Pepsi).

Does KAM mean that you cannot serve both? In some industries, large customers, and particularly those with dominant market positions, may try to keep their key suppliers out of their competition. This is done through suggestion, influence and pressure (not by contractual demands!).

The reasons are clear: if a close relationship is to form, where sensitive information will be exchanged, then there must be some security. For the supplier, there may be a need to make choices – one or the other – and the KA selection process is one of the tools for aiding such decisions.

In many cases there will not be a need to make such a stark choice as 'one or the other', but there will be a need to recognize the sensitivities of customers. The common solution is to ensure that the KA teams serving such competitors are not composed of the same people. In this instance (perhaps the only justifiable occasion), the building of some walls within the supplier's own organization may be of benefit rather than a barrier.

An important health warning

This process is about getting you and your team to think. It should not be done as guesswork, or in five minutes on the back of an envelope. It is about understanding how and why you should deal with customers and how that might change over time. It is not about labelling them forever. And yes, of course you can break the rules and the definitions – provided you can explain why.

The KAISM is designed to help our thinking, not to replace our brains.

My own business, a training and consultancy firm, regularly conducts this identification and selection process, and for many years our chosen criteria for the two axes always found a particular customer down in the bottom-left box. The reason was that this customer had their own in-house training organization, never an attractive proposition for a supplier of training and a hard act to be compared favourably against. But we all knew that this was a key development account, so were we doing something wrong in our analysis?

Not at all. We always had to remember that times change and that we should always be asking, 'What if the company should close its in-house training organization?' Then it would be catapulted into the top-right box. But, rather than wait until that happened, shouldn't we be treating it as a key account now, in preparation – perhaps even to encourage them in their decision to close their own operation?

In the event, the company began to wind down their own training operation and our key account attentions began to pay dividends. For a number of years we had a higher strategic intent about the company than they had about us and wondered if this mismatch was a problem. Sometimes it is, if there is no likely realignment of intent in the future, but sometimes you just have to wait, and prepare – and manufacture your own luck.

Do the analysis ...

...do the mathematics...

...re-engage the brain...

The perfect investment portfolio?

Any successful business will require a mix of customers: key accounts, key development accounts, maintenance and opportunistic, a balance across all four boxes of the matrix.

If all customers were key accounts then, even if the term didn't become meaningless, the effort involved to manage them properly could quite conceivably create greater costs than the income enjoyed. If all were key development accounts then the likelihood of this occurring would be all the greater.

A business with too many maintenance accounts, while enjoying a handsome income, might have cause to worry about the future; might the bulk of their customers actually hold them back? And a business with too many opportunistic accounts, while they may be very profitable, is a business heading nowhere in particular. It is all a question of investment and return.

The fastest return on your investment should come from the opportunistic accounts – don't even think of making a 'jam tomorrow' case to your boss on these ones!

Maintenance accounts should have a fairly fast return; you are after all regarding these as your cash cows (to quote the Boston Box). Key development accounts will be the longest haul, and don't allow your bosses (especially the accountants among them) to impose unrealistic short-term returns on these – that is the sure way to kill the opportunity stone dead.

STEP 4.i: CUSTOMER ATTRACTIVENESS FACTORS

The classification and selection team will need to agree the criteria for assessing the relative attractiveness of customers; we will call these criteria the 'customer attractiveness factors'.

What makes *you* want *them*?

Ideally they will combine factors that assess the long-term potential as well as the short-term realities, and will be a mixture of tangible and intangible, quantitative and qualitative. Most importantly they must be unique to your own business situation. The importance of defining these factors, and then using them as measures, cannot be overstated. If the matrix is to be any kind of guide to allocating resources, deciding priorities, or determining customer relationships, then a great deal of thought should go into this exercise. Don't in any circumstance be tempted to 'steal' someone else's factors as a template!

It is probably true that the most value to be gained from using this classification approach is not in the final outcome, but in the thinking and the discussions that go into its origination. The matrix provides an ideal opportunity for cross-functional teams to meet and discuss, sharing the viewpoints of their different perspectives. As such, this exercise is a key part of gaining cross-business alignment and is of huge value even if the outcome tells you nothing particularly new or startling (though it usually does!).

Choosing the factors

There are many types of attractiveness factor, and we might be helped in our search for the right list by approaching them through five different but overlapping considerations:

- Those that represent 'pure' attractiveness.
- Those that indicate a likelihood of success.
- Those that relate to your long-term business objectives: Where do you want to be in x years?
- Those that help to indicate specific opportunities: What can we get?
- Those that are based on a realistic assessment of our resources and capability.

'Pure' attractiveness

This category includes attractiveness factors such as 'large enough to be worth $1m profit to us'. On its own, this consideration could be dangerously broad or theoretical; if you like, these are judgements made in a vacuum. Often they serve as givens – nobody smaller than this could be considered attractive, but they don't help us distinguish between two of the same size.

Likelihood of success

These factors aim to indicate how likely it is that those pure attractiveness factors could be made real. They help us to narrow the sights. An example might be that they 'share our view of the future technological solutions'. Of two customers that pass the first 'pure' attractiveness test, perhaps only one passes the likelihood of success test.

Business objectives

If your planned source of competitive advantage is to be some unique added-value element in your offer, then you might regard customers that valued that element as attractive. If high-tech solutions to customers' problems is your pitch, then you might expect your most attractive accounts to be those that value such solutions, and are prepared to pay the price. If you want to be market leader by volume then big players may be attractive. If your goal is to be the supplier of highest repute then that might lead you to a rather different definition of an attractive customer.

Specific opportunities

Let's say you see your future in providing services that are currently provided 'in-house' by most businesses. Your most attractive accounts may be those that have a positive attitude towards outsourcing such services – they provide the most likely opportunity.

Resource and capability

Some customers may be beyond your reach – you're not in the right place, you're not big enough, you're too big, and so on. An attractive customer may be one that is easy to gain access to, perhaps because of geography or existing relationships. These are real world assessments.

A sample list

The following list summarizes the most typically used customer attractiveness factors:

- Size: volume, value, profit.
- Growth potential: volume, value, profit.
- Financial stability: will they be there in the future and will they pay their bills?
- Ease of access: geography, openness, and the like.
- Closeness of existing relationships.

- Strategic fit: do they see the world the same way as you? Will they take you where you wish to be?
- Are they 'early adopters': do they pick up on new ideas and products, or do they wait until the market has tested them?
- Do they value your offer? Is it relevant to their needs?
- Level of competition (low being attractive).
- Their market standing: industry leader, credibility, prestige and so on.

A suggestion for 'working the process'

1. Ask each member of the team to list their own favoured criteria. Give them the task of listing at least 12. You might focus their minds by asking that at least six should represent their own function's view and at least six the view of the whole business. (This might have been done as pre-work, but never assume that people will do such things, and of course some will overdo it, turning up with the absolute list, no discussion allowed.)

2. An additional 'flavour' can be had if you ask them to list 12 as above, and then another two, three or four, having put themselves into the shoes of another function, and so on for as many different functions as you might like them to consider.

3. Then put your colleagues into pairs or trio groups and ask them to put their lists together so that they have a composite list of at least 20, viewed from all and every angle. They may need to add some more to get to 20, but don't worry about editing down at this point – that will come soon enough!

4. Now gather the full team and get all of the possible criteria up on some flipcharts. There will of course be plenty of duplication – to avoid this put one pair or trio's list up in full and then ask for anything different from the rest of the group.

5. Now, and only now, add any criteria that may already have existed as a result of business strategy discussions or marketing plans (you will need to investigate whether such criteria have ever been set). The reason for doing this now and not at the start is to allow free thinking – no constraints by what 'them upstairs' might have said.

6. Now comes the hard bit – *'getting it down to six'*. You may like to call on the help of an impartial (but skilled and knowledgeable) facilitator to get this stage accomplished. There are plenty of perils waiting for whoever stands by the chart with the pen. On the one hand they will be seen as taking over. The alternative is for them to take part only as the scribe, and that means one valuable view is lost.

    Most likely of course is that they *will* take over – the power of the pen. In many ways the worst person to be stood by the chart is the boss; it is far too easy for them to impose their views on everyone else.

Why six?

Why this magic number of six factors? If you have very many more than this there are two problems:

- The mathematics of the rating process tends to blur every account into an indistinct middle ground.
- It becomes very hard for others to understand the basis of the analysis, and as this is a crucial reason for doing it in the first place this is fault enough!

If you have too few factors, then there is the danger of being too narrow in your outlook (the peril of sizeism again). It is not obligatory, but you may choose to weight the factors chosen, for a more refined analysis. One benefit of such weighting is that you can maintain the same list of factors over a long period of time but change the weightings to reflect changes in market circumstances or your own objectives and aspirations.

Getting it right for you

Your own business circumstances must determine your selection and the weighting you might give to individual factors. Working with a client in Russia, we spent a great deal of time identifying a list of six factors, but there was one that stood head and shoulders above the others: will the customers pay their bills? It was a crucial aspect of their market circumstance and without it there was little point proceeding – some factors are absolute 'must haves'.

Whatever your final choice, you must be able to apply these factors to each of your customers, measuring them against each other. It will become apparent at this stage why it was so important to segment your market before tackling this process – apples must be compared to apples. It is quite likely that the list of factors selected will need to be different by market segment.

Dulux Paints in the UK supplies to both the DIY market and the professional decorator market, two distinct segments of the decorative paint market. If we just take one of the factors that might determine customer attractiveness, we will immediately see the importance of segmentation; let's consider scale.

In the DIY market, the goal of brand leadership makes the large DIY superstores very attractive customers. In the professional decorator market, a large firm means large-scale contracts, which means pressure on price, so perhaps not so attractive? The real key accounts in the professional market might be identified as the distributors that give access to the small and medium-sized decorating firms. Different segments, different objectives, different attractiveness factors.

The golden rule: segments first, key accounts second

STEP 4.ii: RELATIVE STRENGTH FACTORS

The identification of the factors for the vertical axis is reasonably straight-forward for two reasons:

- You know what they should be because they relate to your own objectives and aspirations.
- They will be the same for all customers in any given segment.

What makes *them* want *you*?

The factors on the horizontal axis are rather harder to identify because here we need to view the world through our customers' eyes. What are their objectives and aspirations, and how does that translate into their rating of suppliers?

Not only are these elements harder to identify (but hugely valuable to know), they will also be different for each customer. Some customers publish explicit lists of vendor ratings while others are more secretive. Some will use 'hard' measures, others will favour more subjective evaluations based on perceptions rather than facts. The horizontal axis is hard work, but will repay the effort handsomely.

Identifying these factors will require great honesty. It is tempting to select all those things that you just happen to be good at, and you will feel very pleased with the outcome, only it will be worthless. The perceptions of different functions within your own business will be of great value to the debate – each will have a distinct awareness of what goes down well and what causes complaints.

The more you know, of course, the better. If you find this part of the exercise particularly difficult then it will at least have highlighted a priority action for your KAM implementation programme – find out.

Given the propensity for most of us to either pat ourselves on the back or whip ourselves unreasonably, it may be valuable to gain some kind of independent insight as a route to the truth in this matter. Consider formal and independent market research into customers' views, needs and levels of satisfaction.

Using research as a way of talking to customers will be a good antidote to one of many a supplier's greatest failings – talking to themselves.

The range of factors (seen from your customers' perspective) might include:

- price;
- service – on-time-in-full measures, just-in-time requirements and so on;
- quality;
- speed of response;
- relationships and attitudes;
- technical innovation;
- investment in the industry;

- value in use – value in the supply chain, total acquisition cost and the like;
- attitude to exclusivity arrangements;
- long-term sustainability;
- trust and confidence – ethical standards and behaviour.

COMPLETING THE ANALYSIS

The weblink associated with this book has a software package that will help take you through the process described here, but it is no bad idea to commence with a paper exercise, however rough, for several reasons: it quickly identifies the black holes in your knowledge of your customers; it makes a team-wide analysis easier to facilitate; and most importantly, it engages the brain rather than your typing fingers.

The two tables shown in Figures 24.5 and 24.6 are designed to help you identify where your customers sit in your portfolio. They will provide a 'first cut' analysis, but you may wish to go further than this. Weighting of individual factors is the obvious next step and it may be that at this point you should turn to the software for help – the sums start to get quite involved!

The KAISM (Figure 24.4) represents the relative positions of customers within a specific market segment. The table shown in Figure Table 24.5 allows

	Account/Customer	Customer attractiveness factor (CAF) scores						
		CAF 1	CAF 2	CAF 3	CAF 4	CAF 5	CAF 6	Total Score
1								
2								
3								
4								
5								
6								
7								
8								
9								
10								
11								
12								

Figure 24.5 _Customer attractiveness factors_

you to rate and compare customers against your chosen list of customer attractiveness factors.

- Enter your chosen customers across the top of the table.
- It is advisable to work with a list of about six factors – of course, more will exist, but this will help to focus the analysis.
- Enter a score from 1 to 10 for each customer, against each attractiveness factor. The higher the score, the better your customer meets that aspiration. Try to set a benchmark of what is 'good' and 'bad' before starting to score, and try to stick to it! (It is all too easy to uprate your 'favourite' customers.)
- Calculate the average score – the grand total of all the total scores divided by the number of customers assessed (This will be used once you have completed the table shown in Figure 24.6).

Next, the table shown in Figure 24.6 allows you to assess your relative strength, using the customer's measures to see how they rate you in comparison to your competitors.

	Relative strength factors	Weight %	Customer/Account:					
			Relative strength factor (RSF) scores					
			Your own business	Comp 1	Comp 2	Comp 3	Comp 4	Comp 5
1								
2								
3								
4								
5								
6								
	Total score:	(100%)						

Figure 24.6 *Relative strength factors*

- For each customer under consideration, identify six relative strength factors (RSFs) that represent their principal needs from their suppliers and by which they would judge you in comparison with others.

- Complete one table for each of the customers selected for analysis. It is quite likely, of course, that each customer will have their own distinct set of RSFs.
- Place you and your competitors across the top of the table and enter a score from 1 to 10 for each supplier against each factor. This is how the customer views you and your competitors, fact and perception – so be honest! The higher the score, the better the supplier meets the customer's needs.

Completing the matrix

Using the information from these two tables, you can place each customer on the KAISM (Figure 24.4)

From the customer attractiveness factors table shown in Figure 24.5, if a customer scores higher than the average score then they will be in one of the two upper boxes; if lower than average, they will be in one of the two lower boxes.

To identify which of the two, use the results from the relative strength factors table shown in Figure 24.6. Where you score better than your best competitor, this indicates the right-hand box, and the left-hand box if you score worse.

'Manual' analysis, or software?

My advice is always to proceed manually until it gets too complicated! In 'manual' mode the brain stays engaged, and the early decisions about factors and weightings will probably benefit. By the time you reach the detailed rating stage you will probably be pleased to use a piece of software to help with the mathematics (see Chapter 33 for more information on the options).

How much effort and how much detail?

It is probably the thinking that goes on around this exercise, rather than the outcome, that is the most important 'result'. That being so, perhaps the main effort should be put into identifying the two sets of factors, customer attractiveness and relative strength. When it comes to the rating, calculations to two decimal places that shift customers a few millimetres on the matrix are unlikely to add much to anybody's understanding.

Where you simply do not know the answers, most likely in looking at your relative strength, make a note to find out. A supreme benefit of this exercise is the demonstration of what you don't and must know. Seek professional advice on how to do market research into customers' needs and current satisfaction – it takes more than the salesperson asking the buyer's opinion.

This is an exercise that should be done repeatedly, each time seeking for more completeness and greater certainty in your assessments. Over time, you and your team will build up a substantially better appreciation of how you view your customers and how they view you.

The debates around the exercise, particularly if done by a true cross section of functions, tell you a great deal about the different viewpoints in the business, and help enormously in the all-important task of getting alignment behind the decisions.

KEY ACCOUNTS AND MULTIPLE BUSINESS UNIT SUPPLIERS

Getting your act together

An interesting challenge for KAM is the situation where the supplier is formed into a number of business units, working independently of each other and selling to common customers. Let's say a packaging company, divided into business units focused on different packaging solutions and materials, has common customers that use a variety of these solutions and materials.

Business Unit Alpha makes high-tech plastic film, and its No. 1 key account – let's call them 'X' – is designated so because its business is developing fast in the pre-packed, pre-cooked food industry where such high-tech films are going to be of increasing importance.

Business Unit Beta makes corrugated cardboard boxes and it also sells to customer 'X', but not in particularly large quantities.

Is customer 'X' defined as a key account for Business Unit Beta? Probably not. Is there a likelihood of 'difficulty' here? Absolutely.

What if Business Unit Beta, having defined customer 'X' as one of its opportunistic accounts, decides to let go a piece of business with 'X'? Perhaps, worse than that, it has to let 'X' down in order to meet the demands of one of its own key accounts? How does Business Unit Alpha feel about this?

Well, maybe it is so separate from Business Unit Beta that it doesn't even realize what has happened. So no problem? What if customer 'X', frustrated by the poor regard the supplier holds it in, chooses to take out its frustration on Business Unit Alpha? Plenty of scope for difficulties.

One 'solution' is to insist that any one business unit's KA must be regarded as the same by all other units. Seems logical, but just wait for the fights to start.

There is a larger question: does the supplier have anything to gain by acting more in concert? The answer to this will come primarily from the customer's perspective. Does the customer buy film and corrugated card, or does it buy packaging solutions?

Some businesses try to solve this problem by using hierarchies of key accounts. They might run as follows:

- the global key accounts that cross all business and regional boundaries;
- the regional key accounts;
- the business unit key accounts;
- the national key accounts;
- sometimes even the local sales representatives' key accounts.

There are two dangers in such hierarchies: confusing yourself and confusing the customer, which is quite enough confusion for anyone!

If such designations also come with clear definitions of responsibilities and accountabilities then they may yet succeed. Who will get first call on the resources available? Where will we aim to forge diamond relationships? How far will we allow the account to drive business decisions? Where does the ultimate responsibility for this customer lie? What is expected from support functions?

SHOULD WE TELL THE CUSTOMER?

KAM has been described as an outward-facing process, but there is one aspect that should perhaps remain internal – these labels of customer categories. Telling a key account their classification is one thing, but how about being told you are in 'maintenance', or are viewed 'opportunistically'?

So do you tell the key accounts? Perhaps it is about timing. If there is a right time to tell, then that is when you are about to do something that makes a difference; something that makes them sit up and take notice. If that time is still some way off, don't give yourself a rod for your own back by exciting their expectations with talk of their top-level status. You commit two sins by such 'careless talk'; first, prompting them to ask to what special prices, terms, services (and all the rest) this label of KA now entitles them, and second, almost certainly preparing them for a disappointment. This is a very quick way to kill KAM before you even start.

APPLICATION EXERCISE

This is a major exercise, best completed by a carefully selected team. Perhaps the most important part of this exercise is the identification of the factors used to judge attractiveness and relative strength.

After that, you can use the online software to conduct what I will call a 'quick and dirty' first cut, comparing up to 10 customers.

- Select six attractiveness factors:
  - Weight these factors.
  - Rate your customers against these factors.
- Select the relative strength factors (factors used by each customer to rate your performance):
  - Weight these factors.
  - Rate yourself against the competition.
- Assess the positioning of each customer on the key account identification and selection matrix:
  - Does it accord with your expectations?
  - If not, do you accept the positioning as indicated?
  - If not, were the factors used (or the ratings) at fault?

25

Customer distinction

In Chapter 24 we walked through Steps 1 to 4 of the six-step customer classification process. We start a new chapter for Steps 5 and 6, largely to make clear the change in the nature of the task and the challenge.

Steps 1 through 4 asked us to think and to analyse, Step 4 in particular asking the questions: who, and for what reasons? Steps 5 and 6 require us to do something about all that thinking, something that will make a difference to our business.

First, to remind ourselves of what these last two steps involve (see Figure 24.2):

- Step 5: Customer distinction strategies.
- Step 6: Communication, alignment and implementation.

STEP 5: CUSTOMER DISTINCTION STRATEGIES

By 'customer distinction' we mean: finding the means to distinguish between the four customer classifications defined by the KAISM exercise (see Figure 24.4). How will our approach to each of the four 'types' differ? Will our level of investment be different, will we approach the customer differently, will our contractual arrangements differ, will we have different service packages, and might even our prices and our terms perhaps differ?

If we end up with no distinction between the four customer types, then, quite apart from having wasted our time entirely, we will be committing three further sins, at the very least:

Three big sins...

- Sin number one: we make it impossible for those involved in servicing the customers to decide how to act, other than to give everyone the same, or to decide on their own prioritization.
- Sin number two: we will suffer from 'service creep'. Perhaps for an initial period, despite our failure to lay down lines of distinction, the key accounts will in fact get the best attention, the best ideas, the best services, indeed the best of everything, but it won't be long before jealous eyes from those involved with non-key accounts start to want the same things for their customers. Before long everyone will have what was once exclusive to the key accounts; so what was the point of setting them apart? Worse, it is very likely that the return on these non-key account investments will be less (and if they are not, then there was something wrong with your initial classification!). Worse still, the level of complexity with which you now burden your business might be fatal.
- Sin number three, and the worst of them all: you will never be able to free up enough time and energy from the non-key accounts to allow you to practise KAM in any meaningful way. It is very likely that the majority of your customers will be in the bottom right-hand box of the KAISM (see Figure 24.4) – the maintenance accounts. The failure to make clear what level of investment and attention is due with these customers will almost certainly mean that the majority of everybody's time will be taken up with these customers, denying you that time and effort for the key and key development accounts.

It is an irony that for many businesses the real challenge of KAM is not to be found in the management of the key accounts, but in finding new ways to look after those customers defined otherwise!

Figure 25.1 indicates the need to 'free up energy' from the maintenance accounts, and to invest that energy in the key and key development accounts. It also indicates the high likelihood that more energy will need to be invested into the key development accounts than the key accounts. This might surprise some in your organization, but a quick analogy with 'life' will make it clear why this situation is so common. Imagine the key development account as a person, a particularly attractive person, so attractive in fact that you feel you would like them to marry you. Unfortunately they don't appear to feel the same way about you, or at least they pay you very little attention (their affections may even be diverted elsewhere...). So you set out to 'court' them, and if we reflect for a moment on our own courting experiences (or others' if you are still too young) then most will admit I

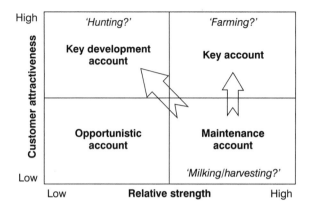

Figure 25.1 *Freeing up the energy…*

think that the efforts expended at this stage of human relationships are always significantly more than once success is achieved and the marriage knot is tied!

Figure 25.1 also suggests three different approaches to these customers, using words familiar to you I hope from Chapter 7. A certain amount of 'hunting' will be required with key development accounts, to open doors, to make a first impression, to achieve some 'quick wins', or just to be recognized. With key accounts the doors are wide open and our reputation is clear, so we move to a 'farming' approach. With our maintenance accounts the challenge is to withdraw resources, and yet maintain the business. If we are successful in this we might see that we are in effect 'milking' such customers, or perhaps a more attractive term is to think of it as 'harvesting'.

We have identified here, in this short comparison of approaches, the first basis of customer distinction. We must now look to the rest.

Determining the distinction strategies

For KAM to be effective, energy and resources must be liberated from the non-key accounts. For each customer type we need to develop distinct sales and service strategies that allow for this reallocation of resources.

First, identify the possible 'bases' for distinction – the things by which you will distinguish your offer, your services and your proposition to each customer type. Any or all of the following may be appropriate bases:

- expectation of ROI – profitability and the time horizon;
- frequency of contact;
- deployment of a team (or not);
- level and depth of contacts;

- involvement of senior management;
- nature of commitment to the customer;
- contracts – *long or short, or none at all;*
- allocation of resources;
- access to resources;
- availability of technology;
- commercial or technical 'openness';
- nature and number of projects;
- provision of services;
- whether we charge for services, or treat them as part of the package;
- terms and pricing;
- scope and detail of the account plan;
- direct supply or use of distributors;
- how the customer views us.

Next, for each possible base, ask how this would manifest itself with a key account, perhaps trying to identify a 'minimum and maximum' range. If the base was 'level and depth of contact', you might for instance require that contact was made with the customer's CEO, or as a minimum, the functional directors or vice-presidents.

Now repeat the same exercise for each of the other customer classifications. Using the same example base, the requirement for an opportunistic account may be no more than contact with the person who places the order.

Table 25.1 shows an example (and it is only that, please don't feel any obligation to copy any issues or points – your challenge is to formulate your own such table) of the finished result.

Outcomes to avoid

As well as the definitions of 'what you will do', there is one further thought you should give to your distinction strategies, and that is indicated by the last line of Table 25.1: what are the 'outcomes to avoid' with each customer type?

Beware of the short-term dangers of reducing resources or toughening up of the stance against maintenance accounts.

Take care not to destabilize the market as a result of short-term opportunistic activities with opportunistic accounts.

Beware the risk of 'over-egging' the package for key and key development accounts. With key accounts the 'cost to serve' (see Chapter 30) must always be in line with the expected return on the investment. With key development accounts take care not to get sucked into commitments that promise no return on the investment. In both case the wisest course of action is to measure closely the individual customer profitability (see Chapter 30 for more on this issue).

Table 25.1 *Customer distinction profiles*

Basis for distinction	Key account	Key development account	Maintenance account	Opportunistic account
Return on investment	Measured over a minimum 2–3 year period 'Lifetime value'	Be prepared to invest up front Have a clear timetable for anticipated returns Conduct regular reviews	Pay constant attention to enhancing profitability Take an 'accountant's' viewpoint on costs	Returns must be instant
At what level must we 'understand the customer'?	Business strategy Vision and drivers Market position View of our competitors Vendor ratings	Prepare analysis using the full diagnostic toolkit	Continually monitor for changes in their business strategy that might cause us to reclassify the account	Current needs
Nature of our contractual commitment	Full contract designed to promote trust and confidence, as a platform for developing full partnership	Take 'letter of intent' approach, outlining aspirations and expectations No financial penalties	Enter into full contract designed to protect current business and build barriers to exit	No contracts
Relationship and level of contacts	Diamond team Contact matrix GROWs for all KA team members	Focus on the key sponsors and influencers Involve senior management ASAP	Seek increasing efficiency of contacts Make greater use of 'inside sales' team	Bow-tie relationship
Account plan	Full written KA plan Focus on long-term growth and profitability	Draft plan Focus on short-term wins	Summary plan Focus on building barriers to exit	No written plan Sales forecast
Customer's perception of us	Their No 1 'helper' A strategic supplier Supplier of >60 per cent share	A bringer of specific and targeted improvements A key supplier	Steady and reliable Eager to keep our business	Commercially astute 'We can do a deal with these guys'

continued

Table 25.1 *Continued*

Basis for distinction	Key account	Key development account	Maintenance account	Opportunistic account
Allocation of resource	Agreed internally on an annual basis Agreed with customer against clear returns	Allocate resources against clear and realistic targets Timetable of ROI	Continually withdraw resources where there is no negative impact	Sales only
Provision of services	Formally agreed service levels Formal access to R&D	Allocate services against clear and realistic targets Timetable of ROI	provide standard technical service	Always charged at commercial rates
Nature and number of projects	Projects formally agreed by the account team Financial investment where required	Draw up small list of highly targeted projects with clear criteria for success	Provide 'copy/paste' projects	Only short-term projects No financial support
Availability of technology	Full collaboration High speed of delivery	Top speed of delivery Tailored 'new' technology	Limited support on 'modifications' Medium speed of delivery	Existing 'off the shelf' technology No development work
Pricing	Value based	Market based	Value based	Tactical, based on our available capacity
Overall strategy	Farmer Long-term focus	Focused hunter Short-term wins to establish credibility	Seeking 'lock-in' Raising barriers to exit	Opportunistic hunter
Outcomes to avoid….	Higher than justified 'cost to serve' KAM bureaucracy	Getting locked into commitments with little or no return	Becoming complacent Treating the customer as a second-class citizen	Destabilizing the market

Removing resources

One of the toughest things to action is the removal of resources or services from maintenance accounts. They may have been in receipt of these things for a very long time, and will inevitably regard their removal as a form of abandonment; or will they?

The critical thing to understand is, what value do they currently put on each of the activities, services or interactions with you? If it is high then you must of course proceed with caution, but what if it is low? It is not unusual to discover that many of the interactions that were once of high value have ceased to be so. Times change. If that is the case then do yourself the favour (and the customer) of terminating all the 'unwanted Christmas presents'. These things cost you money, they sap your strength, and they no longer impress the customer, or worse, they make the customer question your true understanding of their needs, or worse still, they only go to explain why you are so expensive! All members of the KA team should be charged with continual vigilance in this regard.

Don't give unwanted Christmas presents

STEP 6: COMMUNICATION, ALIGNMENT AND IMPLEMENTATION

Perhaps the most important step of all six: getting the whole organization behind the decisions taken through this customer classification process. Do they understand the need for the classifications and the basis upon which they have been made? Do they understand and accept the implications of the customer distinction profiles? Will they now give full active support to the plans for each customer type, and in particular to those identified as key or key development accounts?

There is a great deal to be done, so much that the whole of Part VIII is devoted to this particular part of the KAM challenge.

APPLICATION EXERCISE

- Brainstorm the means by which you could distinguish between the four customer types described in the key account identification and selection matrix.
- For each selected means of customer distinction, identify the appropriate application for each of the four customer types:
  - Draw up your own version of Table 25.1.
- How will you use this to help free up your energy from the maintenance and opportunistic accounts?
- How will you ensure that these 'packages' are communicated to all those who will be involved in their delivery?

Part VIII

Making it happen: preparing for KAM

26

Sins and requirements

To repeat: the challenge of KAM is not in the concept or theory, nor in the tools and processes to be used, it is squarely in the task of practical implementation. It is the long list of things that can get in its way that present the main problems, the vast majority of which are internal. It is rarely the customer or the competition that prevents you from making KAM work; it is your own organization.

THE SINS

The following list of 'deadly sins' is compiled after many years of encountering pretty much the same obstacles almost everywhere I go. In fact, the day that I meet an organization that suffers not one of these sins is the day I hang up my trainer's boots.

In life there are said to be seven deadly sins; pride, covetousness, lust, envy, gluttony, anger and sloth – we may encounter some of those in our pursuit of KAM, but there are many more besides:

Problems with leadership and organization

- inertia and complacency – no 'burning platform';
- unclear (sometimes conflicting) goals;
- top management short-termism;

- unrealistic expectations regarding the timing and scale of the return on the investment;
- abandoning the concept in times of crisis;
- the 'silo mentality', with managers as 'barons';
- clashes of objectives, priorities and performance measures across functions;
- inappropriate operational excellence;
- functions not talking to each other;
- competition between business units for the same customer;
- disputes between business units (whose key account is this anyway?);
- too many key accounts;
- inadequate customer classification (see Chapter 24);
- inadequate customer distinction (see Chapter 25);
- service creep (see Chapter 25);
- no plan for freeing up the energy from non-key accounts (see Chapter 25).

Problems with skills and capabilities

- resistance from the sales team.... a preference for 'hunting' (see Chapter 7);
- insufficient authority for the KA managers and KA teams;
- inappropriate skills in the KA managers;
- inappropriate people or skills in the supporting team;
- a non-streetwise supporting team;
- poor plans for personal development, recruitment, or succession planning.

Problems with IT and systems

- too much IT – the straitjacket of processes and templates;
- too little IT – inadequate means of analysing, recording and communicating;
- existing systems no longer appropriate but too deeply imbedded to change.

Problems with measuring profitability

- inadequate measures of customer profitability;
- no process for assessing investment propositions.

Problems with KA plans

- no formal, written KA plans;
- the 'telephone directory' plans;
- the 'top-secret' plan;
- KAM as a planning bureaucracy;

- the failure to include the people (contact matrix and GROWs);
- the failure to identify the value proposition.

Problems with tracking the progress

- failure to measure the impact, positive and negative;
- failure to measure or communicate successes;
- no plans for developing capabilities.

Some of these 'sins' have been discussed in earlier chapters (as noted above). The majority of the remainder will be dealt with in the following chapters (27 through 32).

It is a daunting list, but can be made more manageable by a few simple questions: from which do you suffer, and about which you can do something? Nobody will be unlucky enough to suffer them all, but a company completely free of any of these sins, even after consistently applied efforts, I have yet to meet. Don't get hung up about curing everything before you start; rather like Alcoholics Anonymous, recognizing that you have the problem is half the battle.

Sign the pledge...

Making it happen is not about seeking perfection; rather, it is about establishing priorities, and working with what you have. KAM demands a high degree of realism, and the wisdom to know when change is necessary and when to just get on with things.

THE REQUIREMENTS: *MAKING IT HAPPEN*

Figure 26.1 repeats the KAM model already encountered, now surrounded by the range of actions, capabilities and processes required for KAM to truly come to life. Each of these areas of requirement will be dealt with in the following chapters (27 through 32).

Figure 26.1 *The requirements for making it happen*

APPLICATION EXERCISE

- Assess your own company's current KAM performance against the 'sins' listed in this chapter:
  - Do you suffer any additional 'sins'?
- What are the three most serious obstacles to your own progress?
- What actions are required to clear these obstacles?

27

Leadership and organization

LEADERSHIP: MANAGING CHANGE

Without leadership from the top, the very top, KAM will falter at each of the hurdles, and a fall will become increasingly likely. But what does 'leadership' mean?

There are more books written on this question than on almost any other facet of business management, very often from the perspective of one or more 'corporate heroes'. I don't propose to go down the 'do it their way' route, but to limit my advice on leadership to a 10-point list of (perhaps rather obvious) requirements, all based on the principles of change management:

- Have a clear picture of why KAM is required – and communicate it.
- Create the vision of where you want to be through the practice of KAM.
- Communicate that vision, ensuring full alignment across all functions.
- Identify the obstacles and establish a list of critical success factors (CSFs) by which to guide the removal of those obstacles.
- Ensure the right organizational structure.
- Ensure the right capabilities, and provide sufficient authority for those that need to act.
- Have the right performance management process in place – targets, monitoring and rewards.
- Celebrate and promote the successes (establish winning approaches) and learn from the setbacks (modify the approaches).

- Institutionalize the new approaches.
- Be involved, as a leader, and as a team member.

The burning platform

One of my clients refers to the 'burning platform' as a means of identifying and describing the 'burning need' for KAM. The notion is, the more dire the outcome of failing to practise KAM (the hotter the platform), the more likely people will be to respond and pursue the necessary changes with alacrity. It's an approach.

Others feel that people don't change when they are caught like a rabbit in the headlights. They argue that the best way to manage change is by simple and modest steps, almost imperceptibly, not by urgent calls to arms. It's another approach.

You must take your pick, or more likely, find the appropriate middle course between these two 'poles'. What is certain, whatever your approach, is the need to have clarity on why KAM is so important. There will have to be an internal debate, involving the full spectrum of interested parties, and yes, the urgency of the need must be apparent. Urgency is fine; it just doesn't have to be handled as an emergency (unless that is genuinely the truth of the matter!).

We have just described the first step of a model that you will recall from Chapter 23, the 'change equation', illustrated again in Figure 27.1.

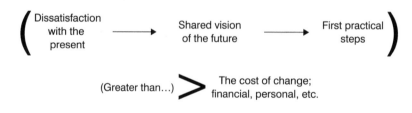

Figure 27.1 *The change equation*

It is necessary to establish a level of dissatisfaction with the current situation if you wish people to go through the efforts that KAM implies. Complacency is the biggest sin at the outset, given the inertia of all your existing approaches and processes, processes that may still be working well enough for now.

Where complacency exists – and the worst kind is reflected in that most awful of all comments: 'If it ain't broke, why fix it?' – then it will be necessary to project this feeling of dissatisfaction into the future: not just, 'What's going wrong around here today?' but also, 'What's going to be even worse tomorrow?'. (Incidentally, the best response to that awful phrase is: 'if it ain't broke, it will be…')

There may be all sorts of reasons for dissatisfaction; the following lists just some of the most typical:

- losing customers;
- falling sales;
- falling profits;
- competitors gaining ground;
- failure to seize new opportunities;
- growing customer dissatisfaction;
- an unresponsive organization;
- internal squabbles over priorities;
- rising costs of selling, with inadequate returns;
- failure to penetrate the customer's decision-making processes;
- failure of new product development;
- failure to secure key supplier status;
- not getting on the customers' radar screens.

Vision and goals

Stirring up doom and gloom is not of course the aim; thoughtful concern would be a better target. Scared or depressed people are no easier to change than the smug and complacent ones. Dissatisfaction is only the start of the change process and you will soon be an unwelcome Cassandra if that is all you generate. The next step is to work on the thoughts of how things might be, to establish and communicate the shared vision of the future.

The key word here is 'shared'. There will be alternative views, but there must ultimately be one agreed vision. More internal debate, perhaps even argument, with patience and diplomacy ever to the fore. The aim is the alignment of all functions behind an agreed vision, which might suggest compromise, but do try to avoid the mediocrity and mutual dissatisfaction of compromises made for compromise sake. Sometimes leadership involves forcing the issue.

Goal 'hierarchies'

There will be goals for the business, goals for KAM, and goals for individual key accounts. They must all join up, of course, and sometimes it may help the process of goal setting for KAM to start at the two ends (the business, and the individual accounts) and aim to meet up in the middle. Does that sound lazy, or fatalistic, or being led by your customers rather than your own good sense? If so, just remember that if KAM is about customer focus, then shouldn't the results of that focus be played back into your strategic direction? We are of course in the land of the chicken and the egg, but that is the eternal reality of strategy formation.

Cross-functional alignment

KAM cannot succeed as a sales initiative. The vision must be business wide, relevant to all functions. Everyone, whether sales, customer service, marketing, finance, production, distribution, legal, HR and all the rest, must be able to answer:

KAM is not for sales alone

- What will KAM do for us?
- What must we do for KAM?
- What will KAM do for the customer?
- What must we do for the customer?
- What will KAM look and feel like?
- How must we change?

One of the biggest obstacles to cross-functional alignment is undoubtedly the matter of performance measurement. Different functions use different measures.

A production manager might be measured on 'occupacity' – the ability to use the plant to ensure maximum output. A key account manager might approach that manager with a 'customer-focused' request – to produce a modified product. Let's say that this might involve closing the production line, a re-tooling, a relatively short production run, another close down, another re-tooling, and then back to where we left off. Should the key account manager be surprised if the production manager treats the idea as a joke?

The head of logistics might see the world differently again. By their very nature, logistics and distribution functions crave regularity and order. Customer-focused key account managers who come with short-notice orders (which might be helping the customer out of a big hole and so winning bags of loyalty) are not always welcomed.

Might the solution be found in the world of professional basketball? Anyone that follows professional basketball will know about the host of statistics that surround the game. There seems to be a measure for every single aspect. Players' performances are measured with merciless accuracy – that is the nature of the professional game.

Learning from the world of professional basketball…

Two measures stand out – 'baskets', and 'assists': that is, how many times they put the ball through the hoop, and how many times their 'play' helped another player put the ball through the hoop. Couldn't some functions be measured on 'assists'?

The critical success factors (CSFs)

Despite the advice from some business 'gurus' that the role of leaders is to foment upheaval and chaos, it is usually best to avoid revolutions wherever possible, and in the field of KAM very much so. The key accounts are your most important customers, and they don't want to be on the receiving end of any such 'upheaval and chaos'; they would almost certainly rather it was 'business as usual'.

Sticking with our change equation (Figure 27.1), aim to agree the 'first practical steps' to get things moving. These do not have to be dramatic – almost better if they are not. The agreement of a list of those things most vital to our success (the CSFs) often provides such a first step.

Again, a fully cross-functional debate will be required, and at a senior level. Repeat the urgency for KAM, present the vision again, and then aim to identify the obstacles to that vision (see Chapter 26's list of 'deadly sins'). Now you can turn to those things that must be in place for the obstacles to be overcome and for KAM success to blossom.

CSFs: an example list

The following is a list of CSFs, identified by a real business at the early stage of embracing the KAM philosophy, based on a full examination of the obstacles to progress and success. (Please note: it is not given as a template, but solely as an example of how such a list might look.)

- KAM must be a cross-business process, supported at senior levels, with objectives and responsibilities that supersede those of individual functions or departments.
- Everyone must understand and share the purpose and objectives of KAM.
- KA teams must have the capabilities and resources to focus on the customer's processes and the customer's markets.
- KA teams must have sufficient authority to develop value propositions designed to increase customer prosperity and secure key supplier status.
- Team members must have the right skills and understanding to carry out a customer-intimate role – interpersonal skills and commercial awareness are top priorities.
- There must be a system for cross-business communication (including the customer) and the necessary skills and disciplines to make it work.
- We must all understand the dynamics of team working.
- We must have enhanced skills of project management.
- Attention to detail. We require relevant, customer-focused operational excellence from all functions.
- There must be a system for measuring progress on the KAM journey and for assessing the benefits to our customers and ourselves.
- We must be able to measure customer profitability.
- There must be written and easily updateable KA plans.

Ensuring the right capabilities and sufficient authority

This aspect of the leadership task will be covered in Chapter 28.

Performance management

Much time and creative thought has been given by sales managers to the reward and recognition of their salespeople, using every kind of package from straight salary to 100 per cent commission, and all stops in-between.

Reward in the KAM environment requires a new kind of creativity. The solutions must be designed to suit your own circumstances, and must above all else be designed to support the business objectives, but the following four questions might stimulate your own debate:

- On what criteria should rewards be based?
- Do you reward the KA manager or the KA team?
- Given the 'rarity' of good KA managers, how do you keep them in place?
- What is the value of sales awards?

Reward criteria

Sales volume is unlikely to be the best measure, although it is certainly the easiest. Better measures will be those that emphasize the key account as an investment. Profitability is therefore to be preferred, but it is much harder to measure (see Chapter 30).

There should also be measures that relate to the nature of the task, such as building the relationship. Customer satisfaction ratings should also be included. Of course the best measure of all is to track what progress is made towards the objectives set down in the key account plan. This linkage of reward to objective setting, planning and successful implementation will also help establish the responsibilities of KAM on the same level as business management, which is precisely where they should be.

The KA manager or the KA team?

This one is very simple: it must be the team. This requires the formal creation of a team with clear goals, roles, obligations and work plans (GROWs – see Chapter 8) for each member and for the team as a whole. Up until the point that such a team exists, the reward might be related in part to the KA manager's ability to form the team.

Keeping them in place

The Royal Air Force has come up with a neat solution to a problem not so dissimilar to that for keeping able and ambitious KA managers in place. This isn't raised as a suggestion so much as a means to simulate your own debate.

If you joined the RAF to fly planes then you could do so up to the rank of squadron leader, but after that if you wanted promotion you had to take a desk job. This was a significant problem for those who had joined the RAF to fly.

The solution was to allow those officers who wanted to continue flying to continue moving up a salary ladder that might ultimately see them paid the same as those in ranks well above them, while still remaining themselves at the rank of squadron leader.

R&D functions often practise something similar, for those people that want to 'stay by the bench'. The so-called 'scientific ladder' allows for increases in reward without the need for a move into general management.

Could a 'sales ladder' do the same for KA managers?

Sales awards

I confess to not being a great fan of such things, my experience being that even when KAM is the preferred methodology in a company the award too often goes to the salesperson that won the most exciting piece of new business that year – a hunters' charter.

In the KAM environment, you might like to consider two changes. First, give the award to a KA team, not to an individual. Second, consider giving the award to the KA team that has retained the most business in difficult circumstances – a real test of KAM farming skill, especially in a mature market.

Handling success and failure

Sir Winston Churchill's view was that 'success is about going from failure to failure without any loss of enthusiasm'. Rudyard Kipling described success and failure as 'those two impostors', the handling of which proved you to be a 'man'. Perhaps there is some truth in both these thoughts for those involved in KAM.

Celebrate success at every opportunity, and use it to guide the creation of new approaches and processes. Learn from the failures, modifying the approaches and processes as you proceed.

Most importantly of all, don't leave these examples of good practice and lessons learned as isolated anecdotes, but aim to institutionalize them as the formal approaches and processes for KAM.

Being involved

Leadership in the KAM arena implies involvement. Senior managers must be involved in setting the strategy, in removing the obstacles, and as active members of KA teams. They may also perform the role of senior 'mentors' for the KA managers, helping them through those difficult moments of cross-functional tension, providing the boost to authority that such moments demand (you might call it 'knocking heads together' if you prefer).

ORGANIZATION AND STRUCTURE

The mortal enemy of KAM is the silo-based organization. Figure 27.2 illustrates what we might call the 'no chance structure'.

What hope is there for a KA manager, buried at the bottom of the hierarchy, to build and lead a truly cross-functional team? It can be done of course, and there are examples of KA managers working hard, against all the odds, and still pulling off minor miracles. One such described the experience to me as something of a cross between an army assault course and an on-the-job MBA. So there are heroes, but isn't there a better way than to have to rely on such rarities?

If teams are to be truly cross-functional, if the functions are to be aligned behind a customer-focused vision, if performance measures are to be based on customer satisfaction, and if the business decision-making process is to be driven by customer requirements, then isn't all of that going to turn the organization upside down? So why not do it?

Figure 27.3 shows the comparison between a traditional hierarchy and a possible KAM driven hierarchy – the organization has been turned upside down. In traditional hierarchies, the management sits at the top and the people with customer contact sit lower down, often at the bottom. In a KAM hierarchy, the people with customer contact (whether salespeople, customer service, distribution or whoever) are placed right at the top, with the lines of management beneath. If you can't be rid of silos, then at least turn them in the direction of the customer.

So what? The message is perhaps mainly symbolic, but well expressed by one new manager when he took over a major company that he felt was arrogant and distant from its customers. This was how he addressed his first meeting with the senior management team:

> 'If in your job you don't actually meet with customers, then you had better make damned sure you support someone who does.'

In time it becomes more than symbolism as KA teams are empowered to act on behalf of their customer.

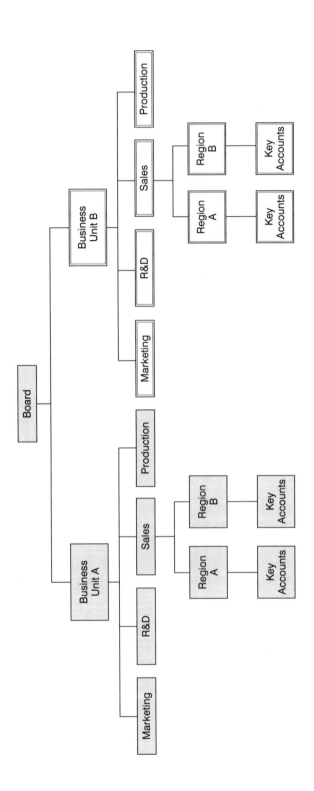

Figure 27.2 *Silo-based structures*

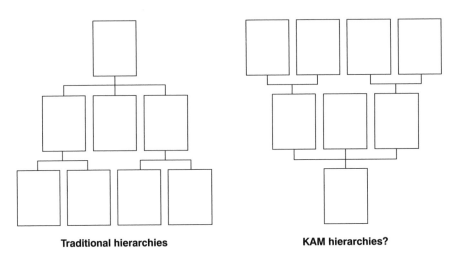

Traditional hierarchies

KAM hierarchies?

Figure 27.3 *The organization turned upside down*

The point being made with upside-down structure charts (or perhaps we should start to call them right-way-up charts) is that the management structure should exist to service those who service the customers. The same point can be made for the functions: they exist for the customers, not for their own definitions of operational excellence.

Letting the customer be your guide

The perfect structure is not possible, there are too many conflicting interests for that to be so: the eternal battle between external needs and internal preferences. You must make your choice as to whether you favour one side or another in this battle, or can find a 'right down the middle' compromise, but if KAM is to be a genuine part of your business you might need to lean towards allowing your structure to develop on the basis of the customers' view of the world.

Customers will have little sympathy for structures that might mean something to the supplier but have no positive benefit for them. Worse, if they see the supplier's structure as an obstacle to their progress then the writing will be on the wall. It is interesting to note that whereas in the past a good supplier would always try to secure an 'organogram', or structure chart, of their customer, it is now quite normal for the customer to ask its supplier to provide details and explanations of *their* structures. This is so that they can judge how easy it will be for them to do business with the supplier, and assess what level of importance they will have in the supplier's organization. If they see something like that shown in Figure 27.2, what do you imagine they will conclude?

Learning from your customer...

311

Businesses that are responsive to their markets will already be guided by their customers when it comes to determining their own structure. If the customers demand low, and steadily decreasing prices, then a structure that helps promote internal cost reductions will probably have developed. If the route to lower prices is through economies of scale then manufacturing will perhaps take a lead role, driving the business through forecasting and supply chain processes. The sales effort will be focused on volume, in a business driven by operational excellence (see Chapter 18 for an explanation of the 'operational excellence' driver).

If, on the other hand, the customers demand high-tech products with 'added-value' services, then we might expect to find R&D in a more prominent position, working in close collaboration with sales. We might expect a business and structure driven by product leadership and/or customer intimacy (see Chapter 18 for an explanation of these two drivers).

Multi-business, multi-unit, multi-site suppliers might find some sense in having separate sales teams for the same customer, but often the customer does not see things the same way. Duplication of contacts is bad enough, but if this complexity also leads to different terms, conditions, service levels and the rest, then the customer will not be satisfied. The pressure will be on to change the organization in response to customer demand – not a bad motivation, but it is always best if the organization can pre-empt such demands and look at their own organization from the customer's perspective first.

The matrix structure

Figure 27.4 illustrates the almost inevitable matrix 'structure' that emerges from the practice of KAM. It is neither regular nor uniform, but depends on the involvement of different functions in different accounts. Whether this becomes the basis of an actual structure, or simply illustrates some different internal relationships, will be entirely the choice of those involved, and there is much to be said in favour of either outcome.

It is probably fair to say that as a structure it will not be liked by those who crave neatness in such matters, but if the task is to find something that is effective then it certainly deserves some serious consideration.

Evolution not revolution

The peril with changing organizational structures is that in the pursuit of new objectives you can easily risk losing whatever worked before. In view of this, evolution rather than revolution may be no bad thing. Figure 27.5 illustrates a typical evolution.

If we go back 30 years we would find many companies structured along geographical lines. Perhaps they moved away from that basis, moving

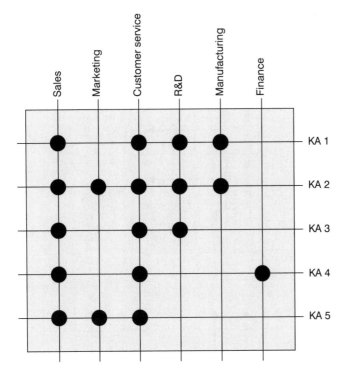

Figure 27.4 *The inevitable matrix*

towards a business-unit-led structure – the predominant format for much of the 1980s and 1990s. Today we see those structures morphing once more, towards market segment or channel-based organizations. It is not too hard to see how the next shift might take them into key-account-led structures.

KAM and downsizing?

Some businesses see KAM as an opportunity to reduce the size of the sales force, replacing regional structures of field-based reps with a small team of KA managers, perhaps supported by a customer service office of inside-sales people.

If this is an opportunity for you, take care that your thinking is led by the nature of the market and its demands, and not by your desire to cut costs. **Be very, very careful...**

Pharmaceutical companies have made drastic cuts to their sales teams in recent years. Some justify the cuts by reference to insupportable cost structures and the need to protect the bottom line. Others argue that the cuts reflect the changing demands of the market and a move away from call-rate driven sales towards a more efficient account management basis. Assuming that both are right in their analysis, I leave you to decide who has the better motivation.

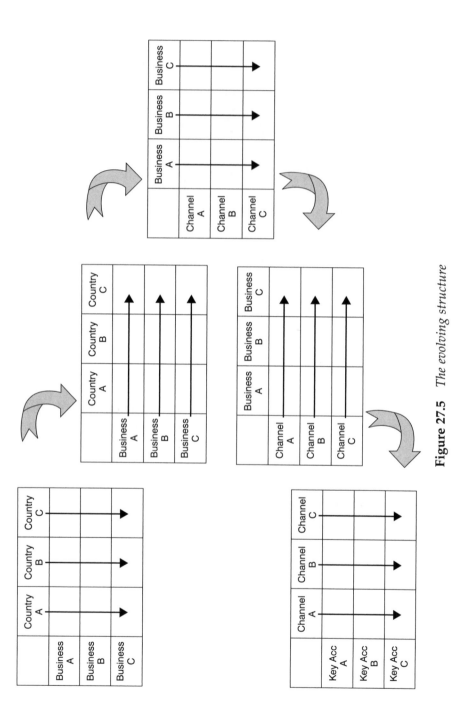

Figure 27.5 *The evolving structure*

314

APPLICATION EXERCISE

- Assess your own company's leadership performance against the 10 requirements listed at the beginning of this chapter:
  - What needs to be improved?
- Identify the CSFs (the factors critical to your own success) appropriate to your own circumstances:
  - Do these suggest major or minor change?
  - How will this change process be managed?
- What are the most important aspects of *performance management* to be considered for your KAM strategy to succeed?
  - Will this involve major or minor change?
  - How will this change process be managed?
- Assess your own structure and organization:
  - Is it appropriate for the KAM challenge?
  - If not, what needs to change?
  - How will this change process be managed?

28

The skills required

We come now to what I once heard a senior manager dismiss as the 'soft stuff', as if it was a minor frill placed on top of the 'far more important' tools and processes. I would rather call it the 'hard stuff', inasmuch as it is one of the hardest parts of the whole KAM package to get right, and without the right skills in place no amount of tools or processes will advance you an inch.

There was a time when the question of what skills are required was asked only of the KA manager. Many an HR manager was given the impossible task of tracking down the kind of superhero capable of handling every part of the task, solo. The error made was in thinking the KAM task a simple extension of the traditional sales task.

The following list represents the range of skills required in what we might call a 'traditional sales professional':

- product knowledge;
- interpersonal skills;
- presentation skills;
- negotiation skills;
- self-organization;
- time management;
- territory management;
- independence.

It is quite possible to find individual possessing all of these skills, or at least to regard the 'full set' as trainable. Let us now turn to the skill set required for the KAM task – and please note that this list is a very much a top-line summary:

- strategic thinking;
- strategic influencing;
- business management;
- project management;
- team leadership;
- team working;
- innovation and creativity;
- coordination;
- managing change;
- managing diversity;
- coaching;
- 'political entrepreneurship'.

Do you have what it takes?

What becomes clear when we consider the KAM task is just how multi-faceted it is. Do you honestly expect to find anyone who is good at all this? And if you do, what will you have to pay to keep them?!

Fortunately this is not a problem you need think about; the solution is not to be found in superheroes, but in a team. The KA team should be constructed with care, not only to take into consideration the customer contact strategy required (see Chapter 8) but also the mix of skills required in the team. We will see a little later that there is also a third consideration, that of each team member's 'team role'.

Looking to the team for these skills does not mean that KA managers can simply get on with what they always used to do as 'lone' sales professionals. If they do indeed come from that background then they are about to be faced with a very significant change in their role. To use a musical analogy, they must be able to put down their violin – whatever their virtuoso ability – and pick up the conductor's baton. Their role is to conduct the orchestra. Their ability to motivate others, to delegate tasks and to coordinate a team-sell becomes paramount.

Given that nature of their new 'conducting' role, there are of course some 'must have' skills for the KA manager (not everything can be delegated to the team!). These will of course depend on the circumstances, but in most cases I have found the following three to be the top priorities:

- team leadership;
- coaching;
- political entrepreneurship.

The 'must haves'...

TEAM LEADERSHIP

This is not about being the boss, but it is about having authority. Wielding authority as a result of your job title (what we might call 'given' authority) is a relatively easy task, but to have and to demonstrate authority through your behaviours and attitudes ('earned' authority) takes skill.

There are many ways to earn authority; the following lists some of the more important in the KAM environment:

- Demonstrate knowledge, but be honest about what you don't know; 'bluffing' is the fastest way to be found out.
- Consult the experts, and demonstrate your ability to listen.
- Involve senior management, but don't let them steal your clothes; you remain the conductor of the orchestra.
- Demonstrate confidence, but always be realistic; 'boosting' is another sure way to be found out.
- Demonstrate 'inclusive leadership'; show interest in, and empathy for, the views of others; actively seek diverse opinions; explain your decisions.
- Coach, don't tell.
- Demonstrate structure in your thinking and organization in your planning; a well-prepared KA plan is very important in this respect.
- Give regular feedback, communicate progress, don't hide from bad news and setbacks.

What sort of leader?

Figure 28.1 shows the 'leadership spectrum', a choice of approaches ranging from being 100 per cent directive to acting as the master of empowerment. The choice of where to pitch can only depend on your circumstances, but there is a good chance that at the early stages of KAM you will need to stand somewhere 'left of centre', aiming to move to the right as fast as circumstances allow.

Team dynamics

There are dozens of different models for team working. I have chosen two as being of particular relevance and use in the KAM environment: the team role model of Dr Meredith Belbin, and the notion of the 'team clock'.

Belbin team roles: the team in practice

The KA team 'in practice' must be more than a collection of job titles. To work as an effective unit, bearing in mind the almost inevitable personality clashes, the competing egos, the politics, and the shrinking violets who

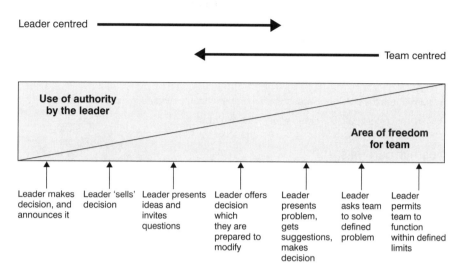

Figure 28.1   *The leadership spectrum*

contribute nothing but in fact know all the answers, the KA manager will need to give consideration to what Dr Belbin calls the 'team roles'.

There are nine roles identified in the Belbin model, each having a distinct and valuable contribution to make to the successful working of the whole team. Each role has its positive qualities, and also what Belbin calls its allowable weakness – the price you pay for the strength. Figures 28.2 through to 28.10 summarize these points.

The 'ideal' team will need to contain all roles, but that does not mean you need a team of nine – each team member will probably display two, or maybe three of the roles within their make-up and personality.

The teams to avoid are those made up of the same type – a group of perfectly cloned statistically minded analysts might get on well together, but they will never complete the task in hand. Similarly, a room full of hard-driving, objective-led extroverts might make a lot of appropriate sounding noise, but come to an agreed conclusion? No chance.

Some simple questionnaires can help the team to identify the roles most likely to be played by each member, and once that is done a little analysis should follow:

- What roles, if any, are missing, or under-represented?
  - What will be the implication of that for team performance?
  - What can you do to compensate?
- What roles are 'abundant', perhaps even over-represented?
  - What will be the implication of that for team performance?
  - What can you do to mitigate that?

THE *COORDINATOR'S* CONTRIBUTION

- Coordinates the way the team moves towards group objectives
- Make best use of team resources
- Recognizes team strengths and weaknesses
- Maximizes the potential of each team member through encouragement
- Acts as a focal point for group effort in tough times

POSITIVE QUALITIES

- Welcomes all contributions on their merit
- Listens without prejudice, remains focused on the main objective
- The team's ringmaster

ALLOWABLE WEAKNESSES

- Is unlikely to be the most creative member of the team

WHAT TO WATCH OUT FOR

- Obstinacy vs. determination

Figure 28.2 *The coordinator*
from the work of Dr Meredith Belbin

THE *RESOURCE-INVESTIGATOR'S* CONTRIBUTION

- Explores and reports on ideas and developments outside the team
- Creates external contacts
- The best person to set up external contracts

POSITIVE QUALITIES

- Capacity for contacting people and exploring anything new
- Enthusiasm and a source of external ideas
- Ability to respond to challenge
- The team's detective

ALLOWABLE WEAKNESSES

- Low boredom threshold, needs stimulus of others, may spend time on irrelevancies

WHAT TO WATCH OUT FOR

- Too much involvement in own ideas rather than those of the team

Figure 28.3 *The resource investigator*
from the work of Dr Meredith Belbin

THE *SHAPER'S* CONTRIBUTION

- Directs the way in which team effort is channeled
- Focuses attention on objectives and priorities
- Results oriented and competitive
- Pushing through change

POSITIVE QUALITIES

- A readiness to challenge politics and inertia
- Tough on complacency and self-deception
- The architect of the team

ALLOWABLE WEAKNESSES

- Prone to provocation, irritation and impatience

WHAT TO WATCH OUT FOR

- Arrogance and pushiness
- Steamrolling colleagues into a course of action

Figure 28.4 *The shaper*
from the work of Dr Meredith Belbin

THE *COMPLETER-FINISHER'S* CONTRIBUTION

- Ensures nothing has been overlooked
- Checks details
- Maintains a sense of urgency
- Invaluable where accuracy and deadlines are important

POSITIVE QUALITIES

- Capacity for follow-through
- High standards in quality and delivery
- The team's workhorse

ALLOWABLE WEAKNESSES

- Tendency to worry about small things
- Reluctant to let go

WHAT TO WATCH OUT FOR

- Getting bogged down in details

Figure 28.5 *The complete finisher*
from the work of Dr Meredith Belbin

THE *IMPLEMENTER'S* CONTRIBUTION

- Turns concepts and plans into practical working procedures – does what has to be done
- Carries out agreed plans systematically and efficiently

POSITIVE QUALITIES

- Organizing ability, practical common sense
- Self-disciplined, hard-working, trustworthy
- The process controller of the team

ALLOWABLE WEAKNESSES

- Lack of flexibility, unresponsive to new or unproven ideas

WHAT TO WATCH OUT FOR

- Criticising others for their lack of pragmatism
- Getting stuck in a rut

Figure 28.6 *The implementer*
from the work of Dr Meredith Belbin

THE *MONITOR-EVALUATOR'S* CONTRIBUTION

- Analyses problems, evaluates ideas and suggestions
- Enables the team to take balanced decisions
- Checks and balances

POSITIVE QUALITIES

- Judgement, objectivity, discretion, hard-headedness
- The team's conscience

ALLOWABLE WEAKNESSES

- May lack inspiration and ability to motivate others
- Can appear aloof and even negative

WHAT TO WATCH OUT FOR

- Criticising others too frequently
- Lack of awareness of the big picture

Figure 28.7 *The monitor evaluator*
from the work of Dr Meredith Belbin

THE *TEAM WORKER'S* CONTRIBUTION

- Supports other team members
- Builds on suggestions
- Compensates for other team members' shortcomings
- Fosters a team spirit
- Ensures internal communications are kept up

POSITIVE QUALITIES

- Ability to respond to people and situations
- Enthusiasm
- The team's 'glue'

ALLOWABLE WEAKNESSES

- Indecisive, especially under pressure

WHAT TO WATCH OUT FOR

- Stress, especially within internally competitive teams

Figure 28.8 *The team worker*
from the work of Dr Meredith Belbin

THE *PLANT'S* CONTRIBUTION

- New ideas and creativity
- A creative approach to problem solving
- Challenging the status quo

POSITIVE QUALITIES

- Lateral thinking
- The 'spark' of the team

ALLOWABLE WEAKNESSES

- Inclined to disregard processes and protocols

WHAT TO WATCH OUT FOR

- Handling criticism badly – switching off
- Becoming an ivory tower

Figure 28.9 *The plant*
from the work of Dr Meredith Belbin

THE *SPECIALIST'S* CONTRIBUTION

- Specific skills and work-related capabilities

POSITIVE QUALITIES

- High level of functional skill and knowledge
- Professional standards
- Commitment
- Pride in their work

ALLOWABLE WEAKNESSES

- Lack of interest in other's roles

WHAT TO WATCH OUT FOR

- Can become too single minded
- Slow to change if their specialization is threatened

Figure 28.10   *The specialist*
from the work of Dr Meredith Belbin

For help on how to assess the Belbin team roles and apply the model to your own team, see Chapters 28 and 33.

The team clock

You are perhaps already familiar with the terms; 'forming', 'storming', 'norming' and 'performing', as applied to team working. Figure 28.11 illustrates these four stages of team development around a clock face.

All teams must go through these four stages, from initial 'forming', where everyone is nervously polite and not much gets done, through the painful but necessary 'storming' stage where arguments abound but the resultant friction helps to start things moving, on to the stage called 'norming' where team rules start to be established, and on (it is hoped) to the 'performing' stage.

Identify where your own team stands at present – at what time of the clock? What are the limitations of this position? Where would you like to be within three or six months – at what time of the clock?

COACHING

It has already been noted that among the challenges of the diamond team approach are that few if any of the supplier team members will work

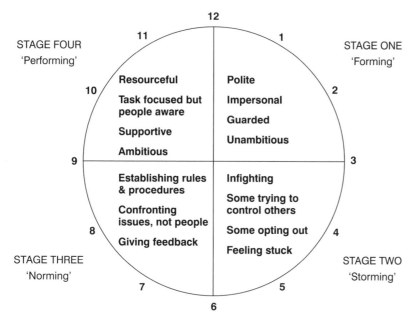

Figure 28.11 *The team clock*

directly for the KA manager, they may also be senior to the KA manager, and given their individual speciality they will very likely be more knowledgeable and expert. The use of the contact matrix and GROW mechanism (see Chapter 8) is only part of the answer; of much greater importance will be the ability of the KA manager to coach the team members.

Coaching is a big topic, too often ignored, and very likely to be one of your higher priorities when it comes to training and development. It requires professional training (see Chapter 33) with plenty of skills practice, so I will limit myself here to just one observation. Sales professionals often think they will be good coaches because they are good talkers, good presenters and good persuaders. Unfortunately this misunderstands the whole basis of coaching! For a start, coaching is far more about listening than telling, but more importantly than that, it starts from an important assumption that is quite different from 'selling'. **A truly vital skill**

Selling begins with the assumption that the seller has something or knows something worth giving, and that the buyer (listener) should pay attention! Coaching starts with the assumption that the listener (coachee) has something to give, and should be encouraged to do so. In the KAM environment where we are speaking of 'expert' team members, coaching must also start from the assumption that the coachee will be better (ultimately) at the task in hand than the coach (is Tiger Wood's coach a better golfer than Tiger Woods?), and that the coach is simply trying to extract that expertise.

This is a skill requiring patience, tact and the ability to suppress one's own ego – quite a challenge for many a sales professional!

POLITICAL ENTREPRENEURSHIP

Perhaps the most vital skill of them all?

All this talk of leading, of managing team dynamics, of coaching, all of this must go on within a complex organization – your own. At the same time, it is conducted in such a way as to be relevant to another complex organization – the customer's.

All of this calls for a high degree of political awareness and diplomatic aplomb. The KA manager must know when to push and when to retreat, when to insist and when to parley, when to pacify and when to throw an appropriately managed fit.

The skill of political entrepreneurship is perhaps the most important of the three under discussion.

The 'entrepreneurial' part of the combination is about having a commercial sense. It is about being able to see opportunities and chase them, which sounds like the territory of most sales professionals, but there is something more. The KA manager (and their team) must be able to make the right judgements about those opportunities, based on their impact on the whole business. This takes us beyond the 'nose' of the sales professional and on to the 'brain' of the business manager. Indeed, it might be said that the KA manager is not a salesperson at all but a business manager, or even an investment manager.

The 'political' part of the combination does not necessarily come so easily to the sales professional. Salespeople are often in a hurry, and might at times be likened to bulls in china shops. Their political skills will perhaps come through experience, though this is where the availability of a senior manger as coach and mentor will be of great value.

SOME FREQUENTLY ASKED QUESTIONS

Hunters or farmers?

Referring back to a discussion started in Chapter 7, what we have been describing will sound far more like a farmer than a hunter. Must we conclude at last that the role of the KA manager is not for the hunter?

I have met successful KA managers whose 'hunter quotient' was very high, but they had one particular capability: a high degree of self-awareness. If you know that you are a hunter, then you can build a team around you that has much more of a farmer hue. The Belbin roles discussed above may also be useful in this particular pursuit.

Do key account managers have to be salespeople?

In short: no. As has already been said, they are perhaps first and foremost business managers. Indeed it is often true that when the role of selling is lifted from their shoulders (by appointing non-sales professionals to the role), they can operate with greater freedom, creativity and vision. The key to this scenario is of course to have sales professionals in the team.

There is a simple rule: appoint the person best suited to the task, not the person next in line for promotion. It is a similar rule to that too often ignored: appoint the person who will have the right 'chemical reaction' with the team and the customer, not the person who lives closest to the customer's head office.

Does this mean the death of the traditional salesperson?

Of course not. There continues to be a role for the traditional hunter with all those customers classified as something other than key accounts. In multi-site key accounts there may still be a requirement for sales professionals at a local level. Moreover, the hunter's skills will often be welcomed within a KA team. Perhaps the greatest benefit that such hunters will bring to KA teams will be their resolution to keep pushing.

Should key account managers be senior managers?

Why not? If they can commit the time, this can be a successful approach, particularly where there are significant internal barriers to progress. But take care not to turn such senior managers into salespeople, or to allow them to be sucked into the daily detail. Again, as with the preceding question, support such a KA manager with sales professionals in the team.

There is a counter-view that says senior managers will be better acting as coaches, mentors and enablers. I can only say that I have seen both scenarios work.

In South Africa, Kohler is a leading supplier of packaging materials, and is organized into distinct business units focused on each main packaging technology, such as card, film, can and so on. When Kohler decided that they needed to appoint KA managers to coordinate the activities of these separate units, in front of customers like Nestlé that made use of all of the units, the appointments were made at senior levels, for example, plant manager or divisional director. The role was one that required knowledge and experience of the inherent barriers and an authority to overcome them.

Directors as KA managers

> For some new appointees, the 'sales' orientation of the new role seemed a problem at first. Either it raised new expectations of them or, for others, it might have appeared a downgrading of their seniority. In fact, as far as the top management at Kohler was concerned, the role of KA manager was among the most important in the company and would be rewarded accordingly. The message finally got through, and most senior managers were keen to be involved in the new direction.

Training or recruitment?

Many businesses have looked at their existing sales force and found it wanting, turning instead to outside recruitment. While this might secure the necessary skills, it should be noted that it doesn't always make for an easy initiation for the new recruit. The existing salespeople probably see the role of key account manager as their natural next step and may be less than cooperative with anyone who bounces them off the promotion track. Given the likelihood that your existing sales professionals were taken on because of their strong independence and hunter characteristics, external recruitment is going to be a tough message to get over.

That warning having been given, it is certainly true that recruitment is often more successful than training (and I run a training company, so that is said between gritted teeth). This is most often the case where traditional approaches have become so ingrained as to be almost impossible to eradicate. I am reminded of the tale of the sports commentators in South Africa.

The tale of the sports commentator

Sport was not broadcast regularly on South African television until well into the 1970s – radio being the normal medium. When TV started to broadcast more frequently, it needed commentators, so it took them from the radio – well-known and respected voices. There was, however, a problem. After years of reporting every move on the pitch and every swing of every club, bat or racquet, the radio-trained commentators found it hard to adapt. Quite simply, they spoke too much and soon infuriated the audience who could see quite plainly what was going on with their own eyes. The solution, at least in this case, was new people with new perspectives and different skills.

The pharmaceutical industry experiences this problem more than many. Having focused for so long on 'call rates', territory 'coverage' and 'detailing', pharma companies find the shift towards any form of Key Account Management is a tough one to make. Unfortunately, for many of the larger ones the current trend is very much about downsizing the sales team and in such an environment taking on new talent can be a serious 'political' problem.

The key to good recruitment is having clarity about what you are looking for; it is all too easy to 'take a shine' to someone, only to discover at a later date that they lack the vital capacities. Interviews and assessment centres should be conducted with care, looking, I would suggest, for the three vital skills noted above – team leadership, coaching and political entrepreneurship.

Is it about skills, attitudes or behaviours?

As well as skills training it will be important to attend to people's attitudes and behaviours. New skills do not appear simply because a job remit changes and a training course is run. Skills do not develop in a vacuum.

Before new skills can be taken on, those involved need to understand what is required of them, why it matters, and how they might benefit from the change. A man who has spent a lifetime in the role of family breadwinner does not become an ideal house-husband just because he loses his job.

Attitudes and behaviours are deeply entrenched and rarely respond to simple exhortations to change. A skill can be learned, but will not be applied unless there is a desire to do so. Men can be very slow at learning how to cook, iron and wash up – much slower than at learning the skills of, say, driving, fishing and gambling!

Attitudes are the most deeply entrenched, and will take longest to change – if at all. Behaviours result from attitudes and, although we can all 'play act' to some extent, our true colours will eventually show through. Skills are merely the tip of the iceberg.

Let us just consider one example, from a salesperson's perspective. A traditional sales representative might have been accustomed, over the years, to receiving annual sales targets, a range of new products and an instruction to go out and sell. In order to succeed (and survive) the following attitudes and behaviours (good and bad) might have been in evidence:

- My job is to make the customer want what we have.
- I work in my own best interests and if that doesn't suit the customer, I will let my company know through periodic sales reports.
- Achieving my sales target is my number one objective.
- I will aim to do this with minimum disruption to my own organization.
- I will do this single-handed (because I have to!).
- If I encounter internal opposition, who am I to argue?
- If I encounter customer opposition, I need to sell harder.
- Success will result from my own energy and my ability to present and negotiate.

The world of the KA manager is rather different. To begin with, it is quite possible that they will be responsible for setting their own targets. On top of this, any new products they have to offer will have emerged perhaps as much as a result of their own lobbying as of any marketing departments say-so. For them, the word 'sell' will have a different ring. Success will depend on a rather different set of attitudes and behaviours:

New ways of thinking

- Not: my job is to make the customer want what we have, but:
  our KA team's job is to develop an intimacy of relationship that allows us to fully understand our KA customer's needs.
- Not: I work in my own best interests and if that doesn't suit the customer, I will let my company know through periodic sales reports, but:
  it is the KA team's responsibility to seek an alignment between our own and the customer's interests (where this is not possible, perhaps the customer cannot be a KA).
- Not: achieving my sales target is my number one objective, but:
  satisfying the customer in a profitable manner is our number one objective.
- Not: I will aim to do this with minimum disruption to my own organization, but:
  we will aim to do this by involving and directing the organization as appropriate.

New ways of behaving

- Not: I will do this single-handed (because I have to!), but:
  the KA team will achieve this.
- Not: if I encounter internal opposition, who am I to argue? but:
  if we encounter internal opposition, we must understand why and seek a way forward, continually aiming to align the business behind our KA objectives.
- Not: if I encounter customer opposition, I need to sell harder, but:
  if we encounter customer opposition, we may well be doing the wrong thing.
- Not: success will result from my own energy and my ability to present and negotiate, but:
  success will result from our ability to work in collaboration with the customer and to harness the resources of our own organization.

THE WIDER TEAM'S SKILLS

What additional skills does the wider team require? It is perhaps ironic that as a training company we have often spent more time working with the team members than with the KA managers themselves.

The most typical skill gaps tend to lie in the following areas:

- 1:1 interpersonal skills;
- persuasion and influencing skills;
- commercial awareness;
- customer focus;
- a *streetwise* sense in front of the customer;
- consultative selling.

To some extent, people from what previously might have been 'back-room' functions will have to take on many of the skills of the sales professional, but it might not be wise to represent it that way!

APPLICATION EXERCISE

- Conduct a skills audit of your own business and/or account team, based on the skills set indicated in this chapter. In particular, assess:
  - the coaching skills of the management team and the KA managers;
  - the 'political entrepreneurship' of the KA managers.
- Where are the biggest gaps?
  - Should these gaps be closed by training, or by recruitment?

Consider a live KA team:

- Where is that KA team on the *team clock*?
  - What behaviours is that likely to generate?
  - What problems or obstacles may be encountered?
  - How should you aim to deal with these?
  - Where would you like the team to be in six months' time, and in a year's time?
  - What actions and behaviours are required to get you there?

Draw up a team charter:

- How often should the team meet?
- What should be the format/agenda/purpose of those meetings?
- How will you ensure the best use of Belbin team roles?
  - What roles, if any, are missing, or under-represented?
    - What will be the implication of that for team performance?
    - What can you do to compensate?
  - What roles are 'abundant', or perhaps over-represented?
    - What will be the implication of that for team performance?
    - What can you do to mitigate that?
- How will you manage communications within the team?
- How should the team be led?

29

IT systems

This will be a short chapter, or at least shorter than you might expect, and not because IT is unimportant to KAM – the truth is very much the reverse – but simply because the pace of change in this field has a way of leaving any detailed discussion of systems or functionalities looking 'old hat', or plain foolish, only moments after going to press. Instead, I will limit myself to the kind of demands likely to be placed on your IT colleagues.

The first point to make is: talk to your IT colleagues early – they will need time to develop the kind of things you will require. Make sure they understand the purpose of KAM, and its scope, and its detail. In short: include them in the team.

TOO LITTLE OR TOO MUCH?

In Chapter 26 we noted two particular sins regarding IT – the sin of 'too little', and the sin of 'too much'.

'Too much IT' usually occurs when you are obliged to shoehorn your KAM needs into some larger 'master' system. The system determines the nature of your KAM. Alongside this sin comes what I refer to as the 'template culture', where everything has to fit into pre-ordained boxes. This is the way to strangle KAM at birth. A key account plan (just to cite one example) must be a living document that reflects the particular issues and

Overkill?

solutions with the particular customer; the process of ticking boxes in a mandatory template is hardly likely to achieve such an end.

If you think you may be about to suffer from 'too much' IT in this sense, then ask why it is necessary to do things this way. Is it to satisfy the management's desire for neat reports? Is it to satisfy the desire for uniformity in an environment that almost demands the reverse? Ask how this approach gels with all those statements from senior management about being customer focused.

Or underkill?

'Too little IT' is just as bad, though for different reasons. This is where the KA managers and their teams are expected to develop professional plans without access to the essential data, or to work in complex (and often remote) teams without adequate means of sharing knowledge or communicating ideas.

Getting it just right is not easy and will only result from much thought and debate. So, and I make no apology for repeating myself, make sure that you are talking with your IT colleagues as soon as possible. The aim is not to get every part of every system in place before the real business of KAM commences, that would be both unrealistic and unwise. Better that you have the essentials in place, using as simple a methodology as possible, and then aim to enhance those methodologies as the KAM journey develops and with it, your awareness of the true needs.

THE VITAL REQUIREMENTS

There are five 'must haves' from IT:

- a means of recording data, reports, comments, snippets of understanding, and other information;
- a means of analysing the above;
- a means of sharing: information (knowledge management), the planning process, and so on;
- a means of communicating within the KA team, and beyond;
- a means of communicating and working with the customer.

I will not go into any details as to what kind of system or level of functionality is needed to meet these requirements (it is enough to say that many thousands of very smart people are working on such things every day), but will limit my comments only to the nature of the requirements.

Whether you seek to develop one system to meet all requirements, or work through a number of different systems can only be a matter of your own choice – the pros and the cons of either option tend to balance themselves out.

Another decision will be whether to purchase or go in for self-development. If you have the resource to do it, then the latter is usually preferable, being far more likely to give you what you require rather than having to adapt your intentions to suit the system.

CRM: CURSE OR SAVIOUR?

CRM (customer relationship management) systems are increasingly common, ranging from simple storehouses of data to systems that 'claim' to create your sales plans. Beware of such claims. How would you feel if the captain of an aircraft you were on was to announce that he intended to allow the autopilot a go at landing the plane? Some things just demand human attention. The 'M' for Management in CRM is perhaps a little misleading. It will still be people who manage the relationship; the system will provide the necessary information.

A good CRM system makes an excellent tool, but a very poor (and usually tyrannical) master. It is rarely the fault of the system that this should be, but far more to do with the attitudes of those that use it. We have a prime example here of the sin of 'too little' or 'too much'.

Underkill? In the too little scenario people have a disregard for the system, regard it as an intrusive burden (big brother set up to spy on honest sales folk) and make no effort to keep it supplied with information. In a short space of time it becomes a redundant repository of outdated information, and people's complaints about its lack of value become only too true. I heard one disgruntled user refer to the CRM system as the world's best, but certainly most expensive, address book.

Or overkill? In the too much scenario CRM becomes the master and its users find themselves spending several hours a day on what can be slavish box ticking. There is sometimes an urge to automate the relationship management process – I have seen one system proudly demonstrated that not only prepared journey plans for the sales team, to be accessed each morning before setting out, but instructed those sales professionals on what they should do and say at each call, on the basis of the recorded sales history and previously logged data on customer needs and attitudes. Clever stuff, but is that what KAM is all about?

Those who want KAM to succeed must find the intelligent compromise between these two extremes. If they do, then they will find that CRM can indeed be a saviour, a means of achieving most of the vital requirements listed above (most CRM systems are designed to meet the first four of these requirements, with perhaps only limited value as a medium for customer communication and working).

A good CRM system well used will be an important asset for any but the simplest of KAM applications. It can be used to capture and pool the data that is usually locked up in so many separate places – the accounts system, the forecasting system, the sales statistics system, the heads of the sales team, and so on – allowing it to be analysed and shared.

Even the urge to automate the relationship management process can be made a good one, if directed at the right customers. Please make full use of human beings for the key and key development accounts, but turn to CRM for help with the maintenance and opportunistic accounts (see Chapter 24). As a means of 'freeing up the energy' from these accounts (as advised in Chapter 25), CRM can be of vital importance.

I cannot advise on the nature or scope of the system itself (do seek expert advice in this area) other than to recommend three tests: does it provide ease of data entry, ease of access for analysis, and ease of sharing across remote teams?

There is in any case something far more important than the specific 'bells and whistles' of the system, something that will make it either sink or swim for you: the people. It is remarkable that companies will invest well in excess of a million pounds in such a system and then spend a great deal of time and money on training people how to use it, and yet spend almost no time (or money!) on ensuring the correct attitudes and disciplines are in place. Without such, even the finest system will founder.

People must be shown the value of the system if they are to participate. They will be asked to spend considerable time inputting data (particularly at the outset) so be sure to let them know 'what's in it for them'. They must also adhere to some disciplines in use, to ensure things are kept up to date, to ensure accuracy, and to ensure responsible use of what can sometimes be very sensitive data.

Analysing the data

The better the CRM system the larger the store of data, which can of course bring its own problems when it comes to data analysis. Prioritization will be important if you are not to disappear down the 'analysis paralysis' tube.

You must of course determine your own priorities, but let me urge two on you:

- Measuring customer profitability (see Chapter 30) – immediate access to a customer specific profit and loss account would be brilliant.
- Customer classification and distinction (see Chapters 24 and 25).

Knowledge management

'Knowing stuff' is one thing, getting that knowledge shared across the organization quite another, and turning that shared knowledge into practical actions is the ultimate achievement. In all but the smallest of organizations some form of knowledge management system will be required.

BP has had enormous success in using its own BP intranet to develop what it calls 'virtual team networks'. This is a knowledge management system, process and culture, all wrapped into one, used to connect business units, project teams, geographical regions, customers and suppliers.

The philosophy of the BP intranet is to allow staff to use it as they wish – creating their own home pages – 'let a thousand home pages bloom'. Since it was launched with a relatively small group of users in 1995 (the pilot scheme saw a £7m investment), very quickly staff have found access to information, expertise and unknown colleagues working on similar issues, and the idea grows, with more people requesting access to the scheme. By 1996 business units had to pay to become involved, and they came in droves, voluntarily.

One of the most ambitious elements, and particularly relevant to the KAM scenario, is the way major projects are being handled through these 'virtual teams'. Major contracts are conducted through desktop conferencing, and suppliers are involved in a highly creative way. Suppliers are asked to form an 'alliance' on a particular project, working together with BP. More than this, the alliance of contractors is asked to manage the project with much less direct supervision from BP than ever would have been the case in the days before 'virtual teams'. This is what BP call 'breakthrough thinking'.

Enhancing the KA planning process

If KA planning is to be a truly team-based activity then the ability to share information will be vital. And it may go well beyond simple sharing. Some KA teams will allow the KA plan to be enhanced by individual contributions, and not necessarily funnelled through the KA manager. Whether you take your own planning process into the realm of 'individual enhancement' (a concept popularized through the likes of the online encyclopaedia Wikipedia) is for you to decide.

Oiling the wheels of KAM

BP's 'Platinum' system, based on Lotus Notes and used in its specialized industrial business unit, provides the account teams with the ability to share and assess:

- customer data, and not just the figures, but also more subjective matter such as needs, motivations, purchasing styles, and key drivers;
- action plans – team, project, and individual;
- performance measures, including the all important cost-to-serve data and the resultant measurement of account profitability.

One of the most impressive parts of the system, perhaps the most important, is the way in which individuals can sponsor changes and improvements to the system itself, improvements found through the experience of their own practical use, now shared as benefits to all users.

Enhancing team communication

Ever hovering behind the glossy façade of a diamond relationship (see Chapter 7) is the possibility of a communications breakdown: the ultimate e-mail nightmare. As more people talk to each other, and more reports of those meetings flow, and more data is gathered and shared, then there is a danger that KAM can become a monstrous bureaucracy.

The technology exists to ease the flow (there are many different e-mail management systems), but as with the discussion on CRM, it's not the technology that matters so much as the people.

Whether e-mail helps or hinders is down to the users. How many messages do you have when you return from a week away? (Going away for a fortnight is now just too daunting!) It wasn't the system that sent you this headache; it was people.

Agree a team communications charter:

- How to handle 'address groups': do we want all communications shared across the whole team or will the unthinking use of address groups lead to overload?
- Confirmations: when someone asks for something to be done, must the recipient reply to say they are doing it, or can it be taken as read?
- E-mail or telephone: what sort of conversations should we try to have by telephone, or videoconferencing, rather than e-mail? (Never try persuasion or negotiation by e-mail!)
- Attachments: take note of the fact that complex PowerPoint presentations and the like can be a big problem for some users – be sensitive.

Learning from the 'greats'...

- Length of messages: messages should be edited ruthlessly. Don't send long rambling 'streams of consciousness'. Of course, this takes time; George Bernard Shaw once sent a long letter to a friend and closed with an apology, 'I am sorry for sending you such a long letter, I didn't have time to write you a shorter one.'
- 'Do as you would be done by': this was a famous piece of advice from Lord Chesterfield to his son in 1747. He wrote a letter of course, but such brevity would have made him a natural for e-mail!

A final thought on team communication. However good the systems and the disciplines, don't allow e-mails and videoconferencing to replace physical meetings. Don't underestimate the social element of the team, or the simple fact that putting faces and personalities to names is hugely beneficial in itself. Any new member of the team tends to remain an outsider until such time as they meet their colleagues face to face.

Working with the customer

Perhaps the most important systems of the lot are those that enhance your ability to work with the customer. As well as the standard operational systems such as forecasting, order receipt, order processing, invoicing and credit control, you may also need systems to facilitate things such as project management or joint R&D.

The key in all of this is 'making it easy for the customer to do business with you'. Out of all the supplier vendor ratings and out of all the criteria in customer satisfaction surveys, it is this issue that comes out most often as the key to supplier success. So, every time you consider a new system that involves the customer, ask the same question: 'Will this make us easier to do business with?'

E-commerce

The purchasing function has seized the e-revolution with both hands and instituted a boggling array of e-commerce possibilities from simple computer-to-computer ordering (EDI) through to telemetry (remote monitoring of customer stock levels and automatic re-ordering), online auctions and extranets (a company intranet that allows access to outsiders – particularly important in a key account/key supplier situation).

The message is clear: suppliers must keep up, or risk consignment to the dark netherworld of the IT illiterate.

Figure 29.1 indicates the nature of e-commerce interactions that might be sought by the customer, depending on their positioning of the supplier (see Chapter 14).

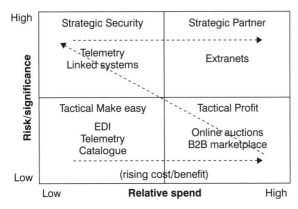

Figure 29.1 *E-commerce solutions based on supplier positioning*

A common challenge for the supplier is, just how far must we open up our systems to the customer? What if the customer wants direct access to your data on stockholding? What if they want to place orders direct to the plant? What if they want to monitor your supply chain?

Will saying 'yes' make it easier for the customer to do business with you? This is the first question to ask, but there is an important follow-up question: are you confident that the customer's intentions are 'honourable'? If they are a key account and you are a key supplier, then unless either side has been lazy with their appellations the answer should be clear. It should perhaps be one of the criteria for identifying a key account that it is a customer with which you would wish to become this intimate.

Forecasting

One final aspect of working with the customer deserves specific attention, for it is the one that causes perhaps the lion's share of the antagonisms between supplier and customer. This is the process of forecasting. Everyone blames everyone else when forecasting goes wrong, and the customer is perhaps the favourite butt of them all.

Forecasting usually goes wrong when it is done in isolation, and most often when it is done by salespeople with insufficient access to the vital data.

The best forecasting systems are ones that involve the customer. The more intimate the customer relationship, the closer you will get to accurate information. Perhaps of more importance, the closer you work together, the more you will know of the customer's doubts – the key to real, long-term forecasting – rather than relying on their public pronouncements, usually about enormous growth! A forecasting system that allows an element of judgement, a 'percentage of certainty' on any particular order for instance, is one that will suit the intimacy of a KAM environment.

Forecasting in the KAM environment must be thoroughly professional. The 'wild blue yonderings' of irresponsible sales reps must be banished for good. Forecasts must be 'owned' by all, the customer, the KA team and the supporting operations team.

APPLICATION EXERCISE

Consider the IT support required for your own KAM strategy:

- Where should you focus your attentions:
  - recording data;
  - analysing data;
  - sharing information – including the KA plan;
  - communicating within the KA team;
  - communicating and working with the customer?

30

Measuring customer profitability

Is it a reasonable assumption that KAM will be more profitable than traditional selling? The only possible answer to this question is: never make such an assumption (!), and for all sorts of reasons.

KAM might not have been pursued principally with that aim in mind – it might have been pursued *in extremis*, as a 'survival strategy'. In such a case, to compare levels of profitability with 'what used to be' may be very misleading. What was is gone, and KAM is now a necessity. Without it, we die.

It may be true that the practice of KAM results in a more efficient use of resources, but does that inevitably lead to increased profits? Consider the tale of the National Health Service.

The tale of the NHS

In the UK in the 1940s, the creation of the NHS was heralded not only as a mark of a new height of civilization, but also as a route to greater efficiency. The planners sincerely believed that the NHS would result in the steadily decreasing cost of healthcare provision. Why? Because the NHS would improve the health of the nation – the populace would therefore require 'less healthcare'.

We now know how things turned out in practice – people expected ever-more sophisticated treatments for an apparently ever-growing range of ailments. It was almost as if the NHS invented a whole new range of diseases!

What is the analogy with KAM? It is possible that the diamond team relationship, while improving the efficiency of relationships, will in itself uncover a whole new range of needs and actions required. This is almost certainly 'a good thing' in as far as it represents 'the truth' and helps to cement the relationship between supplier and customer, just as the NHS really *did* improve the health of the nation. But might the new actions, like those in the NHS situation, result in increased costs and so reduced profitability?

In a sense these possible scenarios are irrelevant, inasmuch as there is only one proper course of action to be pursued, and that is to actively measure the impact of KAM on profitability. We must therefore measure individual customer profitability – this is a rule.

KAM will necessarily involve the shifting of resources (most commonly this means people's time) from some customers to others. What is the impact on profitability where resources are reduced? What is the impact on profitability where resources are increased? Without knowing the answers to these questions, how can you be sure that KAM was in fact a 'good thing' at all?

FOUR 'ALMOST TRUTHS' OF CUSTOMER PROFITABILITY

Here are four 'almost truths' (that is to say, they are very nearly always so) of customer profitability:

- The largest customers (ranked by volume) are rarely the same as the most profitable customers (measured by percentage return on investment).
- The cost of winning new customers, even in a high-growth environment, is almost always higher than you think.
- In the short-term, retaining customers is almost always a more profitable activity than winning new customers.
- The longer you keep a customer the more profitable they become (measured by their life-time value – see below).

Without proper measures of profitability it is all too easy to favour 'big customers' simply for their size, far too easy to favour the 'macho' activity of winning new customers (without a proper understanding of the costs) and far too easy to underestimate the value of customer retention.

The costs of large customers

There is plenty of evidence across a broad spectrum of industries that a business's largest customers are significantly less profitable than the middle-ranking ones. This might be less so in situations where economies of scale are substantial, but even here the big customers are often not as profitable as might be imagined. They get the best prices (often better than their higher volumes actually justify), the best terms, the most attention, the lion's share of resources (especially those expensive people of yours), and so it goes on. When businesses actually commit to measuring customer profitability they can receive some unpleasant surprises in this regard.

Figure 30.1 shows the widening gap between profitable and unprofitable customers in just one sector, the European printing industry, comparing 1985 to 2005. Back in 1985, profit came in more or less equal measure from the largest through to the smallest customers. By 2005, largely as a result of customer consolidations and the attendant price negotiations that drove down prices despite there being no real increases in volume, we see that the largest 10 per cent of customers represent a loss to suppliers.

% of company profit by customer decile (each decile = 10% of customer base)

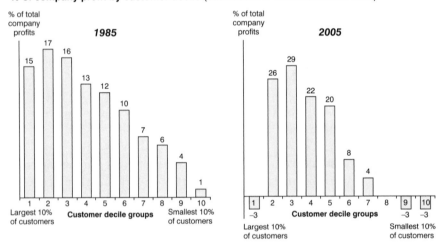

Figure 30.1 *Profitability by customer size*

So why keep big customers? Often because their volume is what keeps your operation turning. This is fine, provided everyone recognizes the reasons for keeping them, and also recognizes the different value of other, more profitable customers.

The costs of winning new customers

Buying your way in

First there are the more obvious costs; the initial discounts given for trial and first orders and the customer-imposed 'start-up costs'. In some markets, suppliers have to 'buy their way in'. This is particularly true for those selling to the retail industry in the United States, where suppliers are very often obliged not only to offer excellent terms, but also to purchase their space on the shopfloor and to buy up any stock of the supplier they may be replacing. Some US suppliers refer to this, rather euphemistically, as 'selling a customer'. Perhaps a more honest phrase would be 'buying a customer'.

The cost story does not end there. When a customer changes their supplier, they might suffer costs in down time during 'swap-overs' or to take account of new specifications and processes. PPG sells paint for repairing damaged cars and needs to offer the ability to match any colour, anywhere, any time – a massive undertaking requiring great skills of colour matching and reproducibility. Any supplier to PPG wishing to replace, let's say, an existing supplier of a particular pigment has to be aware that their product will be used in perhaps thousands of recipes for individual colours – recipes that have been got 'just right' with the current supplier. The tasks of testing and changing formulations can be enormous, perhaps too big for the customer to even contemplate, at least without significant help from the new supplier. All of this will have costs in time and money, borne by both customer and supplier.

There is more. When you win a new customer, do you factor in the costs of people's time, the extra travel, the cost of presentations, meetings and entertainment? An advertising agency can sometimes spend its first year's anticipated profits in pitching to a new client. In addition, if you are a manufacturer, you must keep higher stock levels to service new customers, and there will be an increase in debtors, especially if you offer extended credit as a carrot.

Winning customers feels great, but what does it do for short term profitability?

Do you also factor in the not so obvious cost of devoting less time to your other concerns? What if, while directing your best people to the new pursuit, you took your eye off the ball and lost an existing customer? Then there are the costs of new systems and processes to cope with the new customer, perhaps there are training needs, perhaps new operating procedures, changes to databases and promotional materials... the story goes on.

The value of customer retention

Customer retention, as a stated strategy, is about increasing the security of your position in a world where change happens fast. Customer retention is about acting to ensure that supplier rationalization programmes do not find you the loser. Customer retention is about getting a proper return on investments that sometimes require a long-term payback.

Keeping a customer might be the best thing you ever do for profitability

There are many reasons that profits improve the longer you keep a customer. Here are just a few:

- Gradual increases in volume may not be matched by discounts for that volume.
- Operating costs are reduced as the supplier grows more experienced in servicing the customer.

- Forecasts become more accurate, which bring efficiencies for production and distribution.
- Better relationships develop, which result in better customer intelligence.
- What we learn from this customer is of benefit in dealing with others.
- The customer brings new business through referrals, or the evidence of their own success.
- There is a reduction in the costs of chasing and re-winning lost customers.

FA Reichheld, quoted in *Relationship Marketing For Competitive Advantage* gives estimates of how much profits might improve if a business was to improve its retention rate by only 5 per cent. Industrial distribution companies might see a 45 per cent improvement, while car insurance firms might expect 84 per cent, with advertising agencies seeing the best impact at 95 per cent.

Lifetime value

Investments should be measured over their life – Key Accounts are some of your most important investments

Given that retention is so important to profitability, we should consider measuring customer profit on what we will call a 'lifetime value' basis. This means going beyond the normal annual evaluation, and adding up the profit cumulatively year after year. By this method it becomes very clear that every additional year of retention means a yet more profitable customer. The comparisons with customers that might bring higher margins but move on to rival suppliers after relatively short periods of time can be very illuminating.

Figure 30.2 shows how reductions in customer defections (or improvements in customer retention, whichever way you prefer to see it) increase

Customer defection rate	Average customer lifetime	Annual profit	Profit over a customer lifetime
40%	2.5 Years	1,000	2,500
20%	5 Years	1,000	5,000
10%	10 Years	1,000	10,000
5%	20 Years	1,000	20,000

Figure 30.2   *Lifetime value*

lifetime value. The defection rate indicates what percentage of your customers cease doing business with you in any given annual period. It is simple to see how by halving the rate of customer defections you can, in effect, double the lifetime value of your retained customers.

This is, of course, something of a simplification. Perhaps your defecting customers were the least profitable – maybe that's why you let them go – but the principle is worth remembering: it is the lifetime value of a customer that counts, not just this year's results.

GIVING DISCOUNTS FOR VOLUME

How much more volume do you require if you give a 5 per cent discount on your price but wish to end up with the same cash profit? 10 per cent? 50 per cent ? 100 per cent ?

It all depends of course on your current gross margin. Figure 30.3 shows the relationships between margins (the top line) discounts (the left-hand column) and volume increases required (the corresponding box).

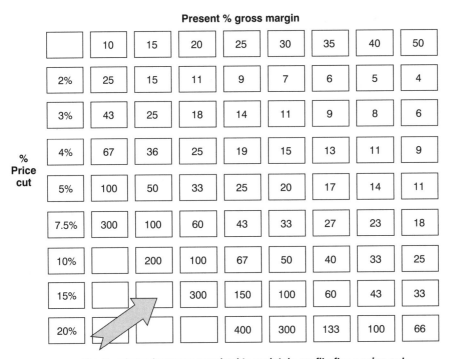

Present % gross margin

% Price cut	10	15	20	25	30	35	40	50
2%	25	15	11	9	7	6	5	4
3%	43	25	18	14	11	9	8	6
4%	67	36	25	19	15	13	11	9
5%	100	50	33	25	20	17	14	11
7.5%	300	100	60	43	33	27	23	18
10%		200	100	67	50	40	33	25
15%			300	150	100	60	43	33
20%				400	300	133	100	66

The % volume increase required to maintain profit after a price cut

Figure 30.3   *Discounts for volume*

For a supplier making a gross margin of 20 per cent, a discount in price of 5 per cent will require an extra 33 per cent volume for cash profit to remain the same as before the discount. (This calculation doesn't take account of any resulting economies of scale, nor of the notion of marginal pricing and 'contribution to overheads', but even so, the figures are rather arresting.)

Buyers have the mathematics of the relationships between price and volume engraved on their hearts, which is why they are so keen to learn their suppliers' profit margins: it puts them in the driving seat for all discount-for-volume negotiations. Sales professionals are too often rather less well informed. Do they even know their margins in the first place (let alone the mathematics of the relationship to price and volume)?

There are two common reasons why sales professionals are denied this information:

- Their business systems are not able to measure profit down to individual customer level.
- The measurements are made, but sales professionals are not trusted with the information for fear that they will tell the customer.

How can KA managers be expected to operate with any degree of proper judgement if they are denied this basic information? And we are only talking here of profit at gross margin level (revenue minus cost of materials): what about the measure of profit after a proper allocation of all other costs and overheads?

MEASURING PROFIT AFTER *ALL* COSTS

It is not enough to pretend that you are measuring customer profitability 'after *all* costs' if those costs are not properly or accurately allocated. We are talking here of the sin of 'marmalading'. This is where the overhead costs are spread 'evenly' across all customers, regardless of each customer's actual use of particular services or facilities.

The tale of the 'marmalader'

Figure 30.4 shows the start point of a business that is killing itself because of the laziness of marmalading. The company has four customers with a combined gross profit of 290, and shows a net profit of 50. The marmalading of the 240 overheads indicates a loss-making customer – Customer D. The decision is taken to cease doing business with that customer.

Customers	A	B	C	D	Total
Gross profit	100	80	60	50	290
Overheads	60	60	60	60	240
Net profit	**40**	**20**	**0**	**(10)**	**50**

Figure 30.4 *The sins of 'marmalading' – part 1*

Unfortunately, overheads do not reduce immediately by the 60 units that had been allocated to Customer D. But perhaps they do go down by 30 and people give themselves a slap on the back for a smart decision. The new situation is as shown in Figure 30.5.

Customers	A	B	C	D	Total
Gross profit	100	80	60	50	290
Overheads	60	60	60	60	240
Net profit	**40**	**20**	**0**	**(10)**	**50**
Gross profit	100	80	60	xx	240
Overheads	70	70	70	xx	210
Net profit	**30**	**10**	**(10)**	**xx**	**30**

Figure 30.5 *The sins of 'marmalading' – part 2*

The company is still in profit, but Customer C is now a loss-making customer and the troubled board meets to decide action. 'Concentrate on profitable customers,' they say, and Customer C is quietly dropped. But, unfortunately, the overheads do not reduce in line, as demonstrated by the new situation shown in Figure 30.6.

Customers	A	B	C	D	Total
Gross profit	100	80	60	50	290
Overheads	60	60	60	60	240
Net profit	**40**	**20**	**0**	**(10)**	**50**
Gross profit	100	80	60	xx	240
Overheads	70	70	70	xx	210
Net profit	**30**	**10**	**(10)**	**xx**	**30**
Gross profit	100	80	xx	xx	180
Overheads	90	90	xx	xx	180
Net profit	**10**	**(10)**	**xx**	**xx**	**0**

Figure 30.6 *The sins of 'marmalading' – part 3*

I think you can guess what happens next.

The moral of the story is clear; decisions about customers and resources cannot be taken without proper knowledge of their relative profitability. Perhaps Customer D was a profitable customer (taking up very few resources) and it was Customer A that was the problem (the biggest customer getting all the high-cost attention).

The answer lies in some form of activity-based costing, where the costs of activities, people, overheads and the rest are allocated more precisely to individual customers.

Management consultants, advertising agencies, legal firms – these are examples of businesses that will do this calculation to some degree. Why them, and not chemical manufacturers or food companies? For consultants and the like, their product is their time, so that time must be monitored and charged. The outcome is a business that knows where its profits come from and so is better able to make decisions concerning its key accounts. Life is harder for manufacturers with their relative complexity, but that makes it even more important that they aim to make these calculations.

Diamond team profitability

How diamond team 'knowledge' cuts costs...

There are of course additional costs of operating diamond teams compared with bow-ties – people's time being one of the obvious and significant – but it is hoped that there will be corresponding increases in volume, and perhaps price, that will more than compensate. There may also be decreases in costs; Figure 30.7 shows how this might come about.

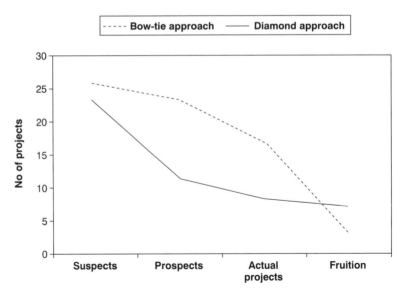

Figure 30.7 *Diamond team profitability*

Imagine a customer that demands a significant number of new products, all of which go through pilot trials but only some of which come to fruition as launched products. In a sales approach based on a bow-tie relationship, the relative lack of knowledge of the customer's business and market might make it difficult to distinguish the likelihood of success for any one project compared with any other. There is a tendency to chase them all, what we might call the 'throwing a lot of mud at the wall and hoping some of it sticks' approach. The costs of such an approach can be very high, and with relatively poor returns.

A 'relative' lack of knowledge and 'relatively' poor returns; to what are we comparing this? If the switch to a diamond team approach improves our knowledge sufficiently to make better judgements about projects then we might find ourselves in the situation illustrated in Figure 30.7. The diamond team are running with fewer projects in the first place, so devoting better quality resource time, so coming out the other end with more successes.

Cost-to-serve models

If you *do* measure customer profitability with any degree of accuracy, then you will be able to construct what we will call a 'cost-to-serve' model. An example is shown at Figure 30.8.

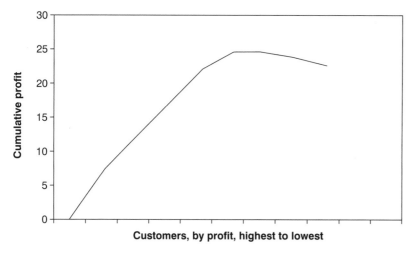

Figure 30.8 *The 'cost to serve' model*

This shows each customer along the horizontal axis, from the most profitable through to the least so, with the graph line measuring the cumulative profit. It is very likely that your business will fit the 80:20 rule in this regard – a small number of customers that account for the lion's share of the profit. It is also possible that you have some customers where you make a loss.

Cutting your losses?

I have one client who has been toying with the idea of telling his staff that, should they receive an order from a customer at the right-hand extremity of the graph, where they lose money, they should send the customer a cheque for $500 and a note saying: 'This is what it would have cost us to service your order, but having saved ourselves the bother here is the money instead.' Needless to say he hasn't done it yet, but it's a thought…

What if you find that those loss makers are your larger customers (and quite likely the ones you have labelled key accounts)? There are plenty of questions, and even more 'ifs' and 'buts'.

How dependent is your business on their volume – does it keep the factory running? Even if it does, is that a good excuse for losing money?

If you cannot bring them to a genuinely profitable level, then their status as key accounts must be questioned.

Another client of mine decided to increase prices to a 'loss-making' key account, knowing that they would lose half the business, but that the remaining half would now make real profit. Having shifted that customer leftwards on the cost-to-serve model, they discovered that it suddenly became more attractive to chase this customer for new projects whereas before they might have seen such energy as throwing good money after bad – a happy ending was in sight.

Creating the model

The process of creating such a model is no simple task, and will involve the support and enthusiasm of finance and IT staff. Most importantly they will want to know why it is worth all the effort. Equally, those people that you start asking to keep some form of record on time spent or costs incurred with specific customers will want to know why – be sure you tell them.

Some businesses will want and need to do this for all customers, some only for the largest, some only for those called 'key' – you make the rules. One option is to select a sample group of customers, deliberately choosing ones with very different profiles of scale and demands, and at least create the model on those. If nothing else it will tell you whether it is worth the effort to ask yet more questions.

APPLICATION EXERCISE

- How well do you measure individual customer profitability?
- If you do not currently measure individual customer profitability, do you have any concerns about your methods for allocating resources or funds to different accounts?
  - How do you know if you got it right?
- What needs improving?
  - What actions must be taken in order to effect these improvements?

31

The key account plan

'No plan – no value proposition – no key account'

Written key account plans are few and far between. It is as if KA managers have a fear of consigning to paper any forecasts, predictions or promises that may come back to haunt them, customers being the fickle sort they are. Considering the size of many key accounts, and their importance to the business, this is of course a serious shortcoming, but it remains true that many salespeople, long used to living by their wits, often seem to find it difficult to conform to their bosses' demands for a formal planning process. Or is it simply that they don't know how to do it – or perhaps a more likely explanation: they see no purpose in it?

THE PURPOSE OF THE PLAN

How big should the ideal KA plan be, that is to say, how many pages long? The answer must have something to do with the purpose of the plan, so let's consider some possible uses:

1. A repository for all the data and information on the account.
2. Getting your own thoughts together.
3. A means of communicating the importance of this customer to the business as a whole.

4. A means of communicating objectives and actions to KA team members.
5. The best way of tracking progress against targets and so determining the success of your efforts.
6. The mechanism for ensuring that the appropriate value proposition is developed, communicated and rewarded.

The first possible use – the grand repository – is not the purpose of a KA plan. Such a database record is essential, but it should not be confused with a document that is focused on action.

The same applies to the second possible use: getting your own thoughts together. This is a hugely valuable thing to do of course, but the plan is the refined outcome of that process, not the history of your thoughts.

A good plan should achieve the third objective, but there will also be other means of raising your customer's profile. The plan will form part of a wider influencing strategy and should be written so that it supports rather than hinders that strategy, but this is still not the core purpose of a KA plan.

It is the fourth, fifth and sixth uses that we should focus on. These are about communicating objectives and actions, providing a way to track progress, and ensuring the right value proposition. Indeed, my favourite definition of what a KA plan is all about is: *'the value proposition in blueprint'*.

If this is the purpose, then the answer to the question 'how long?' must be: 'as short as is possible'. Plans that run to dozens of pages and overflow with analysis and background data are not very helpful in this respect. Such plans are probably written to communicate the importance and expertise of the KA manager (not on our list of uses) and few readers are fooled. That is if they read it at all!

So, the ideal plan should be focused on objectives and the actions required to achieve those objectives, which might have you shrinking it down in your mind to a single page, but we should take care not to limit the scope of our objectives. We mean more than the sales volumes and revenues, a great deal more. Any sales plan will list the figures, but what distinguishes a KA plan is the breadth of its objectives, which go well beyond the figures; there will be objectives for the relationship, objectives for the team, objectives for the business as a whole. This may run to a few more pages than the much requested one side of A4.

A KEY ACCOUNT PLAN TEMPLATE?

There is no generic template or blueprint for a KA plan, nor should there be. Templates, blueprints and pro formas tend to result in the sin of 'box-ticking' rather than thinking. Moreover, templates that come from outside your own business are unlikely to meet the requirements of your own unique situation. Isn't a key account meant to be a customer with whom you aim to work in a different way, a customer deserving of a specifically tailored value proposition? As such, how can the plan be captured in a uniform document?

So I make no apology for failing to provide you with a template in this chapter (it really is for your own good!), but will certainly aim to provide you with a framework for your planning activity.

The very task of designing your own format will in fact be a part of the thinking and planning process, determining what is important to you and what less so (which is why I maintain that it really is for your own good not to have a template). There can be nothing worse than agonizing over a piece of analysis, perhaps even commissioning research, simply to fill in the spaces of an academic model that will never be used. And there will be nothing better than getting everyone in the account team to agree on the things that matter in your business, and what should be included in the plan. Writing the plan should be a team effort, and as such, a source of team cohesion.

Defending templates?

I do hear some alarm bells ringing at this point, and a counter-argument being made. If every customer has their own plan, to their own format, will that not be a problem for all those people that have to support the plans? If there are six key accounts and six different formats, will that not cause confusion? Consider someone on more than one account team, having to recognize and understand two different approaches; what does that do for their own role and contribution? These can be very valid points, and you have a choice to make based on your own circumstances. Which is more important in those circumstances: individually tailored plans based on real differences between customers, or a uniform format that allows the maximum number of people to recognize and understand a common KAM philosophy and to adhere to a disciplined approach?

If you are at the early stages of KAM implementation, then perhaps you might lean towards uniformity with a view to developing common disciplines. If your KAM practices are more mature, then perhaps you might be more confident in allowing a little more latitude.

Perhaps there is a compromise to be found. Perhaps the format can be a menu, in the same running order for all, but without insisting that every 'course' is included. Perhaps the physical appearance of the plans (Excel? PowerPoint? Word?) can be uniform across all key accounts?

It is worth considering the physical appearance at this point, and whether to go for one of the standard software package formats. They each have their pros and cons:

- Word documents: actually, I can't think of any plusses! This format leads to wordy prose, and is a real pain to update.

- Excel spreadsheets: great for the numbers, but can lead to an over-emphasis on this part of the plan. In the wrong hands these can be a nightmare to present, or comprehend.
- PowerPoint presentations: there is always a danger of the oversimplification of bullet points, but this does make the best format for presenting and involving.

My own preference is for PowerPoint, largely because it is the most 'involving' of the formats – Excel in particular can be a very 'private' affair – but you must decide according to your own preferences and requirements.

There has been a tendency of late to allow the IT department to design the format, the idea being that this will result in the broadest access to plans through shared drives and the like. The objective is a good one, but I would object strongly to this vital tool being hijacked, and possibly compromised due to the limitations of technology. At the risk of sounding like a dinosaur, I would rather a humble piece of paper.

A final point on this 'choice': if the decision is to go for uniformity simply so that the bosses have an easier time of reading and monitoring, then I'm afraid I'm very much in the anti-uniformity camp.

SOME 'MUST HAVES'

So, no blueprint, but there are perhaps a few things that just have to be in the plan:

- goals and targets;
- people;
- projects and activities;
- resources, risks and contingencies.

Goals and targets

Without these, there is no direction, no hope of a common approach and no way of judging success. There should be targets for a number of things, and not just the obvious ones of sales revenue and profit. They include targets for how the relationship should progress, targets for communications, targets for progress on key projects and targets for customer satisfaction ratings to name but a few. Just because some of these may be hard to quantify, that does not make them unimportant.

People

People are at the heart of KAM and so must be at the heart of the plan. People are what will make KAM work, and what distinguishes it from ordinary selling; so don't forget them in the plan. Perhaps the most important part of the plan, the absolute heart, will be the identification of the customer's decision-making process, the members of their DMUs (decision-making units), and who in the KA team will be responsible for the all-important points of contact. For me, the contact matrix and the GROWs (see Chapter 8) are the most important items. A KA plan without a contact matrix is a plan that is unlikely to be implemented. A KA plan *with* a contact matrix *alone* is perhaps already more than half a plan.

The contact matrix is often the most important difference between a sales plan and a KA plan

The GROWs identify one part of each individual's contribution to the KA team; the customer-specific goals and roles, and the all-important obligations to the team, but there is also another contribution to be considered: the contribution of each individual to the effectiveness of the team, as a team.

Dr Meredith Belbin has done a lot of work on this second kind of team role: the way people behave as team members, and the value that their different styles can bring. A KA team could do worse than going through the Belbin team-analysis process as a means of discovering their own team make-up (see Chapter 28).

Projects and activities

This is the nitty-gritty of what is going to be done by the team, with clear plans for each project. The range of possible projects is of course huge, from internal projects focused on removing obstacles or improving capabilities to externally orientated projects focused on customer relationships or value propositions. Whatever the project, there are some vital ingredients:

- Objectives: who is responsible, timetable, milestones of progress.
- Critical path analysis.
- Measures of success.

Critical path analysis is simply the practice of laying out the timetables of activities and noting the interrelationships between them – some activities will depend on others having been completed. As a result of this analysis, you can prioritize what must be done first in order for others to follow and so on: the critical path.

Resources, risks and contingencies

One of the most important reasons for writing a KA plan is to identify the resource required and to put up a case for winning it. Resource needs may appear in many guises: new people, additional skills, more access to IT support, greater R&D involvement, expansion of production capacity, investment in new technology and so on. It is only when we know the resources required to achieve objectives set that we can make a full judgement as to the value and priority of a particular key account, so this is an important element.

Putting the case is only the start. Of course, the aggregate resources required by all the key account plans must be assessed before projects and activities can commence. Next – resources may be allocated, but will they bring success? Will the new plant be able to produce to the quality required by the customer, and in time? Will the investment in e-commerce be enough to satisfy the customer's demands for transactional efficiency?

Every expansion of resource carries an attendant risk, a risk of failure, of higher expense or of any other kind of shortfall, and the KA plan must assess that risk and propose an appropriate contingency in the event of any such shortfall.

A SAMPLE RUNNING ORDER

Having said there are no blueprints, regard the following with care. It is no more than the headings of a 'typical' key account plan. The exact order, and the weight given to one section against another, will depend to a great extent on the current level of your relationship. If you are at the bow-tie stage (see Chapter 7) then the plan will lean heavily towards exploration and information required. If you are at the diamond team stage (see Chapter 7) then the focus will be more on projects and activities.

The sample running order given below might suit a supplier that has moved beyond the one-on-one or the one-on-many relationship, and is just entering into a diamond team relationship with their customer. Let's also suppose that they have a history of writing plans heavy on long and worthy analysis with little practical application, so the focus here is very much on action:

- The key account team: core and full.
- Executive summary.
- The profit plan: current profitability and future target.
- Opportunities and objectives: including the competitive position.
- The contact matrix and GROWs.
- The value proposition: the positive impact on their total business experience.

- Projects: project teams and milestones.
- Resources required: actions required by management to commit resources.
- Implementation timetable.
- Appendices: analysis and information.

Analysis or action?

At the early stages with a key account it may be important to show a good deal of the analysis that has been done in the body of the plan itself, in order to ensure understanding and to win support within the suppler business. As the relationship develops and matures, so much of this analysis might 'withdraw' by stages to an appendix. To some extent it is the length of time that the account has been managed that will determine what is analysis and what is action.

Some typical pieces of analysis might include the following:

- The KAISM analysis (see Chapter 24).
- Historical account profitability analysis: lifetime value analysis (see Chapter 30).
- The market chain: value and decision hotspots (see Chapter 5).
- The customer's purchasing strategy (see Chapters 11 to 14).
- The customer's business strategy (see Chapters 15 to 18).
- The shared future (see Chapter 19).
- Customer's decision-making process: DMU analysis (see Chapters 6 to 8).
- Activity cycle analysis (see Chapter 21).
- Proposal analysis (see Chapter 23).
- Belbin team roles (see Chapter 28).
- The KAM health check (see Chapter 32).

Information

Keeping these kinds of things in an appendix prevents the plan from becoming a glorified telephone directory, or a historical record:

- address book;
- customer's organization charts and contact profiles;
- customer's performance – sales, growth, shares, profitability, financial status;
- our sales performance – history, current, forecast – share of business;
- product listings;
- competitor profiles.

SHARING IT WITH THE CUSTOMER?

Could you, or should you present the plan to the customer? With a few subtle edits, this should perhaps be a definite objective (at the right time), and having the confidence to do this will be evidence of a good and healthy relationship. Some customers may even ask you to present your plan, as a means of testing your capabilities and your commitment.

As ever, there can be no rule about this, only an observation that the most successful supplier–customer relationships do tend towards some form of joint planning.

LUCK OR JUDGEMENT?

So, you have a plan. Add to this a few bucket-loads of energy, a great deal of resolve, not a little patience, and finally that old stalwart of all successful business activities – a little piece of luck. But don't wait for fate to intervene. Figure 31.1 shows why time spent in the early days on analysis and planning will pay off in the long run, preventing you from wallowing in a morass of argument and painful rethinking.

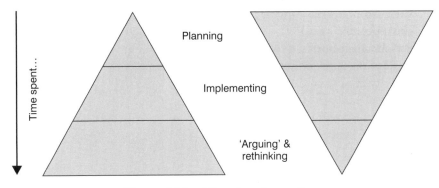

Figure 31.1   *Why planning matters*

Just as importantly, good planning will allow your team to recognize good fortune when it smiles on you, to know it for what it is, and to be best placed to turn it to your best advantage. I never wish my clients good luck on their KAM journey, I wish them the best luck that they can make for themselves.

Making your own luck…

A FEW LAST TIPS

- Don't write *War and Peace*, and avoid anything looking like a telephone directory
- Keep it updateable (that means keeping it short and to the point, and preferably in a medium that makes revisions easy).
- You don't have to write it in one sitting; the best plans will form over time, perhaps a long time.
- Start off with some strong comments on direction, goals and targets; people reading the plan will want to know where you are headed (but note the final tip in this list).
- Stress the actions resulting from the plan and who is responsible for them.
- Prepare it as a team effort (it is true that committees should not write novels, but the KA plan is a practical tool, not a work of art).
- Make it available to the whole business; stamping it 'Top Secret' is unlikely to be of much help to those who will make it reality.
- Include an 'executive summary' of the key points: direction, benefits, actions and requirements.
- Provide the background information on the account in an appendix to the plan, otherwise pages of data start to obscure the direction and the actions.
- Focus on actions, not analysis. If you feel the analysis is important to develop understanding or to win support then fine, otherwise put it in an appendix.
- Avoid unsupported hype.

APPLICATION EXERCISE

- Draw up a running order for an 'ideal' KA plan appropriate to your own business circumstances:
  - What will be the ideal account plan format?
  - What IT support will you require?
- How important is it for you to have uniformity of plan design across all key accounts?
- Will you share your KA plans with the customers?

32

Tracking progress

Fight short-termism from the very start...

Senior managers are often impatient; their short-termism with regard to KAM was one of the deadly sins noted in Chapter 26. On the one hand KA managers must persist with arguing the case for long-term investment, but on the other hand, the 'political' part of their 'political entrepreneur' make-up (as discussed in Chapter 28) will be telling them that they must supply the bosses with some short-term wins. It's a very common dilemma.

The problem can be avoided if, at the very outset of the KAM journey, time is taken to consider how progress will be tracked and reported, to the satisfaction of the short- and the long-term thinkers.

The market is awash with software tools ranging from project management to CRM (see Chapter 29), each of which may give some help with this task, but the simplest methodology remains, not to put too fine a point on it, simple:

- Set clear objectives for KAM, by customer, and for the whole KAM journey, in each case noting the current position and the expectations, perhaps to include:
  - financial expectations (sales volume, value, profitability);
  - product expectations (ranging, NPD, shares);
  - project expectations (timetables);
  - relationship expectations (bow-tie to diamond);
  - customer and market knowledge expectations;

- security and status expectations (key supplier status and so on);
- customer satisfaction;
- implementation timetable of the KAM process (CSFs, customer classification, KA plans, and others);

- Establish clear roles for the KA manager(s) (their GROWs).
- Establish clear roles for members of the KA team(s) (their GROWs).
- Measure progress against these objectives.
- Identify personal or team development required to ensure full capability against their roles.

The most important step is the first one; without clear objectives any tracking of progress will be subjective, prone to anecdotal references, and very likely guilty of the sin of blowing in the wind: – 'however things are, now is where we planned to be…'

Make sure that the objectives set are SMART: specific, measurable, achievable, relevant and timed.

Make sure that the objectives set reflect the timing required for results to flow. The political part of your make-up will ensure that you include a good balance of short- and long-term objectives.

MEASURING THE TANGIBLES

Some of these expectations lend themselves to quantifiable analysis – the financial measures of course, with the measurement of customer profitability being a particularly important one. Take care not to shoot yourself in the foot with this one however.

Remember that KAM is an investment, and that the returns on that investment will not be instant. Profitability may actually dip in the first instance, and this should be accommodated in your objectives and expectations. Do not allow managers (or accountants) to pull your precious new plant out of the ground every five minutes looking for the development of roots – they will kill it within the day! It is of course much the same situation that faces marketing professionals managing a new product launch: the product life cycle (PLC), if measured against profit and not sales volume, will almost inevitably show an initial dip below the line (see Figure 16.3). You could do worse than seek their advice on how they manage the expectations of their bosses in this regard.

Customer satisfaction surveys provide us with another important measure, with many sophisticated tools available, though professional expertise should be sought in this area. Tempting though it may be to send salespeople out with home-grown customer questionnaires, a host of factors conspire to make such exercises next to useless (not least the salesperson's determination to get a good report!).

MEASURING THE INTANGIBLES?

It has often been said: 'If you can't measure it, you can't manage it', and that is a regularly abused and misinterpreted piece of advice. Some might interpret it as meaning that things that cannot be measured are by definition of no significance and so of no value. It may be a great relief to those that think this way not to have to worry about relationships, about trust, about the quality of communications, and a whole host of other vital but hard-to-measure ingredients of good KAM practice. A relief perhaps, but a huge disaster looming.

Respect personal judgements

Allow room for a certain amount of gut-feeling and faith. Personal judgements are not irrelevant simply because they cannot be entered onto an Excel spreadsheet.

Having said that, relationship management *can* be measured. Use the 'KAM journey' model illustrated in Figure 7.3 to identify your starting point and your desired destination at various points of time in the future. Use the different relationship models discussed in Chapter 7 to describe your expectations – bow-tie, one-on-many, cotton-reel or diamond team. Look for the existence of a contact matrix populated with GROWs, as illustrated in Figure 8.13, as evidence of professional management of the relationship.

'Trust' is a little harder, though customer satisfaction surveys can tell us much about this. The analysis illustrated in Figure 8.9, considering the customer's perceptions, can be used to compare 'what was' with 'what is now'. Certainly we are still in the world of perceptions and judgements, but we are encouraging a discussion along formal and 'measurable' lines, rather than relying on gossip and anecdote.

COMPARING KEY ACCOUNTS?

Dangerous. One KA manager has secured key supplier status and has doubled sales, while another is still struggling to penetrate the decision-making process and sales growth is non-existent. Does this make the first KA manager the better of the two? There are too many variables to be sure about that.

A better comparison would be in the way they have used the tools and processes of KAM. Do written KA plans exist? Is there a contact matrix? Does the KA team meet with sufficient regularity?

MEASURING THE IMPLEMENTATION OF KAM

The following question is often asked of marketing managers: do we judge the success of a marketing strategy by the business results, or by the professional adherence to the marketing planning process? It might seem at first glance that the former is the only right answer, and ultimately it must be, but along the way should we not be asking if the process is being managed properly? If we don't then we risk once again that sin of 'blowing in the wind' (see above).

In measuring the success of KAM, we must look at more than the business results; we must also track the professional application of the agreed KAM tools and processes.

Set an implementation timetable as part of the objective-setting process outlined above. It might look something like the following:

- Phase 1: Establish the KAM steering team.
- Phase 2: Determine your expectations from KAM.
- Phase 3: Identify the obstacles.
- Phase 4: Identify the critical success factors (CSFs).
- Phase 5: Ensure top management support and cross-business alignment.
- Phase 6: Develop the necessary support systems.
- Phase 7: Customer classification, customer distinction, and KA selection.
- Phase 8: Identify the KA managers and potential teams.
- Phase 9: Develop the relevant skills and capabilities for each KA team.
- Phase 10: Prepare key account plans (first draft).
- Phase 11: Track progress (the 'performance map').

If this timetable seems too skeletal for your tastes then feel free to add as much flesh to its bare bones as you like, only take care not to strangle the child at birth through over constraining 'bureaucracy'.

THE PERFORMANCE MAP

If we accept that the tools and processes of KAM are good and necessary, then should we not track their usage, and should we not conclude that proper professional usage will be evidence of success to follow? If you answer 'yes' to this question, and if you can persuade your bosses to do the same, then the 'performance map' tool will be of interest to you.

Figure 32.1 shows a performance map, laying out in logical sequence (left to right) the individual processes and tools that make up the full KAM package. A circle represents each individual tool or process.

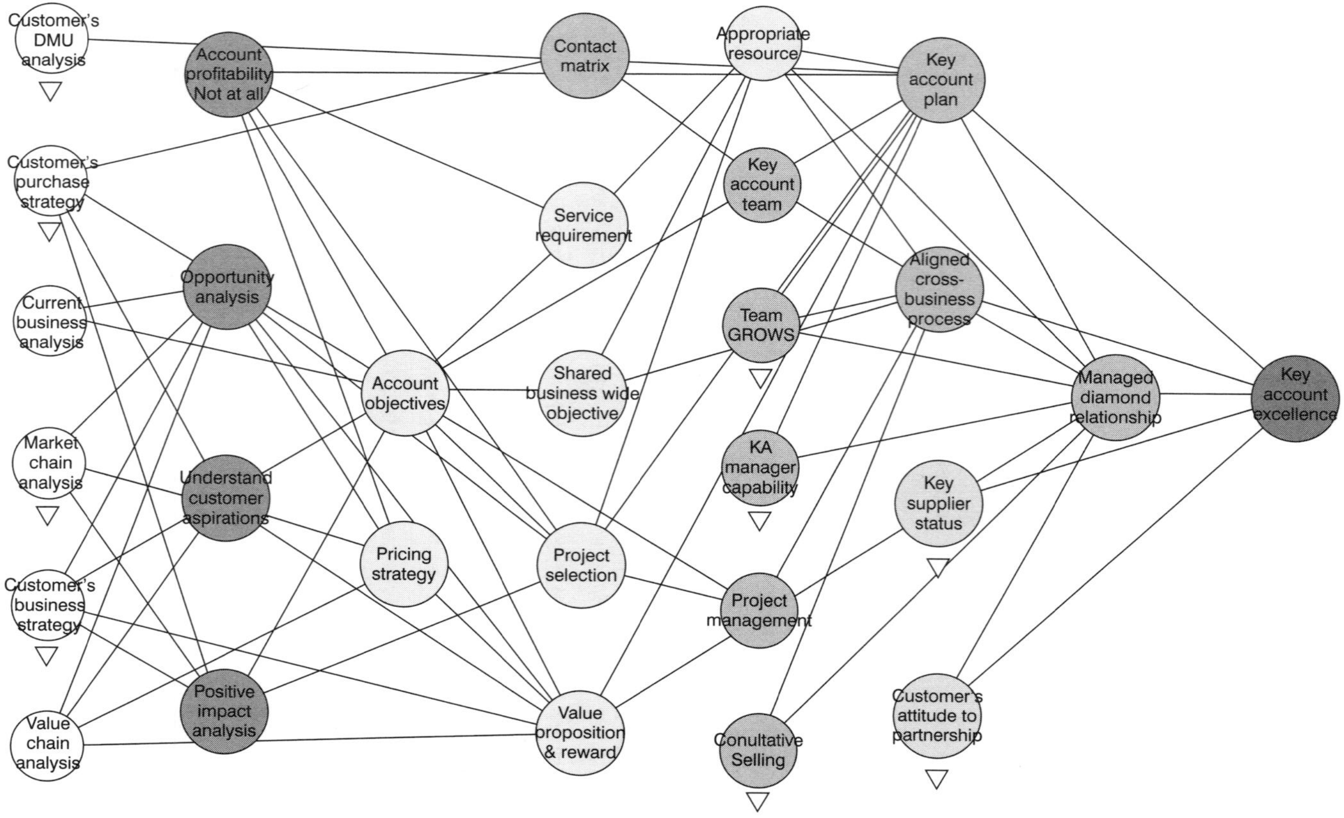

Figure 32.1 *The performance map*

You will of course need to identify which tools and processes to include on your own map, as they suit your own particular circumstance.

An important feature of such a map is the way in which tools and processes relate to each other and contribute to each. Those on the left are necessary building blocks for those on the right.

Having constructed the map, the next step is to conduct a questionnaire of all those involved with KAM as to the current position against these tools and processes. Have we worked through each one – not at all, partially, mostly, or fully?

Given that they build from left to right, claims to have fully implemented a tool or process to the right while answering 'not at all' to those contributing from the left should lead to some raised eyebrows!

Using a software package (see below) the results can be shown as a series of coloured lines coming out from each circle: green indicates that the tool or process has been implemented, red that it has not, and a grey line that it is only partially so. An added sophistication is to indicate by the thickness of the line the relative importance of each tool or process.

The result is a snapshot of progress, whether for an individual KA team, or for the whole KAM journey. If the exercise is repeated at regular intervals then progress can be tracked through the changing colour schemes on the map – red turning to grey, and then to green.

Software and questionnaire

The weblink associated with this book contains an example questionnaire, almost certainly too large for anyone's needs, but the aim has been to cover all the bases; feel free to edit.

A software package is available for constructing a full performance map, and using it to track progress over time. See Chapter 33 for details on how to find more information on this.

THE KAM 'HEALTH CHECK'

If the performance map seems too complex for your needs, then perhaps the simpler KAM health check will be more to your taste.

Recent years have seen a boom in 'well man', 'well woman' and 'well baby' clinics. Their main purpose is prevention rather than cure, based on regular check-ups. Perhaps you should start a 'well KA' clinic in your organization.

The weblink associated with this book contains an example KAM health check questionnaire, and as with the performance map questionnaire please feel free to edit. Indeed, the effort taken to identify your own questions can in itself be a health promoting exercise, and it may be worth doing just that before turning to the example on the weblink. To get you started, the following categories of questions are the most frequently used:

- internal support and capabilities;
- KA team dynamics;
- customer relationships;
- supplier status;
- customer knowledge;
- project management;
- account profitability.

HOW WILL YOU KNOW WHEN YOU GET THERE?

Most journeys have a final destination, but not this one. There is no final arrival, no perfect state of KAM; the whole thing just keeps turning. This can be frustrating, and potentially hard to manage, but far less so than what went before. Someone once said to me that the best thing about KAM was the way that they didn't feel, each 1 January, that they were starting again, which was how it had felt when they practised traditional selling.

With KAM, patience is a true virtue

So, if there is no end-point, the best that can be done is to note where you started, where you are headed, and to keep a log of the journey, holding frequent reviews to see if course changes are required. Use the performance map, or the KAM health check, or your own 'patented' methodology (often the best), but whatever you use, don't be bullied into short-term knee-jerk reaction. KAM takes time, and you (and your managers) need persistence and patience.

APPLICATION EXERCISE

- In your own circumstances, what are the key performance objectives to be monitored and tracked:
  - Business performance?
  - Customer performance?
  - Team performance?
  - Individual performance?
- What is the appropriate time horizon for each of these measures?
- How will you track the implementation of the KAM strategy and processes themselves?
  - How could you use the performance map approach?
  - How suitable is the performance map questionnaire to be found on the weblink associated with this book?
    - Redesign as appropriate.
- Complete the KAM 'health check' (on the weblink associated with this book):
  - What are the key actions required to 'improve your health'?

33

Getting further help

Throughout this book, references have been made to seeking professional help and advice, whether with your analysis of customers and markets, the targeting and selection of key accounts, the identification of team roles (Belbin) or practical implementation through planning or training.

The author of this book is a director of INSIGHT Marketing and People, an international training and consultancy firm that specializes in all aspects of KAM implementation. We deliver training around the globe (this book has been translated into more than 10 languages), for clients in the broadest possible range of industries, and would be pleased to receive any enquiries for further help or advice on any of the issues raised.

Please contact:

INSIGHT Marketing and People Ltd
1 Lidstone Court
Uxbridge Road
George Green
Slough
SL3 6AG
United Kingdom
Tel: +44 (0)1753 822990
Fax: +44 (0)1753 822992
e-mail: customer.service@insight-MP.com
website: www.insight-MP.com

THE WEBLINK

- The full set of figures used in this book, in PDF format.
- The performance map questionnaire (see Chapter 32)
  (*For further details on the full performance map software please contact INSIGHT at the address shown above.*)
- The KAM health check questionnaire (see Chapter 32).
- A simple KA plan template (see Chapter 31).
- A blank contact matrix and GROWs (see Chapter 8).
- A basic KAISM tool (see Chapter 24).
  (*For a more sophisticated version of this tool please contact INSIGHT at the address shown above.*)

THE INSIGHT KAM TRAINING PROGRAMME

Insight offers a full programme of in-company training, including the following:

- the KAM masterclass;
- senior management alignment and the KAM Implementation process;
- customer classification and distinction;
- KAM for KA managers;
- leadership and coaching for KA managers;
- KA team workshops.

THE GLOBAL CHALLENGE

There is one challenge that has not been tackled in any depth in this book, and that is the task of practising KAM on a global level. All of the concepts and tools discussed here will have relevance in that arena, but the additional issues are too great and too significant to be dealt with in anything other than a full book of its own. I recommend you to my own title on the subject, *Global Account Management*, also published by Kogan Page.

Here you will find the additional issues illustrated in Figure 33.1 covered in full detail. The only comment I will make, in closing this book on KAM, is that to describe global account management (as I have heard it described) as simply 'KAM with time zones', is to make the same mistake as describing flying as simply 'walking, but with wings'.

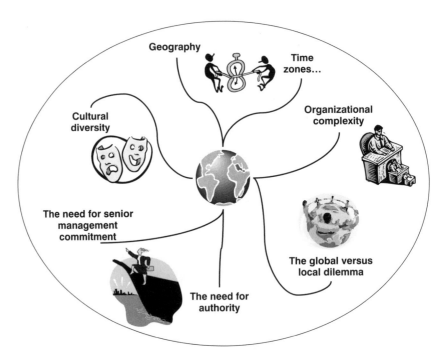

Figure 33.1 *The particular challenges of global account management*

FURTHER READING

There are of course other books that will help you with both your investigations and implementation. In addition to these I highly recommend a regular reading of the business pages of whatever newspapers you favour – you will find these peppered with case studies, good and bad (the latter often being the most useful!).

Cheverton, P (2000) *Key Marketing Skills*, Kogan Page, London

Cheverton, P (2007) *Global Account Management*, Kogan Page, London

Cheverton, P; Stone, M; Hughes, T and Foss, B (2007) *Key Account Management for Financial Services*, Kogan Page, London

Miller, RB; Heiman, SE and Teleja, T (1987) *Face to Face Selling*, Kogan Page, London

Miller, RB; Heiman, SE and Teleja, T (1988) *Strategic Selling*, Kogan Page, London

Payne, A; Christopher, M; Clark, M and Peck, H (1995) *Relationship Marketing For Competitive Advantage*, Butterworth Heinemann

Treacy, M and Weirsema, F (1995) *The Discipline of Market Leaders*, Harper Collins

Index

activity based costing   350
activity cycles   236–46
adopter's curve model   102–03
Aldi   188
AMEX   153
Ansoff Matrix   192–96
Apple   242
Asda   189

B&Q   20
behaviour   329–30
Belbin, Meredith   318, 358
Belbi team roles   318–24
bow-tie relationships   76–78, 194–95
BP   9, 232, 337
Branson, Sir Richard   195
British Gas   185
British Telecom   68
business strategy analysis *see*
      strategic supplier status
buyers   95–97, 133–37

Cadbury's   189
category management   245

CFCs   121–22
chains (value)   37–51, 59–60
change equation   254
change management   253–55,
      302–09
CICS questioning strategy
      257–58
coaching   324–26
Coca Cola   172, 189, 220, 274
competencies   316–31
contact matrix   86, 108–10
contact strategies   91–113
   adopter types   102–03
   buyer role   95–97
   buyer type   99–101
   contact matrix   108–10
   dissatisfaction   101
   DMUs (decision making units)
      92–94
   GROWs   110–12
   influencer matrix   97–99
   influencer wheel   97
   levels of seniority   103–04
   power   101

receptivity   101
supporters   104–05
cost to serve models   351–52
cotton-reel relationships   71,
    80–83
CRM (customer relationship
    management)   335–36
cultural matching   214–15
customer classification   263–85
customer distinction   287–93
customer intimacy   208–16
customer relationship management
    see CRM

deadly sins   297–99
Dell   203
diamond teams   83–89, 350–51
Disney   244
DMUs (decision making units)
    92–113
Dulux   20, 279

EasyJet   203
e-commerce   170, 175,
    339–40
economic buyers   100–01
entry strategies *see* contact
    strategies

farmers: as a style of selling
    68–70, 289, 326
fmcg   9, 53
food industry   220
GE   213
global account management
    373–74
GROWs   86, 110–12

Hewlett Packard   177, 220
Hogg Robinson   153
hunters: as a style of selling
    68–70, 289, 326
ICI   134

identification of key accounts *see*
    key account selection
IKEA   209
implementation timetables   367
influencer matrix   97–99
influencer wheel   97
INSIGHT   372
Intel   168
interpersonal skills   114–20
IT systems   333–40

journey   71–75

KAISM   269–85
Kellogg's   220
key account management
    bow-ties   71, 76–78, 194–95
    competencies   316–31
    contact matrix   86, 108–10
    contact strategies   91–113
    cotton-reels   71, 80–83
    definitions   16–21, 23–33
    diamond teams   71, 83–89
    DMUs (decision making units)
        91–113
    GROWs   86, 110–12
    health checks   369–70
    implementation timetables   367
    investment   16–21
    journey   8–9, 12, 71–75
    KAM model   31–32, 65, 227–28,
        263–64
    making it happen   297–74
    managing the future   23–28
    objectives   24, 29–30, 364–65
    one-on-many   71, 78–80
    opportunity chain analysis
        37–51, 59–60
    organization and structure
        309–14
    performance management
        307–09
    Performance Map   367–69

plans   354–62
profitability   342–52
reasons for: 9–12
rewards   13–14
rules   3–7
selection   263–93
sins   297–99
skills and competencies   316–31
team dynamics   318–26
timetables for implementation
   367
tracking progress   364–70
value chain analysis   37–51,
   59–60
key account managers   316–31
   coaches   324–26
   political entrepreneurs   326
   seniority   327–28
   skills   316–31
   training   328–29, 373
key account plans   354–62
   template   355–57, 359–60
   tips   362
key account selection   4, 263–93
   attractiveness factors   276–79
   customer classification   263–85
   customer distinction   287–93
   KAISM (Key Account
      Identification and Selection
      Matrix)   269–85
   investment portfolio   275
   key accounts   271
   key development accounts
      271–72
   maintenance accounts   272–73
   multiple business unit suppliers
      284–85
   opportunistic accounts   273
   relative strength factors   280–81
   segmentation   265–67
   selection team   267–69
   six step process   264
key account teams   318–26

Keynes, John Maynard   28
key supplier status   131–80
knowledge management
   336–37
Kohler   327–28

lock in   241–42
Lycra   168

making it happen   297–74
   burning platform   303–04
   change management   302–09
   critical success factors   305–06
   coaching   324–26
   cross-functional alignment
      305
   IT systems   333–40
   leadership   302–09
   organization and structure
      309–14
   performance management
      307–09
   political entrepreneurship   326
   requirements   299–300
   sins   297–99
   skills   316–31
   team clock   324–25
   team dynamics   318–26
   team leadership   318–19
   vision and goals   304–05
Marks and Spencer   172, 231
Mars   53
McDonalds   211
MCI Worldcom   68
Mercury   68
Microsoft   242
milk round: as a style of selling   67
Miller-Heiman   99
money-making-logic   205–06

Nestlé   53
NHS   4, 46–47, 342
Nokia   18

one-on-many relationships   71, 78–80
open book trading   173–74
operational excellence   208–16
opportunity chain analysis   37–51, 59–60
opportunity networks   46–51
opportunity snails   52–61
organization and structure   309–14

packaging industry   42–43, 58–59, 127–28, 284–85
paint industry   47–49, 158, 206, 279
Pepsi   274
Performance Map   367–69
performance management   307–09
Pfizer   9
pharmaceutical industry   4, 46–47, 58–59, 87, 195, 328
political entrepreneurship   158, 326
Porter's 'five forces'   187–88
Porter, Michael, and competitive advantage   202–07
PPG   345
Procter & Gamble   4, 172, 177, 220
product leadership   208–16
product life cycles   196–200
profitability   342–52
   customer retention   345–46
   costs of large customers   342–44
   costs of winning new customers   344–45
   cost to serve models   351–52
   diamond teams and profitability   350–51
   lifetime value   346–47
   measuring total costs   348–50
proposal analysis   253–57
purchasing revolution   10, 133–40
   balance of power   162–63
   buyers   95–97, 149

centralization of purchasing organization   152–59
corporate purchasing   152–53
corporate purchasing service   153, 155–56
e-commerce   170, 175
key supplier status   131–80
Kraljic Matrix   161–62
lead buyers   152
lean supply   146–47
managing suppliers   160–80
open book trading   173–74
risk management   174–76
sourcing teams   146
spend mapping   164–66
supplier positioning   160–80, 230–31
supplier rationalization   150–52
supply chain management   141–48

questioning strategies   257–58

RAF   308
recruitment   328–29
relationship management   65–120
   bow-ties   71, 76–78, 192–94
   contact matrix   86, 108–10
   contact strategies   91–113
   cotton-reels   71, 80–83
   diamond teams   71, 83–89, 350–51
   DMUs (decision making units)   91–113
   farmers   68–70, 289
   GROWs   86, 110–12
   hunters   68–70, 289
   interpersonal skills   114–20
   milk rounds   67
   one-on-many   71, 78–80
   rapport   116–20
   trust   89

risk management   192–96
Ryanair   203

Sainsbury's   4, 171
segmentation   265–67
selection of key accounts *see* key
   account selection
selling skills *see* skills
service creep   288
shared future analysis   217–22
sins of KAM   297–99
skills   316–31
SMART objectives   365
snail model   52–61
SNAP model   184–85
solution selling   10–11
specifiers 'buyers'   100
sponsors   99–100
strategic supplier status   183–23
   competitive advantage   202–07
   cultural matching   214–15
   diagnostic toolkit   189–90
   growth and the product life cycle
      196–200
   growth and risk management
      192–201
   money-making-logic   205–06
   shared future analysis   217–22
   value drivers   208–16
supplier positioning   160–80,
   230–31
supply chain analysis   44–45
supply chain management   141–48
SWOT analysis   217

targeting   263–93
team dynamics   318–26
   team charter   332
   team clock   324–25
   team leadership   318–19
Tesco   4, 18, 231
timetables for implementation   367
Toffler, Alvin   205
total business experience   227–35
tracking progress   364–70
training   328–29, 373
trust   89

Unilever   4, 53
user 'buyers'   99–100

value and value in use   143–44
value chain analysis   37–51,
   59–60
value drivers   208–16
value propositions   143–44,
   227–58
   activity cycles   236–46
   cost in use   250
   lock in   241–42
   making the proposal   253–58
   measuring the value   248–51
   proposal analysis   255–57
   total business experience
      227–35
Virgin   195–96, 244

Wal*Mart   9, 18, 177, 188–89, 203
Weirsema, Fred   208